¡Venceremos?

Perverse Modernities

A series edited by Judith Halberstam and Lisa Lowe

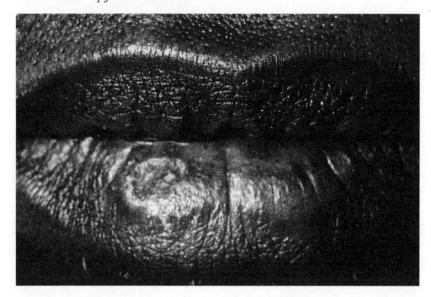

¡Venceremos?

The Erotics of Black Self-making in Cuba

Jafari S. Allen

DUKE UNIVERSITY PRESS   DURHAM AND LONDON   2011

Published with the assistance of the Frederick W. Hilles
Publication Fund of Yale University.

Printed in the United States of America on acid-free paper ∞

Designed by Nicole Hayward. Typeset in Scala by Achorn International.

Library of Congress Cataloging-in-Publication Data appear on the last
printed page of this book.

Frontispiece: © René Peña, *Untitled*. From the series Man Made
Materials, 1999. Courtesy of René Peña.

For Nehanda—
with my love and gratitude

Contents

Acknowledgments

MY PRIVATE PLEASURE (and terror) in this text derives from the love and effort of collections of individuals and institutions.

First, no one is able to do ethnography without people who share. This book would not be possible without people who opened their hearts and minds and their homes, meetings, social circles, and favorite haunts. My gratitude goes to those who opened their mouths to tell their own truths and to those who opened doors to archives and to new experiences. I hope this small offering of the faithful reporting of my truth of this experience will be received with the respect and love it is offered.

Three roads of Ellegua/Eshu opened the door to Cuba to me. If you want to do ethnographic research, go find someone as knowledgeable and generous as Danny Dawson. Such individuals will introduce you to their equally generous friends like the eminent painter and Cubanista Ben Jones, who will then send you to "the field" with an introduction to someone who knows everyone and everything (and has a provocative opinion on it all) such as Tomás Fernández Robaina, the heretical patron saint of black Cuban studies.

Thank you to my friends and family who were not sure that Cuba was really a research site, but listened and loved anyway: Gera Peoples, Tayari Jones, and James Reynolds (whose memorable visit to Havana precipitated an international incident), and Sacha Vington, for his love and encouragement.

Books take a long time to find the bookshelf and your hands. Through research, moves around the country and around the world, near death and death, and relationships ending and beginning, real life and academic life go on—and with as much style as one can decently manage, my thanks to Paulette Young; to my family, especially Barbara Smith and my sister, Yvonne Robinson, for her prayers and for the camera equipment that made the photos possible; to my brothers, sisters-in-law, nieces, and nephews, for wondering aloud (and with some irritation) when the book would be finished.

My thanks also go to my circle of writer friends and fellow travelers who celebrated every completed revision with me and who reminded me that even academic books must be *written*: Marvin K. White, Steven G. Fullwood, Matt Richardson, Martha Ramos Duffer, Sheree Ross and Miramar Dichoso, Ana Maurine Lara, and Sharon Bridgforth. Thanks also to Davarian Baldwin, Rosamond King, Michele Brown, and Bayo Holsey, who witnessed the seeds of this project. Marc Perry, whose account of this same period of time is forthcoming, provided crucial friendship in the field, as did Pablo Herrera Vetia, Ivonne Chapman, Joseph Mutti, Llane Alexis, Sue Herrod, and a number of folks whom I will not name. My thanks go to Nehanda Abiodun, freedom fighter, revolutionary mother-sister of Havana and Harlem, and exemplar of Oshun, to whom this volume is lovingly dedicated; and to Assata Shakur, whose courage and determination is legendary. These women exemplify Che Guevara's contention that "a true revolutionary is motivated by deep feelings of love." Those privileged to see and experience this as exemplified in these women are changed forever.

Enormous thanks go to the members of my dissertation committee: my chair Sherry B. Ortner along with Steven Gregory, Robin D. G. Kelley, Carole Vance, and Nadine Fernandez. They are role models of the highest order, and I earnestly hope that this book honors their work and their time. And to the mentors and senior scholars who have not yet read a word of this work but have carved out space in academe for this to live—I sincerely hope that you see in this book, glimmers of your own work on behalf of new eyes, insurgent voices, and progressive politics. Thank you.

This work was transformed by the effort and grace of my brilliant Duke

University Press anonymous readers, including Martin Manalansan, who eventually "outed" himself as a reader. My eternal gratitude is yours. Having René Peña's *Solitario* grace this cover is a dream come true. Thank you for the inspiration. The Perverse Modernities series editors J. Halberstam and Lisa Lowe, along with Ken Wissoker, deserve every kind word already uttered in print about their enthusiasm, generosity, and professionalism: thank you.

The African–New World Studies Program at Florida International University gave me a home close to the Caribbean in every way I needed it to be: thanks to Carole Boyce Davies, Rosa Henriquez, Jean Rahier, Keisha Abraham, Kameelah Benjamin-Fuller, and the visiting scholar Rhoda Reddock. Thanks also to Nathaniel Belcher who opened his home to me, Jody Benjamin, and John King—all of whom made my life in Miami sunny.

My love and gratitude also go to Edmund T. (Ted) Gordon and Daisy Garth Gordon and to Charles R. Hale and Melissa Smith. At the risk of embarrassing Ted in print, I must say, without hyperbole or drama, that this work— and the work of a growing number of emerging scholars—would not be possible without his revolutionary love and work on our behalf. Thank you to my friends and former colleagues at the Department of Anthropology and the John L. Warfield Center for African and African American Studies at the University of Texas, Austin: especially Juliet Hooker, Pamela Haith, Stephanie Lang, Jennifer Wilks, Jemima Pierre, Shirley Thompson, Stephen Marshall, Ben Carrington, Gloria Gonzalez-Lopez, Frank Guridy, Deborah Paredez, Jossianna Arroyo-Martinez, Tiffany M. Gill, Simone A. Browne, Eric Pritchard, Christen Smith, Kamran Ali, Kamala Visweswaran, and Joni Jones Omi Osun. And to my brother, whom I would call my collaborator if it would not implicate him in the errors and foibles of this book: *muito obrigado* to João Costa Vargas.

Say it plain: Research (and writing) is also a matter of money. Thank you to the National Science Foundation Graduate Research Fellowship; the Columbia University Graduate School of Arts and Sciences Minority Affairs Office, under the direction of Sharon Gamble; the Rockefeller Foundation's Diasporic Racisms Project, and the University of Texas, Austin, Center for African and African American Studies, both directed by Edmund T. Gordon; and the Yale University Office of the Provost, which generously supported my final trips and the Yale Humanities Center's Frederick W. Hilles Publication Fund which supported the preparation of the manuscript.

I have drawn inspiration from my new colleagues in the departments of African American studies and anthropology and the program in lesbian, gay, bisexual, and transgender studies at Yale University, especially P. Sean Brotherton, Kamari Clark, Elizabeth Alexander, George Chauncey, Terri Francis, Enrique Mayer, Emilie Townes, William Kelly, Robert Stepto, Michele Stepto, Alondra Nelson, Marcia Inhorn, Glenda Gilmore, Hazel Carby, Inderpal Grewal, Barney Bate, Khalilah Brown-Dean, Michael McGovern, Eric Harms, Jonathan Holloway, Gerald Jaynes, Doug Rogers, and Karen Nakamura. Thank you for your warm welcome and generous spirits.

I have come to the end of this long-but-still-too-abridged list of institutions and people who have helped to make this book real. As usual, despite all of the wonderful things these folks have contributed, and despite their high expectations and sage advice, there are missteps, flaws, and perhaps even failings here. They are mine alone.

Thank you is of course inadequate to say to my parents, James Herbert Allen Sr. and the late Geraldine L. Allen. My parents are my first and most solid *foundation* of support. Always. Words fail to convey how profoundly I miss my mother. At the same time, I take inspiration from all that she gave to me before leaving in the middle of the research process. *Mojuba* to all of my ancestors, known and unknown.

Finally, to love and live in partnership with an artist is to recognize that time spent in thought, music, verse, fabric, or canvas *doing your work* is not really time spent away from your lover. I cannot repay the time I borrowed from my one and only, Phillip Kirk Alexander, to give to this book. Without Phillip, huge parts of this work, and my own sensibilities, would have perished long ago under a terrifying mound of grief, drafts, anxieties, drywall, and dishes. For this, to you: my love and reciprocal care of the beauty you create.

Invoking "a larger freedom"

¿Venceremos? (Will we overcome?*) ¿De verdad?* (Really?)
I asked seventy-year-old Señor Leudis Ferrer as we sat
together in a small park just beyond the Plaza de la
Revolución in Havana. From the first moment of contact with Cuba, one is struck by this social ethos—
¡Venceremos! (We shall overcome!)—and its stark
contradictions. Free and universally accessible education and healthcare, and one of the highest rates
of literacy and lowest incidence of infant mortality in
the Americas, are just a few of the gains of the Cuban
Revolution of 1959. These accomplishments seem
especially glaring against other realities such as the
widespread shortage of medicine and access to technology, the cultural inequality of women, the marginalization of blacks, and prejudice against sexual minorities. Political disillusionment some fifty years after
the triumph of the Revolution is just as formidable
a threat to the promise of a people's revolution as is
the unilateral blockade of Cuba by the United States.

In practice ¡Venceremos! is less an objective declaration of unqualified victory than a prophetic hope for
the future. And while it is debatable to what degree
Cubans believe in slogans like ¡Venceremos! that pro-
claim the eventual victory of the downtrodden brave
enough to resist, it is clear that this seemingly quix-
otic rhetoric and the political education it represents

has conditioned subjectivities of "entitlement." Cubans feel that it is their birthright to enjoy human security (e.g., free healthcare, education, and subsidized food and housing), as well as to express themselves freely as human beings, even if material realities and political exigencies find them merely subsisting in spaces of lack and uncertainty. This central contradiction of Cuban life is observable in realms of class, race, gender, and sexuality, and is the space in which this books enters; to query *how* and to what extent, in fact, *we will overcome*.

While the stories and analyses here—chronicling racial, gender, and sexual hegemonies and (dis)articulations, are resonant with the experiences of marginalized populations in various places around the globe, what is different in Cuba is this dogged assertion: "¡Venceremos! . . . ¡Adelánte, hasta victoria, siempre! [Ever onward until victory]." It is made explicit on buildings, in newspapers, in theaters, school murals, popular nightclubs, and in the tenacity of Cubans' everyday practices: "No para sobrevivir, pero prosperar [Not only to survive, but to prosper]," Ferrer told me. Writing and living in the United States—post–civil rights, post–Black Power, post–women's liberation, post–queer liberation—in this dawning of the "Age of Obama" in which we are met with "hope" and our own stark contradictions, and find ourselves still reeling from lost political ground following the center's precipitous shift rightward, I am also compelled to have faith. As Señor Ferrer put it, "we must . . . there is no other solution." Thus this book, which critically engages seemingly intransigent racial, sexual, and gender apparatuses that frustrate the hope that even socialist revolution would cure all forms of inequality, is in some ways "a testament of faith and idealism." It insists that we must listen to the margins and look to the interstices of human subjectivity for the realization of the promise of freedom. In this critical ethnography of changing gender, racial, and sexual meanings among contemporary black Cuban men and women, I argue that gendered, raced, and sexed self-making in Cuba is impelled not only by interaction with foreigners and global discourses but most pointedly by individual and group desire for a *larger freedom*.[1] This is made legible and within reach by the Cuban Revolution of 1959. For my respondents, however, this longing is also constrained by the Cuban state, which has seen itself as too embattled to afford "openings" in which its citizens—especially gender-insurgent women, blacks and "queers"[2] who had already been cast as "other"—consume liberally and improvise *new* collective subjectivities.

In order to better read the texts and contexts of this moment, this book points critical social and cultural analysis in the direction of the bedroom, the street corner, and the *bembe* (religious ceremony). The politics of this project insists on recording the real while also mining those spaces for moments, experiences, and roadmaps toward freedom. Here, I am concerned with the proliferation of diversity and difference, and the recognition of a variety of politics—and politics of resistance—that emerge out of contestation and change. What calculus emerges when raced and sexed categories of, for example, nonnational, deviant, nonethnic racial subject, or merely other, are compounded? What are the sites, modalities, and limits of agency and resistance in contemporary Cuba?

While a number of scholars have focused on black resistance, queer subjectivities, Afro-Latin American and Caribbean culture and politics, or the political economy of Cuba's Special Period in Time of Peace, this book intervenes at the nexus of these themes in order to consider the dynamism and political potential of gendered, sexualized, and raced self-making. I seek to reframe a few key concepts and present alternative readings of scholarly debates and popular understandings through illustrating the uses of erotic subjectivity. Erotic subjectivity includes and goes well beyond associations with sexual identity. Here I follow Audre Lorde, for whom the erotic is "a lens through which we scrutinize all aspects of our existence, forcing us to evaluate those aspects honestly in terms of their relative meaning within our lives" (1984: 57). I will introduce the self-making practice of "transcendent erotics and politics," which my respondents deploy to play various "serious games"[3] more effectively. Transcendent erotics and politics is a triune concept—ranging from momentary transcendence experienced in flashes of self-awareness, love relationships, or *communitas*, to transgression of the hegemonic rules of a particular public, to the potential transformation of standard practices of the public. I offer this view as a way of posing the relationship between individual infrapolitical gestures (Scott 1990) and the intention to build community.

The Special Period

Recently, the vexed homecoming of global capital to the shores of Cuba—which I want to call re-globalization—has brought material hardship and existential quandary to the country. For blacks, and non-heteronormative individuals, "deviant" erotic and political possibilities expanded during Cuba's Special Period in Time of Peace. This was a result of a conjuncture of forces, including a greater array of choices, less or different capacity of state and cultural institutions reeling from these changes to repress those expressions, and powerful global forces exerting their own hegemonies on local ones.[4] The Special Period's social rupture began as small cracks, which had been forming in Cuba's racialized heteronorm for a number of years. The Special Period pressurized these cracks, making them cleavages that would have to be addressed. Blacks, gender-insurgent women, and non-heteronormative men had already been discursively cast, in cultural and political realms, as particular types of deviant others whose putatively scandalous, unruly, and potentially "dangerous" erotic subjectivities had to be dealt with in order to constitute a healthy independent Cuban nation and make (and protect) proper Cuban subjects. Moreover, these groups have been the objects of policies and campaigns enacted to contain, reeducate, or eliminate othered subjectivities. Today the state asks black Cubans in particular to hold the ground won by the Revolution *on their behalf* by continuing to adhere to socialist mores and to persevere through material shortages and privation. At the same time, however, (re)globalization of the island creates spaces in which individuals may respond more centrally to market drives and globally valued styles, attitudes, and personal and organized politics. This makes the position and potential *politics of deviance* (Cohen 2004) of black (and) queer subjects especially problematic and promising.

Encountering Cuba

But despite everything I now know, I would forever remain on the side of Revolution. Forced to choose, I would side with a flawed or even failed Revolution rather than the sort of nightmarish society in which I was born and raised, and which I would wish on no one. I would always share a foxhole with those who revolt against oppression. To me, they were kindred souls, even when I would have to mobilize every atom of my body to oppose their revolutionary despotism.

—CARLOS MOORE, *Pichon: Race and Revolution in Castro's Cuba: A Memoir*

As Cuba recovers from the Special Period in Time of Peace—brought on by the dissolution of the Soviet Union, long-term state inefficiency, tightening of the United States blockade, and larger processes of globalization—the country is attempting to reenter global currency on its own terms. However, this move seems contingent upon taking up positions that sharply diverge from those codified in the early years of the Revolution, including limited neoliberal reforms, a greater openness to global social and cultural expressions, and the exploitation of Cuban culture and tourism as principal development strategies. The implications and effects of this are myriad for the Cuban state and for Cuban subjects. In this book I describe and theorize some of the ways that black Cubans (re)interpret racialized and sexualized interpellations of their identities in the current moment. Here I pursue the relationship between Cuban socialist praxis, global flows that challenge these ideologies and practices, and the freedom dreams of ordinary black subjects. These are stories about complexly articulated subjectivities, which are on one hand constructed through the material (and) erotic desires of the powerful, and on the other hand are also (re)made by individuals and collectives. That is, while working within hegemonic "common sense," folks also come to experience, and in many cases also cognitively recognize, forms of consciousness and politics that run counter to it. These forms of consciousness and politics are motivated by their own material (and) erotic desires and informed by their own theoretics.

What follows reflects my own research experience of moving in and between a number of connected scenes, neighborhoods, and social spheres, as well as intellectually moving between distinct theoretical, thematic, and historical frames. My research for this project required various levels of inquiry, and it absolutely depended upon the openness and depth of feeling engendered between my respondents and myself. This was not only to help me to understand what I saw and what was said, but, in fact, to see what was happening around me, to attune my ears to meanings as they were expressed; and finally to help me to know the ways that I have myself coproduced particular expressions, meanings, or assumptive logics in each of a variety of scenes in which I have participated. Ojalá (with blessings, I hope), my interpretations do these folks the honor and respect they so richly deserve. This book reflects ethnographic research undertaken in Cuba over a period of more than four years, within and between sites such as semiprivate parties of gay men (twenty-peso parties); HIV education activism; lesbian performance and incipient organizing; hip-hop and la monia (soul music from the United States) parties and concerts; sex work and other informal services targeting foreigners; and informal transnational black consciousness networks. These sites have been cast as oppositional to the bedrock Cuban revolutionary doxa of nationalism, heterosexual reproduction, and the "hyperconscious negation" (Vargas 2004) of race and racism. And while these scenes of subject formation through pleasure, politics, expressive culture, and "getting over" may seem incommensurable at first, they are inextricably linked in the histories, lived experiences, and bodies of my research respondents. Without this articulation, one cannot productively talk about strategies of the less powerful, or about what any one of these putatively disparate sites means for contemporary Cuba, and black and non-heteronormative subjects. This volume therefore crafts a thick description and critical theorization of the everyday through a combination of historical, literary, and sociocultural analysis, including, most centrally, the experiences and reflections of black Cubans.

When I first arrived in Cuba in summer 1998, Señor Ferrer and many others schooled me on the rhetorics and practices of Cuban masculine sexualities. He held me in thrall as he talked about his childhood in Oriente (the easternmost province of Cuba) and the halcyon days in Havana at the triumph of the Revolution of 1959. This was also my first lesson in "correct" masculine behavior in Cuba. Ferrer instructed me in the correct way to sit; to offer a compliment, a seat, or a hand to a woman; and how to strive to be the most gracious among other men, which includes buying rum and talking the loudest to be heard over the other men, without becoming vulgar or coarse in mixed company. Similar rules of polite masculine behavior apply in my own United States and Caribbean black working-class and middle-class milieus, so I passed easily; that is, I did until he offered me a Cuban cigar. "No. no. no. *chico* [boy] . . . *m'hijo* [my son], . . ." not like that, he admonished— disappointed: "You don't want people to think you are a homosexual because you smoke like a woman." Masculinity studies, social theory, and sexuality studies of Latin America and African diaspora literature reflected only a small fraction of the promiscuous interplay of politics, gender, sexuality, and racialization that I encountered during that preliminary trip and throughout my research. I was fortunate to be led to streets, bars, theaters, kitchens, beaches, museums, and crowded *solares* (tenement housing complexes) by Cuban friends, comrades, and hustlers. Women's accountings of men's sexualities along with the interpretations of women's behaviors and sexual "natures" by the men who alternately loved, passionately pursued, studiously allied with, or repeatedly mistreated them convinced me that the story of gender cannot be told from only one side. The more deeply I became involved in the complex personal lives and communities that had conditionally welcomed me, including the home space made for me by United States black and New Afrikan sister political exiles in Cuba, the more I was privileged to participate in women's gatherings and to observe performances and transnational exchange among women, which in turn provided crucial counterbalance to my black queer feminist analysis of gendered and sexed power conjunctures on the island.

Here I move between scenes of idyllic domesticity to the gritty margins—the generative spaces of multiple contact and possibilities. In residing in four or five different locations in Havana and Santiago de Cuba I sought an array of individuals to illustrate various facets of contemporary urban Cuban life. My respondents are relatively cosmopolitan subjects who introduced me to their friends, families, and associates, through whom I was able to make other acquaintances and contacts.[5] My fieldwork involved observational participation and "deep hanging out" with individuals who took me into their homes and their street corners and bars, to their UJC (Union of Communist Youth) and FMC (Federation of Cuban Women) events, and to their concerts, art openings, shopping trips, doctor appointments, unexpected visits to police stations, university classes, baptisms, saint's days, spiritual cleansings, dates, parties, and meals with family. Local readings of my own racial/color, sexual, and class positionality varied only slightly. My phenotype—clearly "negro" on the otherwise elaborate Cuban scale (or as a close Cuban friend remarked, "negro! negro! negro!"—reportedly commenting not only on my dark-brown skin color and rounded nose but, as he saw it, my predilection toward fiestas and good rum)—along with my gender and youth (at least at the outset of the project) consistently activated reactions that provided insights absent from other ethnographic accountings of Cuba and Latin America more broadly.

While my friend's emphasis on excessive, stereotypical blackness illustrates that my color, physical features, and hair texture provided very little room to claim those measures of hybridity, for a few respondents and observers who were invested in traditional rules of black respectability I became *negro fino*, that is, a "fine or well-educated and well-mannered black man" because of my relatively high class status as a North American who had traveled to Cuba for research. This local reading of my race and color may work similarly apropos of sexual orientation or preference. On arrival to the field, I initially chose to "come out" only to those respondents who themselves identified as homosexual in order to prevent the lines of communication from closing after my disclosure. This decision, however, became untenable to me as I developed closer relationships with people with whom I worked. I asked myself how I could justify asking people intimate details about their sex lives, and not share any of my own. One night, during a long conversation with two heterosexual-identified men about women, sex, and relationships, I decided I would disclose my own sexual gender preference. Before I could say anything, twenty-nine-year-old Leonid finished his point about male polyamory in relationships by saying, "It is that way with women. And I guess with men too, right Jafari, *you know* . . . ?" I found that the respondents who were interested already *knew* because, apparently, gaydar is diasporic. I had made no pretension to having a wife or girlfriend, and though I often went to parties with folks who identified as heterosexual, and danced sexually suggestively with women (as is appropriate in those settings), these gestures did not leave the dance floor except in the most clearly mutual "joking relations" with women with whom I was close. What may have been the clincher, however, was the fact that I was so curious about gender relations, sex, and women's equality. As Leonid told me later, "Here, *hombre-hombres* ["real" men] do not talk about this." He then emphatically granted another tenuous exemption, similar to the way negro fino allowed a temporary, contingent reprieve from some of the insults and inconveniences of "negro" on occasion. Authoritatively, he said: "Not that you are a *loca* [sissy]. You are still a man"—explaining, as if he were offering a compliment, that he would "not be able to tell" just by looking at me.

Thus, this work is a chronicle of crossings.[6] It is animated and enabled by my own subject position as black and gay. But most centrally it is motivated by my own human longing for the larger freedom that my research subjects seek in, for example, religious ceremonies in which we encountered our ancestors, *orishas*, and ourselves; at all-night parties where Cuban rum flowed freely and complex interpersonal dramas and tragicomedies unfolded; and within the transnational political solidarity movements of folks who "are trying to fight a Cruise missile with a slingshot."[7] All of these folk continue to press on. Aligned in some ways with Ruth Behar's notion of the "vulnerable observer" and "anthropology that breaks your heart" (1996), this work expanded my heart and changed me forever. Owing to this background, the book resists simplifying the complex. In this work, I attempt to mirror cultural strategies of multivocality, syncretism, complexity, and serious play—which are so much a part of the constituting process and cultural ethos of the black diaspora and Cuban culture. These strategies also mark my own complex position as a critic of the ongoing Cuban Revolution, who is at once invested in the social welfare projects and international solidarity it has championed, and the various movements, projects, and improvised tactics of those working toward a larger freedom than perhaps any state can offer.

Scholarly Crossroads and Political Minefields

The analytical framework I use in this book is indebted to and closely aligned with literatures in the social sciences and the humanities, across regions and theoretical orientations. I attempt to address the gaps between scholarly fields by weaving literatures on Latin American gender formations and sexual culture(s), racialization and blackness in the region and diaspora, and critical reflection on black subjectivity and resistance, into the fabric of black feminist, black queer, and queer of color critique. Rather than present a formal review of these disparate literatures or rehearse familiar arguments, here I will broadly outline what is at stake in various fields in order to give a sense of the cumulative force (and risks) of combining them. Some of these literatures and politics closely articulate to form productive points of analysis, while the high-stakes disarticulation of others suggest provocative entry points for new formulations.

In this book, interstitial analysis emerges through close attention to lived experience.[8] Thus, we must push beyond a few influential and important scholarly works and political positions. My work in this book privileges the up-close ethnography of everyday practice,[9] which demonstrates, for example, that race is (still) lived—alongside and inextricable from gender, sexuality, and class. It focuses on living black subjects as complex, contemporary decision-making men and women rather than as reproduced folklorized "Afro-Cubans" rendered as objects within political and cultural myths.[10] Here I attempt to set aside the falsely dichotomous rancorous debates between Havana and Miami. Factions on both sides of Cuban and Cuban American ideological, intellectual, and political debates are seemingly loathe to acknowledge the fact that complex narratives of race, gender, and sexuality go to the heart of current skirmishes on the future of Cuba (and the ongoing Cuban Revolution). Moreover, this work challenges the celebration of a so-called universal "global gay" subjectivity (Altman 1996). Despite the seemingly totalizing force of the demands of heteronormativity and of various iterations of global capital, desire drives individuals in unexpected ways. The actions that this impels should be read in their particular historic and cultural contexts and through the intentions of folks on the ground. My objective here is not to "explain" or fully describe blackness or sexuality or gender in Cuba, and neither do I wish to provide a concretized monolithic truth. What I seek is a sort of genealogy of the possibilities of the present moment.

A number of my earliest Cuban interlocutors graciously led me to flashpoints of Cuban culture—rumbas, baseball games, dominoes, and Santeria, for example—in order to help me in my quest to understand Cubanía. A few of these interlocutors have been surprised by the smallness and ordinariness of the scenes I chose to report and analyze here. At the same time that one of my respondents, Amílcar, was incredulous when he sensed that an entire day spent learning about Afro-Cuban religion with his uncle, a celebrated palero, would be less useful to me than the dinner and casual conversation with the family later that night, his advice, in an e-mail one year after we had lost contact in Cuba, said it best:

> Mi hermano, Todavía, no es facíl. [It is not easy, my brother. Still]. Here, we are fucked, but still happy . . . You want to understand our culture, the way we do things here? Study slavery . . . the rumba, literature, but look at all the contradictions too . . . We are freer than most but cannot leave the island. We are richer and poorer. We are African and Spanish. We are Caribbean and Latin American. We are Revolutionary but too traditional. . . . What will come next, when he [Fidel Castro] goes? What will our future be when our father leaves?

In this book I am not only suggesting that we continue to see the complexities of local identification of sexual behaviors and desire, for example, but also that we begin to expand our definitions through deeply interstitial analysis. In one aspect of this, I will argue for the centrality of gender analysis in queer theory. For example, in Cuba, the "dangerousness" and "scandal" of male homosexuality is not men having sex with men—this is understood as fairly commonplace—but rather it is the failure to perform the strict script of masculinity and *hombría* (idealized attributes, rights, and responsibilities of manhood) that is itself classed and raced. Further, while sexual "mixing" among men runs parallel to mixing discourses of race in Latin American studies, it is important to avoid the tendency to separate out homosex as a completely discrete and universally translatable category. I sympathize with the positions of a number of scholars who have provided foundational understandings of (homo)sexuality in Latin America and in the Caribbean.[11]

The discursive disregard for sex between women is likewise about gender as much as it is about sex, evidenced by the misogynist view that "real sex" cannot take place without penile penetration. On one hand, this allows for a bit of liberty to *no dice nada, se hace todo* (say nothing, everything is done) since women enjoy access to each other's bodies for "friendly" physical affection without harsh scrutiny, for example. Still, this angst-filled silence is matched in symbolic violence once it is clear that a woman intends not to follow the gender script. One respondent, Yesileny, confided that her mother—amending a phrase popular throughout Latin America by tellingly leaving out the part about being a *puta* (whore)—announced to her that "a daughter is better dead than a lesbian." Her mother's vile comment was not made in response to any sexual overtures toward other girls by Yesileny, but rather when her mother noticed that she showed no joy or pride in cleaning up after her brothers or helping her mother to wash the family's clothes. That Yesileny "turned out to be a big lesbian with bad hair," she says, is incidental but not unrelated to her rejection of the gender roles that family and society would force her to play. Her so-called "bad hair" (deemed bad not only because of its coarseness but also her apparent disinterest in "taming" it through chemicals or heat, or even keeping it an appropriately "feminine" length) was a scandal closely related to "laziness" in her household. This underscores Tanya Saunders's (2009b) argument about the particular compoundedness of black lesbian identity in Cuba. The lesbian is not only a problem for the state, as M. Jacqui Alexander brilliantly theorizes (1997), but also a figure that does not fit easily into cultural and familial tableaux of women as selfless domestic caretakers—that is, as appropriately womanly. This may in fact prove to be an even sturdier obstacle to erotic autonomy than juridical proscription.

For the less cosmopolitan of my Cuban respondents, the very notion of a sexuality or sexual identity abstracted from other facets of life was anathema.

Those who had been more "exposed" could more or less easily give me a definition that is commonly used in Cuba ("homosexual," "bisexual," "heterosexual," for example). Still, many times this was just an opener; that is, a description that we understood would hold a place for deeper exploration beyond it. What I was really looking for—and looking at, in my observations of people and their various relationships and networks—became clearer when I stopped attempting to abstract the "sexual identity" of the individuals I encountered. I understood sexuality as multiply constituted and dynamic, but I still thought of it as knowable as a discrete unit of analysis. *En la calle* (in the street) and attuned to everyday lived experience, I realized more acutely that my mission to study "sexuality" was perhaps misguided. I needed to be attentive to *desire*, as well as to the interarticulations and expressions of that desire in every facet of life that my friends and respondents would allow me to witness or participate in. Other respondents and friends, who chose for their own reasons to "disidentify" or to push me intellectually and politically, clearly saw this more-nuanced concept of (what we can call, in shorthand) "sexuality" as a deeply personal but also culturally constructed desire, articulated not only to (at least) their gender but their nationality, color or race, and spirituality. Here is where it is useful to employ Lorde's enlarged vision of embodied, even "useful," desire, which is certainly sexual but also gendered and racialized inasmuch as these are also categories of experience that are very much embodied. Following Lorde, my reformulation of "erotic subjectivity" attempts to clarify what Thomas Boellstorff poses as a nettlesome "impasse" apropos of a proper relationship between, for example, sexuality (studies), race (studies), and gender (studies) and questions of "intersectionality, inclusion and difference" (2007: 25), by showing the ineluctable situatedness of desire that is obvious to my respondents, and already well articulated in black feminist, black queer, and queer-of-color literatures.

For outsiders with pretensions to speak for "queer Cuba" as a place waiting to be "discovered" and exploited, Cuban homosexuals, bisexuals, transgender individuals, and other non-heteronormative subjects live their lives in a space that is overdetermined by their own "silence." Yet they do in fact speak: namely by negotiating but not wholly capitulating to notions of what Cymene Howe has called the "universal queer subject" (2002) and gay rights as it has come to be understood in the North. If gay Cubans exist, what do we make of the fact that a gay tourist cannot take a taxi to a "gay bar" in Havana or attend a tea dance—rainbow flags waving in the Caribbean breeze? Is the absence of GLAAD, PFLAG, NGLTF, HRC, GMHC, and LOGO proof positive of the repression of homosexuals by the Cuban state?[12] Is this a distinctive reflection of "machismo" or evidence of Third World underdevelopment? Are the critics of the Cuban state who point out the nation's sad, reprehensible recent history merely doing the bidding of the White House? of global capital? of the "Miami Mafia"? And if blackness is real in Cuba—not the invention of North American black scholars as an extension of Pierre Bourdieu and Loïc Wacquant's (1999) uninformed critique might suggest—how do we account for the lack of the NAACP, CORE, HBCUS, or more relevant to some, BET, on the island?[13] I raise these examples, only partly tongue in cheek, in order to poke a little fun at sometimes well meaning but just as often patently disingenuous casual observers on either side of the Florida Straits that miss crucial social, cultural, and historical difference and complexities for their own narrow ideological commitments or scopic desires.

In this work I take up the challenge to further develop a transnational (or diasporic)[14] black queer theorization[15] that is at once about material effects and resonant affect. My goal is to contribute to the recognition and proliferation of various everyday tools that, like Bob Marley's small axe, might be used in struggles toward autonomy and personal dignity.[16] The forms of black self-making I address in the following chapters are not guaranteed to be effective as a formal political strategy. They are however, what we have at this "stony, contradictory ground of the current conjuncture" (Gramsci quoted in Clifford 2000: 94).

Reading Black Resistance / Thinking New Times

Finally, how do we account for black subjectivity? What difference does blackness or queerness make apropos *resistance*? What is the best way to read and write agency, change, and contingent action? While queer theory[17] has proffered a number of studies in which everyday acts of gender or sexual nonconformity are celebrated, this has always been more complex for people of color. The self-making presented here always takes place in a field in which black subjecthood is in some ways still an open question.[18] To read black (and) queer resistance thus requires a much finer analytic instrument than queer studies, black diaspora studies, or anthropology alone provide. Due to the perhaps inescapable position of the black body in the political economy of the Americas—brought as chattel and constantly reified through representations as such—the question of whether the black can be recognized as a subject is still a vexing one. Ethnography complicates the elegant and useful contending formulations of black agency and resistance (Hartman 1997; Kelley 1998, 1994; Cohen 2004; Hanchard 2006), which seem to be at odds with one another but are revealed on the ground—even complexly, messily, inelegantly— to be facets of a process of (or at least potentiality for) "radical becoming." Small practices of self-making through erotic subjectivity, like the ones that the accounts that follow bear witness to are *political*, in the sense that these actions challenge the allocation of social and material capital, and look toward improving the individual's felt and lived experience. These practices potentially instantiate socially transformative returns to personhood, which theorists of black resistance must recognize.

The Book

In my effort to reflect cultural and state structuration while focusing on individual subjectivities and countercurrents, this work necessarily moves between two impulses or modes of investigation. The first explores ideologies and interpellations: the historical, sociopolitical, and ideological terrain of transitioning (post)socialist Cuba. The second offers close readings of interrelated scenes of Cuba's reglobalization and individual and group responses to it—what I call erotic self-making—entailing individual and collective (re)articulation of race, gender, and sexuality, and the creation of new social and political subjects(ivities). This book is not about black gay and lesbian Cubans seizing power to transform Cuban society, as such. More complexly and precisely, I seek to describe and theorize the creation of intimate spaces of autonomy among a variety of folks whose multiply subaltern identities have found them illegible to state functionaries, and to most scholars.

In chapter 1, "Looking (at) "Afro-Cuba(n)," we arrive in Cuba. Here I undertake the differential politics and ways of knowing entailed in "looking" and "being looked upon." Victor Fowler, in writing on his travels to the United States from the other side of the Florida Straits in "A Traveler's Album: Variations on Cubanidad," avers that the "pedagogical side of the Cuban diaspora . . . [transmits] learning of its norms and civility . . . in which the political-ideological operates . . . as a kind of protective shell around the exile communities, so that it also becomes truth" (2002: 108). That is, to see Cuba from the United States is in large part to see it through the very particularly conditioned perspectives of Cuban American exiles. On this side of the falsely dichotomous debate, members of the Cuban exile community, many of whom identify as white, blame Fidel Castro for the island's ills even as they continue to use powerful lobbying organizations to advocate United States policies toward Cuba that make life extremely difficult for Cubans. The other side is characterized by turning a blind eye to the authoritarian and at times despotic practices of the Castro regimes and counting Cuba's problems to United States imperialism alone. In chapter 1, I offer a very different optic—by maneuvering between a collection of scenes—walking in the cities of Havana and Santiago de Cuba. In the Cuba I experienced, at the level of the eye, antiphonies do not necessarily happily resolve as Fernando Ortiz and others assure us they do. Here, the sweeping panoramas of time and place are often collapsed into snapshots or single moments. As such, I attempt to historicize and theorize the constitution—racialization, gendering, and sexualizing—of space in Cuba. Focusing more particularly, I will also assay a few close readings of these practices and the places in which self-made, ready-made, and remade images are enacted—especially apropos of the tensions between the racialized, gendered gaze of individual Cubans, tourists and other visitors, and state apparatus. After this orientation to current life in Cuba and the high stakes of engaged ethnographic methodology, I take a step back to consider the historical and discursive co-construction of race, gender, sexuality and nation. In chapter 2, "Discursive Sleights: Race, Sex, Gender," I provide a critical intellectual genealogy of pre-revolutionary discourses on race, gender, sexuality, and Cuban nationalism.

In the third chapter, "The Erotics and Politics of Self-Making," I introduce my respondents Octavio, Lili, Coleridge, and Yaineris, who travel through several overlapping scenes in the book. These respondents live in three of the most populous and historically significant neighborhoods of Havana: Cayo Hueso in Central Havana; Vedado, the pre-revolutionary upper-middle-class area, now the arena of various embassies and institutes as well as working people and professionals; and sections of Habana Vieja, or Old Havana, which has been recognized by the United Nations as a World Heritage site and now is being renovated as a tourist zone. These respondents therefore represent in some ways the vanguard of black Cuba—those who are on the "front lines" of contact with foreigners. In this chapter, ethnographic vignettes with dramatic public scenes—ranging from using gender fluidity to lessen the sting of racial terror, to actually embodying the New Man of the Revolutionary imaginary— serve as a foundation for my theorization of black erotic subjectivity, which is introduced here and will be explored in subsequent chapters.

The next chapter's comparison of gender and sexual roles mandated by the Revolution is animated by a question put to me by a United States political exile living in Cuba: "What is gender, politically?" In chapter 4, "De Cierta Manera . . . Hasta Cierto Punto (One Way or Another . . . Up to a Certain Point)," I trace hegemonic forms of revolutionary gender, racial, and sexual hygiene which sought to constitute "family" in particular ways. The chapter focuses on narratives of everyday life through a reading of Sara Gómez's film *De cierta manera* (1974) and the contemporary experiences of my respondents Domingo and Mercedes, who are currently making their way through and *between* the now seriously impaired revolutionary infrastructure. State policies that seek to "protect" and extend heterosexually structured familial relations (even as they may be incongruent with patterns of individual erotic desire) show not only the ways in which the state seeks to structure intimate relations but also points to the irony of how intimate relations and the notion of family is often queered—in this case, without folks "coming out" or leaving their homes.

In "Friendship as a Mode of Survival," chapter 5, I introduce the concept of "In the life, in diaspora." I want to support the claim by Audre Lorde, Chela Sandoval, and others that practices of loving friendship and sexual connection form a powerful tool that *we have now* to use as a way of healing from the multiple and compounded traumas of race/sex terror. This constitutes what Kamala Kempadoo and others look for when they call for "Caribbean sexual resistance," and it evidences Michel Foucault's notion of "friendship as a way of life." The chapter takes up the question of homosexuality in Cuba, after which I will engage friendship as a conduit to a new mode of life. It then moves on to discuss communities of "resistance" and the HIV/AIDS healthcare system, in order to show the complexity of the threats and opportunities in Cuba and throughout the black diaspora. Finally, I summarize with a proposal to enjoin both sexual citizenship and "erotic autonomy" (Alexander 1997), toward a larger freedom.

The male sex-work scene in Havana, and its transnational connections through the traveling bodies and images of black Cubans, are closely read in chapter 6, "¡Hagamos un Chen! (We Make Change!)." As scholars such as Kempadoo and others have shown, sex work takes place throughout the Caribbean and other sites around the globe, and nowhere is this more remarkable than the *ambiente* (environment or scene) of sex labor in Cuba. Here, tourism-related sex labor is one of a growing number of spaces in which commonsense understandings of racial and sexual identity are re-presented and exploited toward related aims of material "survival," commodity acquisition and consumption, and becoming a cosmopolitan subject. The long-ignored dynamics of trade in heterosex is also explored here. The spaces between male heterosexual and homosexual behavior and the distinction between "romance" and commerce are more like dynamic conduits than sturdy barriers.

It would be instructive for activists and students of the black experience in the Americas to see the Cuban Revolution of 1959 as one form of "affirmative action"—for example, universal access to education, housing, and healthcare—as one way to frame the difficult questions around pervasive racial hegemonies and pernicious social practices that operate in silence beyond the pur view of top-down juridical remedies. The systematic and legally mandated and supported systems of racial oppression that have caused real material inequities deserve reparative measures that are just as systematic, established, and protected by law until the material effects of the slave trade are erased by a fully level "playing field." In the meantime, there is much to do. Still, to finally bring Cuba in line with its laudable ideals and de jure equality, black nationalist and queer politics and protest postures are not recommended by my respondents or by my analysis. Rather, we call for a critical engagement with issues of racial, gender, class, and sexual politics on the island, from the bottom. Everyday erotic subjectivities will continue to be deployed as a ground for a liberatory politics and as a way to express and increase personal freedom and thereby influence cultural and personal openings in Cuban society from a position *within* and supportive of the revolutionary process.

Looking (at) "Afro-Cuba(n)"

YOU HAVE LANDED in Cuba—for whatever reason. Undaunted by the noise and gas fumes, the mysterious condensation wafting up from the floor . . . the out-of-fashion costumes of the flight attendants on your Cubanacan flight from Toronto, Nassau, Madrid, or Mexico's District Federál, you have arrived, to see for yourself. If your flight is directly from Miami, you *look*, too, with suspicion at these cousins, nephews and nieces, old friends, old enemies, and the Old Man himself.[1] They regard you likewise, even as they are thrilled to witness your return. Your gaze must also be fixed on what you think of as personal property, which your uncles and grandparents have told you is rightfully yours.

On the long, winding road full of schoolchildren and workers hitching rides and of *vecinos* (neighbors) talking among themselves, you pass a convention center where international fairs host businesspeople from around the world—promising profitable business in this socialist country—and you go by a specialty hospital where individuals come from first-world nations for medical treatments. Perhaps you yourself have come for such cutting-edge therapy. You may notice that you also pass a number of clinics where Cubans attend free of charge, but with little of the diagnostic equipment or cutting-edge technology available in the specialty hospital. The same is true if you are a fan of seafood; the lobster and shrimp you eat at the restaurant or small *paladar* (home restaurant) has been reserved for you—not for Cubans. But, farther along the road, green greets you again and your reverie is broken. You see a few cows, and you also see some wagons—which may have parts used and reused for generations—carrying anything from produce to a volleyball team. And yes, there are the old Chevys and Cadillacs from the 1950s that speak of one bygone era, as well as the old Russian-made cars, Ladas, and heavy Chinese bicycles that recall another. Certainly, some buildings crumble, or seem to. Once-vivid blues and vibrant yellows now in turn are grayish, white, and ochre, battered by sea winds and gas exhaust. But Cuba is not a place in a timewarp, no matter how many times that travelers, exiles, and politicos echo this hackneyed phrase. More accurately, it is the perception of Cuba that is warped.

Then, very suddenly, you see the city of Havana. Avenues widen, and there are more tourist taxis and rented Mercedes. More schoolchildren dressed in their gold, blue, or red uniforms. As you pass the famous obelisk monument to Martí you should start counting, since there are hundreds of busts of Martí in the city. Everyone from communist hardliners to dissidents—in Cuba and in Miami—claim him as their own. You get a bit of a thrill when you catch a glimpse of the sculpture of Che's face on the front of the Ministry of the Interior, with serious-looking young black and brown men and women in faded-green uniforms guarding it.

No matter what has brought you here—socialist solidarity, scopophilic drive, erotic imperative, racialized longing—seeing Cuba is more than merely gazing from the windows of a tourist taxi, classroom, or an air-conditioned Mercedes imported expressly for the comfort of foreigners. To see Cuba, and especially its capital Havana, one has to walk. And *look*—like a friend or foe, CIA agent, meal ticket, solidary compatriot, potential lover, exile, escapee, or expatriate.

Not waiting to be discovered; not unaware of its position in the vast sea; too busy resolving the issues of the hour to be on watch for the "last days": this is another way to see Cuba, a view that is in sharp contrast to the pretension to panorama in which texture, color, sound, and contradiction blur into totalized nothingness. This is the Cuba in which antiphonies do not necessarily happily resolve and where *serious games* most often have no clear winner—a place that is peopled by folks whose style and politics are confounding to those unfamiliar with the riddles of black diaspora. In this chapter, we analyze and theorize the constitution of space in Cuba, demonstrating de Certeau's contention that *space* is constituted by individuals' practices within particular places (1984), *walking* street by street in the city of Havana.

Attempted *Flânerie*

This notion of walking in the city, of gazing upon the city's landscape and human interactions within that landscape, owes much to de Certeau, who held that walking, gazing, and tracking city paths well worn by others helps us to more deeply read and experience the various rhythms of human interaction. The notion also owes a debt to Walter Benjamin's wanderings through the arcades of Paris. Still, not all *flâneurs* (and certainly no *flâneuse*) have unlimited access to gaze—though the city of Havana has long boulevards and promenades that have also inspired poets, novelists, and lovers. This is, therefore, also to say that some walkers are *looked at* very differently. Some *look differently*, too. My own practices of looking, for example, fit uneasily within anthropological traditions in which the privilege to look is assumed and the ways that research subjects look at the researcher are mostly ignored. It may seem to some that late capitalist subjects have all become flâneurs in some ways—cruising the great suburban arcade, the shopping mall, *looking*. Susan Buck-Morss, for example, argues that the flâneur is no longer a singular figure because of the "look but don't touch" (1986: 104) illusions in mass consumer culture, to which Cuba is certainly not immune. If the flâneurs, like the sandwich man and the streetwalking sex worker, survive as ur-forms, as Buck-Morss argues, their enduring significance emerges from the ways in which they are constituted and reconstituted, recognized and misrecognized. Frantz Fanon has already illuminated how troubling this is for the black male subject, and various critics, artists, and policy analysts have further elucidated the ways in which gender and sexuality effectively and affectively limit movements of black bodies through public space.

Men predominate on the streets of Cuban cities and towns. They joke, talk, and play games in plazas, on street corners, and in parks, while women are mostly seen en route to some appointment indoors. Women and girls have less access to life *en la calle* (in the street), which is where money is made *luchando* (struggling or fighting, but most appropriately in this instance, *hustling*).

For women, the street is fraught with contradiction. The double and often triple duty of women who are caring for households, working at state-sponsored jobs or enrolled in classes, and perhaps engaged in other (possibly "unofficial") money-making or money-extending opportunities seem to conspire with historical cultural values to keep all but teenagers and *jubiladas* (pensioners) indoors, if not purposely moving between one point and another, in contrast to the *andanderia* (strolling) of men. While it has been widely held in Latin American and Caribbean literature that masculinity is made en el calle, the street is more productively thought of as the public sphere, which while including the actual streets is constitutive also of state rhetorics and practices and interaction with disparate elements of the plural culture. This is distinct, but not opposite to *la casa* (literally house, but more to the point, the private sphere), which has been said to constitute the realm of feminine interest.

HOW DOES IT FEEL to be an object, *looking*, like a subject? What is the best way to see, and understand, the complex interplay of power in the context of "consciousness, culture and material conditions" (Safa and Nash 1986)? During my preliminary field trips to Cuba, I was intrigued by the ways that I was constantly recognized and misrecognized—thereby requiring my own performance of identification and "disidentification" (Muñoz 1999). The ways I was looked at on the streets of Cuba led me to improvise new ways of seeing and being seen. As a student of anthropology, cultural studies, and Latin American studies, which suggest that it is class that matters in this region, not color or race, I was anxious to finally more fully experience the privileges of my class position during my initial fieldwork in Cuba. At home in the United States, I am aware that my middle-class status is mostly illegible to nonblacks (and I am especially painfully aware that my status as law abiding is invisible to the police). As a young black man in Cuba I was constantly mistaken as Cuban and therefore subject to police surveillance. Every day, near a tourist area on my way to various appointments and errands, I was stopped and commanded: "Dame carnet!" (Give me your ID!). Curious about the treatment of the "profiled" during these encounters, I answered police hails of head gestures, hand motions, and "psssst" in various ways. Sometimes I waited to see if I would be pursued. My performances of WWB ("walking while black") were motivated by my youthful zeal to participate while observing, certainly, but also by my desire to play a different racial game than at home in the United

States. In Cuba, we "talked back" to the police by attempting to cajole, shame, or playfully tease these young men who could easily be our cousins (or *country* cousins—*guajíro-guajíro!* my cosmopolitan friend Ulísis would add). One day Ulísis provided one of the number of extemporaneous performances or creative interpretations I was to hear of segments from Nicolás Guillén's famous revolutionary poem "Tengo." In questioning the young police officer from Oriente who had pulled us over on our way to Guanabo beach because there was a white woman who appeared to be a tourist in the car with us, Ulísis boomed: "Is this not my road? . . . my air . . . sky . . . my beach, my police . . . my country?"[2] Although his performance was entertaining to us, it fell flat for the police officer. In my own experience with the Cuban National Police, my protests were heard until the conversation got involved enough to reach the end of my stretched linguistic ability to sound like an angry Habanero, then dismissed. Still, the game of comparative police surveillance must be more fully qualified and pushed further. There is a wide gulf between the terror one feels and remembers while driving, for example, from graduate school's ivy-covered gates to a tenure-track job in the deepest part of George Bush's Deep South—pulled over at seventy-five miles per hour on a seventy mile per hour road. I know the routine "down South." And following Malcolm X, everything south of Canada is down South. Say as little as possible. Call him or her "officer," "sir," or "ma'am." Move slowly. Try to show your university ID or business card as you slip your driver's license out of your wallet—ever so slowly. To be pulled over by the Cuban National Police on the way to the beach with friends or while interviewing respondents on a street corner or a bar was to be annoyed by the interruption, and saddened by the reminder that the Revolution has yet so far to go. On occasion, I violated the law and good sense by purposely not carrying my identification card or passport and visa. I often dressed like a Cuban. Secure in my exceptional privileged status as a foreign researcher, the chance of unfortunate repercussions following disobeying the police was much lower than in my home country—land of the ubiquitous "stop and frisk" and of multiple blows, multiple shots, irrespective of occasion, nationality, temperament, or status. Yet after several recurrences of this hailing during each research trip, the novelty of being taken for a "native" wore off, and by my next extended trip the weariness of being constantly "profiled" had set in. When I was walking or hanging out in public with black Cuban men I was conscious of having to comply with their personal strategies for dealing with police aggravation. But when alone, I simply refused or *disrecognized* the hail. I ignored the signals, pretended I did not understand Spanish, or merely cheerfully waved "hello" when officers of the Cuban National Police attempted to make eye contact or wave me in. On one or two occasions, on the way into a hotel, I simply flashed my United States passport—ashamed, as if *passing* for a Yuma (American), but having saved a bit of energy. In this instance, my attitude of mutual misrecognition and performance of ignorance, coupled with what an especially savvy Cuban described to me as the distinctive walk of a Newyorquíno (New Yorker), marked me as a privileged foreigner and therefore outside of the purview of certain types of police discipline. This was both a matter of consternation and humor for my black Cuban friends. One night, as we contemplated being approached, yet again, by the police who were watching us, my friends Liolvys and Gerardo expounded theories of their own that were parallel to Louis Althusser's formulation of how ideology makes individuals legible to authority—thereby constructing certain types of persons. Liolvys began by stating, "They think they know you are Cuban so they call out to you 'Hey, give me your carnet [ID],' but if you do not look back or act like you know it is you they are calling, they will most likely not bother you." Gerardo, however, adds a critical piece, which makes this a risky enterprise; namely, the force of the state apparatus associated with interpellation or hailing. As he notes, "Well, yes, but if they do catch you, you have really made them angry because you have had a lack of respect for their right to call you." Laughing, he continues, "Jafari can do this because we will call [our New Afrikan sisters] and Fidel will deliver him back to them. You are our brother, but we are not so lucky. Maybe in New York, you can do the same for us!"

My respondent Arturo, who is thirty-four years old, has also tested the disrecognition of hailing as part of his overall self-making strategy to avoid the inconveniences of being interpellated as black Cuban. When we went out for an evening together in tourist-oriented places, he would borrow my clothing or wear one of the gifts that he had been given by foreign acquaintances. As a French teacher, he also has access to linguistic alterity unavailable to most Cubans. He uses it by speaking French when in the earshot of hotel clerks, bartenders, police, and women he wishes to attract. Arturo instructed me to speak English. One day he joked that I should "try an English accent" to enhance our status. When I replied, "I have an English accent," he corrected me by saying, "Not *American* [mocking my Queens, New York, nasality] but *En-*

glish. British." Instead of being taken as *jineteros* (hustlers) and rudely asked to leave bars, Arturo and I became targets for jineteros, high-priced drinks, and various forms of entertainment. Louis Althusser hopes to convince us that individuals are abstract with respect to the subjects they already are. He sets up a condition that he believes to be commonsensical: "Before its birth, the child is therefore always already a subject, appointed as a subject in and by the specific familial ideological configuration in which it is 'expected' once it has been conceived" (1968: 699). Not only do the police, as agents of the state, scrutinize and interpellate but also tourists, as agents of global capital, do likewise. And families, religious authorities, and cultural gatekeepers also seek to make individuals *subject to* their regimes of control. However, although these expectations and "places" are determined by history and political economy, the individual's arrival to the determined place is not. Individual subjects do not always accept this interpellation. They do not always answer the hail, or may do so strategically or with a particular tactical logic to meet short-term or long-term goals. Strategy, to follow de Certeau, is an action occurring with an already determined sphere of governmentality, as opposed to tactics, which are more clearly done on the fly or in situations where the rules may be more flexible or dynamic. These infrapolitical moves do not constitute revolution or even a movement, certainly. But in any case, the individual's concrete, material behavior is, to the contrary of Althusser, precisely not "simply the inscription in life in lieu of the admirable words of prayer—*Amen, So be it*" (1968: 701).

Black Cubans and Afro-Cuban "Folklore"

Callejón de Hamel, or the Hamel Alleyway, is fraught with contradiction, complexity, and ambivalence. A two-block alleyway in the mostly black Cayo Hueso section of Havana, Callejón de Hamel functions as a tourist attraction for more intrepid visitors who prefer to experience the "reality of Cuban rumba" over the overtly folkloric or "canned" versions of rumba at the Tropicana and other famous performance spaces. This multidimensional multimedia outdoor art space with live music is an important site for the production and practice of "authentic" black Cubanidad on the stage, on the walls, and off of the stage among the young men and (fewer) women who hang out there. Cayo Hueso has for many years been a center of popular African practices in Cuba. One can hear the music of *toques* (Regla de Ocha ceremonies with drums) during several nights of the week, along with popular Cuban music—son, songo, charenga, and timba-global pop, reggaetón, and rap. There is an active and historic Ñañigo *potencia* (chapter) here, and some families maintain ties to *Cabildos de nación* (African ethnic associations), going back several generations. Callejón de Hamel is recognized as special because of its intentional and spectacular marking as an Afro-Cuban space. Salvador Gonzalez, the muralist and sculptor who created the Afro-Cuban religious themed murals in the area, describes it as

> a heavy load of poetic images and sculpture . . . Its walls express in one form or another, the feeling of . . . African culture in our country. You will find here pieces of sculpture, overhanging roofs with many colors, poetry, images. A house that could be a temple or that is a temple for this community . . . it preserves those values which for many are archaic, primitive, but which nevertheless have their origin in one of the oldest cultures on earth—. . . a living ritual, with living consecrated drums, with living elements of a strong cultural identity. (Gonzales cited in Sarduy and Stubbs 2000: 115)

The Sunday rumba that takes place at Callejón de Hamel is an important site for the complex layering of meaning and symbolism, in terms of the Yoruba, Kongo, and Abakuá elements used to adorn the walls, the *yerbero* (herbalist) who sells religious and medicinal herbs, and the playing of sacred *batá* drums. Moreover, this event is attended by tourists eager to experience and consume the "Afro-Cuba" that they project, imbue, or expect. This is not to impugn the authenticity of the representations in Callejón de Hamel. More precisely, I want to highlight not only the artistry of Gonzalez and the talented rumberos but also that of ordinary Cubans who also perform "Afro-Cuba." That is, I want to call Fernando Ortiz's term "Afro-Cuba(n)" into question. The artistic movement known as Afrocubanismo, according to Alejandro de la Fuente, "drew heavily on the 'black motifs' . . . to create new cultural discourses that were widely perceived as authentically Cuban." As he notes further, "What scientists explained in academic lecture halls and journals, writers and artists popularized in literature, painting, sculpture, dance and music" (2001: 96). Here we are most interested in the particular purposes for which the term "Afro-Cuban" is currently used or not used, especially relative to the terms "black" or "black Cuban." As de la Fuente points out, "Afrocubanismo [as both an artistic movement to re(dis)cover essential Cubanness; and as specific reference to folklorized African culture in Cuban] had taken Martí's notion of Cubanness one step further, inventing a synthesis that proudly proclaimed miscegenation to be the very essence of the nation" (142). Thus "Afro-Cuba" is rendered as the *clave* (literally, the distinctive beat in Cuban music kept by striking wooden sticks together) or "deep" cultural base of Cuban society. Still, even as remnants of the *culture* of Africans are celebrated, their violent kidnapping and degradation is effaced. In this way, culture is understood in the old and unreconstructed anthropological sense of what can be observed, authoritatively chronicled, and ossified in a volume or a diorama, rather than as the project of living, laden with the messiness of subjectivity, affect, and material conditions.

While in the United States context, in which so-called race mixture is derided by white fear of hypodescent, in Cuba there is little anxiety around African ancestry. Yet blackness, with its connotation of politics and history—and perhaps therefore requiring recognition and reparation (or uprising)—is potentially destabilizing to the mythology of "mixedness." This is similar to the case in several American contexts in which the accumulated alternative knowledges of antecedent indigenous peoples are rhetorically revered and said to underlie every aspect of contemporary civilization, yet living indigenous communities and individuals are still rendered "uncivilized" and discriminated against. One evening, during an otherwise pleasant *brindis* (reception) following a lecture at the University of Havana, a Cuban scholar who was evidently anxious to disabuse me of what he mistakenly thought of as uniform black American understandings of racial formation and white supremacy, explained to me "slavery in Cuba was not like other places." The lack of sophistication of his remark and its politics should be self-evident to any student of transatlantic slavery. Chattel slavery was *different* in each site, yet it was similar in its historically peculiar racialized degradation terror, trauma, and political economy. Observing "ethnographic privilege," I remained silent to allow him to feel more comfortable, and so he continued. Perhaps in a more personally reflexive move, this white-skinned scholar in his late fifties confided in me, saying "our black servants were like parts of our family," and finally, laughing, "I am sure that I have some African blood running through my veins too." After all, as Cubans say, "*si no* tiene sangre *de Congo*, tiene de *Carabalí*! [if you don't have Congo ancestry, you have Carabalí]." In Cuba, "Afro-" heritage can be claimed by the entire nation and used in various ways according to one's interests, since African cultures predominate in the food, religious practices, art, and music of the island. African ancestry—*roots*—therefore, is not the point. Black identification and living, breathing black personhood, however, are distinct matters, which have tragically limited material purchase in Cuba, as in most parts of the world.

Unlike other sites of tourist interaction in Cuba, in the callejón there is a noticeable lack of police presence or any obvious rationalization of space toward crowd control or maximum revenue. The level of organization and highbrow folkloric performance evidenced at national cultural institutions like the Union of Cuban Artists and Writers (UNEAC) and Conjunto Folklórico Nacional de Cuba (CF) does not seem to obtain here. There are no tickets to purchase and no identification needs be shown to enter. For both Cubans and tourists, this contributes to the feeling of relaxation, freedom, and sense of "everyday life" of the place, and it allows for the participation of many young people who would otherwise not be able to afford to attend or who might have less interest in attending. While CF, UNEAC, and other exhibits and shows by any of the innumerable world-class cultural and performing groups of Cuba attract those with what Cubans call *alta niveles de cultura y educación* (high levels of education and culture; in practice, it is largely white-identified Cubans who are seen to fit this category), the gatherings at Sunday rumba attract *el pueblo*, or ordinary Cubans. For self-identified liberal or progressive cultural tourists and solidarity tourists, Callejón de Hamel is, along with CF and UNEAC, among the must-see attractions of Havana. One can purchase *ron de la calle* or "street rum" from a purveyor who will pour it unceremoniously into one's own plastic bottle. Alternatively, the street's makeshift bartender has cold beer, water, and better-quality national-brand rums for sale. The latter is available at an elevated price.

Sunday rumba stands in marked contrast to the Tropicana-type spectaculars for short-term vacationers that feature a sort of pan-Caribbean experience of *sun, sand, and son* programmed activities. Many of these occur within the confines of an all-inclusive resort—an inescapable symbol of Caribbean postcoloniality, as Jamaica Kincaid (1988) exposes in *A Small Place* (the style of which I attempted to recall at the outset of this chapter). Kincaid might put your trip to Callejón de Hamel this way: You have finally taken our advice and escaped your tour group. Feeling proud to be en la calle alone, you walk away from Coppelia ice cream shop, which you recall from the film *Fresa y chocolate*. Notice the young men and women gathered in front of Yara cinema on La Rampa, crowding into old cars and newer ones, queued up. These are not for tourists—at least not unaccompanied. After you pass the famous Habana Libre hotel, you find your way past Fundación Fernando Ortiz and the University of Havana. Suddenly you find yourself surrounded by Cubans who do not look like those in your brochure! They more closely resemble those depicted on the walls of the Fundación Fernando Ortiz, but are rarely seen in the offices there or at the university. The music you hear in the street may remind you of the radio at home, although the action on the street—at once swift and leisurely, is strange to you. Everyone seems clued in but you. Some sidewalks are clearly hazardous to maneuver—cracks and holes abound. Others are inlaid with strange, beautiful designs. Modernist? Primitive? Seemingly at every corner, you are invited to conversation: *My friend! Where are you from!?* You ignore this and walk over to where you hear the drumming.

STANDING AGAINST THE WALL in front of Salvador Gonzalez's door, Herman, Lao, and I have a good view of the rumba. They are a few years younger than me—twenty-seven and twenty-six, respectively—and they are *moro* and *chinito* by Cuban color/race classification. Bodies closely packed in the intense heat, the crowd is mostly male, and among the Cubans, almost exclusively black. The gorgeous voice of the singer pierces the air—her whole body sings, in Spanish and Kikongo. Drummers glisten as their hands conjure sound from goat skins, their heads turned to the side as if they dare not reveal their faces—eyes full of *aché* (a spiritual power often represented with bulging eyes in Yoruba art). The percussion of *cajones* (box drums), cowbells, and other instruments, and the effects of rum consumed in the middle of the hot day, add to the overall exhilaration. There seems to be nothing more important than this single moment of *buen ambiente* (good feeling atmosphere) and enjoyment with friends. This is a crucial cultural value among Cubans. Still, the difficulty *pa' resolver*—to resolve problems and face new ones presented by material circumstances—lingers just below the surface of momentary forgetting. I know this well and have seen it throughout the black world. So, while I am willing to parse definitions and reach toward specificity and precision vis-à-vis "resistance," I am not ready to give up the assertion that managing *to be*—that is, drawing breath on a beautiful Sunday afternoon with friends—is at some very basic level a resistance in a global political economy in which, as Audre Lorde reminds us, the traded, enslaved, and still marked "were never meant to survive" (1978: 31). Perhaps this is best explored, as Alexander (2005) pushes us to do, in the unseen, unqualifiable, but profoundly experienced realm of the spiritual. In any case, who can afford to ignore this—the spiritual, the affective, the ineffable felt/lived experience—less than black folks and those who theorize their various and often confounding moves toward full personhood? As Lauren Berlant (2000) and Ann Cvetkovich (2003), among others, have shown, feelings—private, shared, and remembered—are also political. For many, including some of my respondents, the ability to feel, perceive, experience, and analyze, including that which lies beyond the material, may be all one has.

Aside from the small number of tourists seated adjacent to the dancing area, the space is crowded—and by mid-afternoon at the height of the rumba and the hottest part of the day it is standing-room only. Cuban rumba, unlike the ballroom type most familiar to North Americans, is a group or community activity usually held in a patio area. Mostly of Kongo origin, rumba is also said to include elements from Iberia (*rumba flemenca* and *rumba gitana*). The instruments include *cajones*, *palitos* (wooden sticks), *shekeres* or *marugas* (shakers), and *batá* drums. It is constituted by three different dance styles— *guaguancó*, *columbia*, and *yambú*. Yambú, the slow-partnered rumba, was less popular at Callejón de Hamel. The *guaguancó* is a danced expression of a popular understanding of heterosexual sexuality in Cuba. Women are acknowledged to have sexual desire and agency, yet at the same time they are expected to protect their "virtue" from putative masculine rapacity. As one rumbera told me, "It (romance, life, rumba) is all a game anyway . . . we (women) want to be caught." In rumba the dancer's center of gravity remains in the hips, and like most West African dance it is done with the knees slightly bent. The woman and man enter the dance floor together, shoulder to shoulder, and commence play in which the man attempts, through thrusts of his pelvis and throwing of his arm or a handkerchief as a proxy, to *vacunar* the woman ("vaccinate"—gesture contact with the woman's pelvic area without actually touching).

For advanced rumberos this action is performed in the most inventive ways possible. For her part, the woman entices the rumbero and wins the crowd's favor with her footwork, undulating hips, flirty countenance, shoulder rolls, and shakes, seducing and mocking her partner. She attempts to protect herself from contact with the handkerchief or being in a receptive position when he gestures a forward pelvic thrust in her direction. As I watch with Herman and Lao on this day, at the end of an especially skillful and spirited dance in which most of the rumbero's attempts *para vacunar* have been thwarted by the charismatic rumbera, the rumbero turns his back to her and most of the crowd while he does a simple step. The drums seem to follow his movements, and he begins to look as if he is contemplating defeat. The band continues. Energy seems to dissipate. Then, in a side shuffle and shoulder shake characteristic of guaguancó, during which the man looks down and occasionally draws figures in the air or on the ground (thereby indexing the secret drawings of the Abakuá in their performances), the rumbero moves closer to his partner and returns his right hand to her shoulder. He seems tired and she seems less enthusiastic. As he lifts his right hand from her shoulder to wipe his sweaty brow, she carefully watches that he does not use this traditional proxy of the handkerchief to vacunar. Just as he puts it away in his pants pocket, she moves further away—triumphant and teasing, with hands on her swaying hips. Then, seemingly out of nowhere and in slow motion, the crowd and the formerly triumphant female dancer see his red handkerchief (from his left hand) reach her pelvic area before she can do the customary turn or cover up to avoid it. He has thus saved face with a tour de force redirection. The crowd responds with laughter, applause, and taunts that he had staked his claim.

The Gaze Looking B(l)ack

Standing outside Gonzales's gallery, across from the stage, I note that he appears to do a swift business selling his artwork to tourists at world market prices and entertaining them with a coterie of young men and women who serve rum and beer in a small patio area adjacent to his home studio. Herman, Lao, and I feel a barrier to walking into this space, although it is only steps away from the throng of el pueblo. If not obvious to foreigners, Cubans are quite clear on the necessity of maintaining particular sites and representations.

"This is for tourists," Lao says quietly while we sit on a curb outside the gallery, "it is fun to do sometimes, but the art and the rumba and the cold beer and all the people are for foreigners who have a week or so here." "We live Afro-Cuban culture every day," Herman says.

As Lao, Herman, and I talk loudly above the din of the crowd and recorded music between live rumba sets, I notice yet another tourist (or anthropologist? or CIA agent?) aiming a camera at us. We must look like a piece of revolutionary prop art huddled together in our various shades of brown skin against the blue, red, and yellow painted wall: Lao's Chinese grandfather asserts himself on Lao's face but not his hair; Herman's curly hair is made coarse by beeswax and styled as dreadlocks; and I wear markers of Lucumí religion around my neck and wrists, Kongo ancestry on my face, and no phenotypical hint of ivory towers or ivied walls. As my friends seemingly unconsciously give a thumbs-up sign for perhaps the third cameraman of the afternoon who has made no attempt to ask our permission to be his or her object; I unconsciously *out* myself and my different relationship to surveillance and objectification by shouting, in English, *I did not give you permission to take my picture! Get out of here!* I want to have said, *Why do you call up images of the tropical black picturesque? You do not know that I am an anthropologist from New York—you don't know me!* This day, with no camera to indicate the class/national/occupational privilege I hold to objectify despite my blackness; no designer eyeglasses marking me as middle class; and no backpack with bottled water, toilet tissue, and a blue passport marking me as a privileged foreigner, I have dissolved into the sea of black men watching women—and more furtively, cruising other men—laughing and joking under the bluest of Caribbean skies and hottest Havana sun. In Cuba, my United States passport and United States dollars—poor by my standards but rich by theirs, was the major separation between myself and my Cuban respondents and friends. Still, the fact that my position in the global political economy is different from that of my respondents did not prevent various forms of identification. My perceptions of the barriers between el pueblo for whom most tourist diversions are places to be seen or heard through fences, or negotiated through hard-won class markers, or alliances with tourists; and people like many of my own respondents and friends who move in and out of these circles, were intensified by both identification *as,* and my own identification *with,* dark-skinned Cubans, who are read as less appropriately representative of Cuba in all but the most folkloric of scenes. I do not want to overstate this, or to give the impression that this identification is complete or unproblematic, but given the paucity of critical scholarly reflection on startlingly stable and consistent color hierarchies across diaspora, this is *more than fair*.[3]

There is no doubt, no ambiguity, as to where my phenotype places me in regimes of racialization. However, enamored of the brilliant and ruthless critique of restrictive versions of blackness offered by (often biracial, light-skinned) black cultural critics; challenged by structurally white, bi- or multiracial, or otherwise light-skinned ethnographers who enumerate various names and ways of Latin American nonwhiteness and nonblackness; and engaging (again, white) theorists who all seemed to point to the postmodern subject's ability to play with "identity," I thought I would give it a try. I too wanted to test the putatively porous boundaries and fissures of "race" and color. While interviewing my respondents on their racial identification and attitudes, I embarrassed more than a few who had to deliver the news when I asked, "What would you call me?" Being "negro! negro! negro!" on the Cuban scale has found me well positioned to see the limits of hybridity and the corresponding "possessive investment in whiteness" (Lipsitz 1998) and lightness, evident not only in popular discourses of belonging, welcoming, and ownership, but also in some well-elaborated scholarly and popular work on black hybridity, creòlité, métissage, metizáje and Afro hyphenations. Deep hanging out with rum, stories, laughter, and the myriad problems of daily life just under the surface—the potential of more, just at the skin level—led me to more fully understand my respondents who use one axis of power (masculinity, perhaps) or another (class and education, talent, charm, or physical beauty, in some cases) to mitigate the daily interruptions and outrages visited upon black Cubans.

As we leave Callejón de Hamel, I buy a few flowers for YaYa and Yaineris, from the cart of the old woman on the corner of Vegía. We had asked our friend Yaineris to meet us here, but she refused to join us before going on to the Sunday *la monia* matinee in Vedado. Too many tourists, she said. And too much *guaperia* (aggressive attitudes) from neighborhood guys she preferred to avoid. Our mutual friend and surrogate mother, YaYa, will offer her sunflowers to Osun. Yaineris will present the white freesia, whose scent immediately conjures for me the sound of bata drums, to Obatala. We walk past the University of Havana, avoiding La Rampa so that I will not be stopped by another set of friends and respondents who will be hanging out there. Lao, Herman, and I meet Yaineris at another friend's home where she had been picking up some art books and a few items recently acquired from the United States for YaYa, who depends on these reminders of home—Lawry's seasoning salt; new books to feed her voracious intellect; the latest *Essence*, *Vibe*, and other magazines, and mixtape compact discs. As we walk toward the matinee, our conversation shifts to the meaning of my recent outburst at the photographer on Callejón de Hamel. Hearing Lao and Herman retell the story, Yaineris turns to me laughing, and exclaims, "Ay . . . Mike Tyson!" More seriously, she then says that this is the reaction she would expect—that a black friend from the United States explained to her that there is a rage felt by black men in the United States, which she thinks is very rarely expressed in Cuba. Herman and Lao disagree. They say that they feel enraged and saddened by many things that they experience, including constant police stops and negative assumptions about their intelligence, morality, and revolutionary fervor. Herman adds, "we try to keep it *tranquillo* [calm, quiet]" because we are already perceived as hot-headed and prone to *guaperia* (aggressiveness). Noting the catch-22 of racist practices and rhetorics that impel a burden of representation on black subjects that makes it hard to express, Yaineris quips, "That's what I mean." The young men seem to take her tacit critique to heart as the four of us continue down the street—uncharacteristically silent. Blocks later, Lao explains to her that I had been frustrated. Everyone agrees that this is a frustrating time and a precarious position to be in—young and black in a world where even though opportunities are wider than they have ever been, those possibilities seem shallow and mired in the stereotypes and prejudices of the past. "They do not really see you . . ." Herman commiserates. His reply to Lao is eerily similar to my previous experiences with Cuban police, when my friend Liolvys, commenting on police hailing, had observed that "they think they know you . . . so they call out to you. . . ." Today, apropos not of Cuban state apparatus but of the gaze of tourists and other outsiders, Herman continues, noting that the tourists "do not really see you," but rather see "a *guayabera* [traditional Cuban shirt], a big smile, a cigar [gesturing with his finger on his hand to indicate "black skin"], some rum and—*bam*—you are a postcard!"

Hailing is not exclusively practiced by police or rude tourists, of course, and we are certainly not suggesting that these practices have similar consequences. Still, it is important to get a fuller sense of how these dramas (and comedies) are closely related ideologically, and how they are complexly played en la calle. When I suggested to my friends that *pirópos*, the common practice of younger men "hailing" women on the street with compliments or suggestions, was likewise an instantiation of power—interpellating women, while they are merely moving from point A to point B under their own power and for their own purposes, as objects of their desire, with no regard to the intention or desires of the women themselves—my reading fell on deaf ears. Incredulous, and eerily reminiscent of the agency constraining Althusser, Gerardo averred, with no apparent irony or self-refection, "but they [women] are always objects of desire in Cuba."

BACK TO THE MALECÓN

On another late afternoon, an attractive woman, about twenty years old and wearing a short dress printed with large flowers, walks by our group of four young men. The conversation stops for a moment. Marcos talks loudly in her direction. He clutches his shirt close to his heart and lies down, suggestively, on the sea wall where we have been sitting, and says, "Mulata fina . . . please, please put your flowers on my grave." She saunters by, unfazed. Playfully, I challenge Marcos's intentions in this corny performance of youthful masculinity by saying, "You seem to be talking just to hear yourself talk, she totally ignored you." "Yes," he replied, "but I made her smile . . . did you see her smile?" In response to Marcos an onlooker quips, "She just has gas!" and we all laugh. This sort of attention to and addressing of women that I am told occurs "on the streets of every city and town in Cuba" would be seized upon as indicative of sexual harassment in many quarters of the United States and other places, but it is not widely regarded as such in Cuba. Thirty-six-year-old Rosa, who described herself as a "real Cuban mulata"—that is, by having long curly hair and golden skin as opposed to the representations of olive-skinned women—seemed to agree. Rosa reported using street propositions as a sort of barometer of the power of her attractiveness now that she was no longer a very young woman. She stated, "If they did not give me compliments, I would wonder what I had done wrong in that moment . . . my hair, my body . . . had I lost my appeal to the opposite sex?"

Two other young men laugh and tease Marcos for his not-so-clever "flowers" comment, which of course did not result in a date or even a backward glance. One suggests she is really "just a *jinetera*" (female sex worker) and therefore not interested in Cuban men. "Or maybe she's just not interested," I say, laughing with the group and mocking his assumption: *She did not turn around, or say anything.* "They never do reply, do they?" I ask. His weak retort, "Maybe once or twice, but they like to hear them and that is what we do," was met with silence. I remind them that days ago, on our way back from a party in Santo Suarez, a woman, responding to Gerardo's leering proposition, "*jaba* ["redbone"—a reference to her light skin] . . . it is a nice evening for love," stopped suddenly near the wide intersection of the street. She had placed her hands on her hips and looked back at him blankly, silently challenging him, until he babbled something about revolutionary love and referred to her as "comrade." This sent all of us, including the woman in question, into parox- ysms of laughter. Savoring the victory, and not to be outdone by the boys in this improvised street performance, she strode away with a long kissing of her teeth, side glance, and theatrical wave of the hand. "Why do you keep try- ing?" I asked, returning myself to my anthropological mission. It seems that like the rumba, in which the movements seem to suggest the woman's coy acceptance of the attention, with the man constantly trying to win a strike by gesture, this too is a male performance—a homoerotic street game. Masculine performance is still a major criterion for according respect on the street. Cool cordiality to (heteronormative) men and passing comments to (heteronorma- tive) women instantiate gender divisions and help to place men on hierar- chies of respectable or reputational masculinity. *Transformistas*, transsexual women, butch or transmen, and effeminate men are targets of taunts and sometimes threats and are seen as, a priori, unrespectable. Beyond the pale of masculinity, they are not accorded the cool cordiality that men receive but rather a level of scrutiny and public comment even higher than that of young women. While in the rumba, men show their physical virtuosity through a se- ries of intricate steps and flourishes, pirópos allow for the verbal performance that finds the most successful of the men the individual who can say the most clever (or in some generally frowned upon cases, most vulgar) comment. The end in mind is not to introduce oneself or to make a serious intervention or offer toward the woman, but instead to impress other men. I relayed these stories of street games to Señor Ferrer and to Compañero Lozano, the father of my respondent Domingo. They both remembered this being a pastime from when they too were young men, but they say, of course, that they were much more finessed with their comments in their day. Besides, Compañero Lozano remarked, until the late 1970s, women who were well brought up would not walk in the street by themselves, and therefore would not be subject to the scrutiny and hailing that he now finds so distasteful. "Young people have changed," lamented Compañero Lozano. He was especially concerned with the "disturbing" way that young rappers in his neighborhood dressed. He worried that their style was too showy and surmised that Yankee conspiracy had captured them.

CAFÉ CANTANTE

I had seen this young man before. Short in stature but with a solid frame, he wore a red oversized Mecca-brand jersey that looked even more oversized on him, along with a red bandana and white jeans, which were in fashion in New York City at the time. The *pièce de résistance* was his pair of sparkling-clean white tennis shoes with fat red laces, old-school New York City style, á la Run DMC's "My Adidas" video. As if to exemplify well-paid athletes and hip-hop entertainers, "diamond" earrings glimmered from his ears and a gold tooth shone from his winning smile. That night at Café Cantante, as we waited (and waited) for the hip-hop show featuring Obsesión and Double Filo to begin, when the strobe light caught him one could almost hear the high-pitched "bling" sound exuberantly resonating from the earlobes of this proud and impeccable youth. Flossin' (by now an outdated hip-hop neologism, but important in the 1990s and still relevant), that is, generally showing off materially valuable goods to increase prestige, "reputation," and desirability—is an important *weapon of the weaker* (James Scott 1985) in its inversion of "public transcripts" that interpellate certain groups as less worthy or appropriate to use *things* and style for their own pleasure. Folks told me that this young man had friends in the Bahamas who traffic these (bootleg) items from Miami to Nassau to Havana. As such, he was a sort of walking billboard for the things he sold to other Cubans. His appearance, ability to pay for beers for himself and his friends, and his knowledge of the latest United States adolescent lingo, made him an attractive figure to his peers. Although he could not claim the lyrical or MCing skill of the rappers who (eventually) performed that night, he displayed another sort of hip-hop authenticity, which likewise has quite a bit of purchase among young Cubans forging new "homeboy cosmopolitan" (Diawara 1998) subjectivities.

As Peter J. Wilson avers in his classic study *Crab Antics: A Caribbean Study of the Conflict between Reputation and Respectability*, Caribbean society is steeped in hierarchy, reputation, and respectability, mediated by class, consumption, and color. He writes, "Since lifestyle is an important factor in translating economic differentiation into public status, wealth does no good 'squatting'" (1973: 33). That is, in contexts in which nearly everyone is poor, social class status cannot be reckoned so much through real property or investments, for example, but more by what one *has on* and how one looks. Success, therefore, whether *real* or merely the affect of sartorial choice or borrowing—and regardless of whether it necessitates other sorts of material sacrifices—must be worn and consumed in various ways, including in the form of new or fancy clothing and jewelry, accessories, and treating one's friends to parties and evenings out. That night, I heard "flossin'" translated by a young black Cuban man for another as *a way to show that one has good clothes and shoes and that one lives a good life and shares with one's friends*. Flossin', and the less outdated concept of *swag(ger)*, which is all about performing (again, with appropriate costume) confidence bordering on arrogance, corresponds seamlessly with local understandings of appropriate masculine behavior in which the manliest among men is not only sexually prolific but also self-assured, well-groomed (not *micky*, or fussy, which would be seen as slightly effeminate) but always well put-together, convivial, and magnanimous. While for Cubans like Señor Ferrer and Compañero Lozano, who came of age in the 1960s, 1970s, and 1980s, gender roles were played on the Cuban revolutionary stage and thus required adherence to the styles and rhetorics of the country's leaders, these days younger men and women take their cues from and play to various others inside and outside the island. Some of these are illegible to the state and to their families, while others are clear and threatening to narrowly drawn ideals of Cubanía (essential Cubanness), revolutionary fervor, or social respectability.

Everything Old Is New Again

The space economy of capitalism that exploits the natural resources of poorer nations to maintain and enhance rich ones is not new (Mintz 1985; R. Williams 1961; Wolf 1982). In recent years it has exploded, however, in a process that has come to be called globalization (Appadurai 1996; Gupta and Ferguson 1992; Hall 1980, 1990; Harvey 1989; Lavie and Swedenburg 1996). This process—itself one condition of postmodernity—has not only sped up the circulation of capital, goods, and especially information, but also has morphed categories that we thought we knew. We would do well to reconsider the notions of "socialist," "postsocialist," "consumer," and "agent." In spite of the United States embargo on Cuba, multinational corporations and pockets of capitalist production have appeared in this socialist nation, thereby (re)-conditioning desire, consumption, and production. Tight controls on the sort of representations and images from which one could profit (in the sense of material and cultural capital) have been relaxed as resources for surveillance have diminished. At the same time, the reglobalization of Cuba since roughly 1989 has introduced a spectacularized "free market," where commodities of race, sexuality, modernity, and personhood circulate widely, but also in a predictable array. Everything old is new again, with particularly postmodern twists. During the 1990s, Cuba was "opened up" to a global market hungry for more "new" (yet old) images and sites for desire and consumption. Cuban people—especially blacks who had been shut out of other avenues—were likewise opened up to greater varieties of expression. At the same time that the Special Period played havoc with the economy of the Caribbean nation reeling from the end of its alliance with the recently defunct Soviet Union, it also forced a wider opening of spaces of individual production and trade, and concomitantly, new or renewed avenues of intellectual, ideological, artistic, erotic, and stylistic practice. This is not to say that Cuba had been "isolated" previously. Certainly, the entire Caribbean region had already been "global" since at least the inception of the transatlantic trade in kidnapped and tortured Africans. And neither do we want to claim that one day everything changed in Cuba. Signs of the changes of the Special Period began to appear as early as the 1980s. Moreover, "the rules" were never evenly or completely applied. But before the 1990s, access to foreigners—and therefore migration and cosmopolitan identities—was more or less closed to black Cubans unless they were entertainers, artists, or athletes. Black Cubans, their images, and cultural products, now more frequently circulate beyond the island (but still mostly within these categories). At the moment, just as "before the Revolution," not only is Cuba "cool" but black Cubans are again considered "hot" in the global marketplace of images and experiences of pleasure. Neither the trope of Cuba as a sensual or otherwise erotic/exotic playground, which has historically driven most forms of tourism, nor the notion of Cubanía on which this depends, can be sustained without the working and performing bodies of black Cubans. While globalism is most often cited as crushing local culture and cultural production in the wake of its homogenizing influence (Harvey 1989; Jameson 1991), in nations that depend upon the production and commoditization of difference as a condition for their participation in the global economy, globalization has contradictory effects. For example, for Special Period black Cubans, local identities seem to be coming unmoored from narratives of progress and personhood that had seemed stable. These narratives were figured in pre-revolutionary periods through thrift and racial uplift, and in revolutionary periods via socialist praxis. Personhood was first imagined as abolition of slavery and then as people-of-color autonomy.[4] Following this, the Revolution of 1959 offered an attractive unmarked personhood. Today, the market seems to be calling for something else—for export, "traditional" Cuban representation, while it offers representations of cosmopolitan black urban youth culture for consumption in Cuba. But still, sites of official and unofficial cultural tourism where "images, styles, and representations are not the promotional accessories to economic products, they are products themselves" (Jameson 1991: 87) are ironically also sites where projects that run counter to objectification and commoditization occur—like friendship, play, love, and desire. Reglobalization has not only brought tourism and the importation of a wider array of (life)styles and commodities, but for black Cubans it has also meant more opportunities to inhabit and perhaps be remunerated for performances that northern subjects expect to see, or those that stimulate their own imaginations. Although "afro-kitsch" representations and tropicalist negrophilic desire is (re)produced in these spaces,[5] attention to personal agency and cultural tenacity of the so-called natives reveals not only various levels of self-making strategies at work but also pleasure and joy through cultural expression. Following Robin D. G. Kelley, "though they may also reflect and speak to the political and social world of black communities, expressive cultures are not simply mirrors of social life or expressions of conflicts, pathos, and anxieties" (1998: 41).

Discursive Sleight of Hand

Race, Sex, Gender

2

> I am interested here primarily in what we might call discursive and iconic fortunes and misfortunes, facilities, abuses, or plain absences that tend to travel from one generation of kinswomen to another, not unlike love and luck, or money and real estate.
>
> ——HORTENSE SPILLERS, "Interstices: A Small Drama of Words"

AMALIA AND I ARE PREPARING supper together in the kitchen—once the pantry of the large in-town house of a wealthy family from Cadíz, currently rumored to be living in several homes in Miami that recall the former grandeur of this one. Located in the Havana neighborhood of Santo Suarez, the large house, now much in need of repair, is subdivided into four one-bedroom apartments with three to five family members living in each. I have brought *quimbombó* (okra), garlic and onions, and some locally made tomato paste from the *agromercado* (local agricultural produce market), which I purchased in Cuban pesos for this meal with Amalia's *compañero* (companion or lover) Dani and other friends. The frozen chicken parts and enough cooking oil to last a few weeks, however, meant walking several blocks farther to a store that trades in U.S. dollars and paying about the same amount one would pay in the United States.[1]

Before folks trickle into her home to talk, laugh, drink, sing, and then drink, laugh, and talk some more well into the night, I chat with Amalia, who is fifty-two years old, about men and sex and the economics of men and sex. While talking over the daily chore of separating dry rice and beans from the small stones and sticks that end up in the mix, she waxes poetic when I make a joke about the fact that although *no hay* (there is none) and *no es fácil* (it ain't easy) are repeated in Cuban households as if catechism, there is reportedly never any lack of sugar in Cuban households, just like it is said that there is never a lack of sex between lovers here. The following moment in my conversation with Amalia illustrates common sense articulations between racial, color, regional, and gender differences. This will bring us to a consideration of the foundations of racial, gender, and sexual ideologies, and the disparate intentions these ideologies serve.

AMALIA: . . . *!Azúcar!* [we both laugh at her imitation of Cubana superstar Celia Cruz, and Amalia turns in the cramped cooking space to ignite her butane gas–powered stove] . . . No, we would know that things are really bad if we did not have sugar. . . . Well, here in Cuba it is not like the United States. We are maybe silly because we do not know better than to be happy even when we are miserable. During the Special Period, sugar saved many of my neighbors . . . We *ate* sugar water like in the moment before the triumph of the Revolution when campesinos had nothing but guarapo (sugar-cane juice) to drink. [pause]

. . . Produce sugar, tobacco, and rum . . . and make love. They say we do that very well, right? I am sure that Dani tells you this, and it is true. When you do not have a lot, that is what you do." [laughing] And men like to do it a lot, especially those hot Orientales [people from Oriente, or the eastern region of Cuba], like him.

JAFARI: Really? People from Oriente are more hot? More "horny," [in English] you mean?

AMALIA: Yes. Well [laughing], the weather is hot like Africa, and there is less mixture. Like Africa. It is beautiful there, and simple. Life is not so fast like Havana. People are amiable and laid back and natural. With men from Oriente, I have never had a problem like I have with other men . . .

JAFARI: . . . Why do you say sugar and tobacco and rum like it is a trinity—like that rap song "A lo Cubano"?[2] What relations do sugar and sex have?

AMALIA: [laughing at my awkward construction of "relaciones *entre* de sexo y azucar"] We say that sugar is very important for Cuba . . . and I have said that it helped to keep us alive in times even more difficult than at this moment. It is the most important crop we have.[3]

JAFARI: . . . Oh, I mean to ask why you put them together—sugar and sex. It reminds me of Fernando Ortiz—*Cuban Counterpoint* . . .

Fernando Ortiz did not invent this opposition in his canonical book *Cuban Counterpoint: Tobacco and Sugar,* and neither was he the first to theoretically exploit these "natural" differences. But his analysis does in fact offer a striking metaphorical précis of articulations between and among race, class, gender, and nation in Cuba. The real history of Cuba is (indeed) in the history of its intermeshed "transculturation" (F. Ortiz 1995b: 32). But the complex, even "antiphonal," relationship that Ortiz points out constitutes racial/sexual terror. His concept of transculturation sees back-and-forth transversals of ideas, people, and objects making culture, but it is just as much another theory of mestizáje. The conditions of the production of *Cuban Counterpoint,* in which Ortiz introduced the term "transculturation," in addition to his long list of other books and articles on African culture in Cuba, further illuminate the relationships between what Fernando Coronil would call the occidental world, or the western/northern center, and the Spanish Creole elite. This Spanish Creole elite produced and, as I shall argue, now reinscribes the discursive death of blackness.

Anyone who has attended preuniversitario (high school) in Cuba since the triumph of the Revolution will be able to hold court on the importance of sugar and tobacco as industrial products, touchstones for Cuban culture, and metaphors for sex and sexuality. This is a result not only of the prestige of Cuban tobacco as an export product, and the sheer ubiquity of sugar and tobacco on the island, but also to remind Cubans of the great sugar production pushes, *la zafra,* of the 1960s and 1970s, which included brigades of city people—both Cubans and international solidarity workers—being deployed to the provinces to join in cutting and processing cane. Thus from colonial mercantilism through today, sugar has had special significance to the survival of the island. Amalia is a social worker, and she is therefore somewhat familiar with Fernando Ortiz apropos his work describing African culture and its putative concomitant criminality and lasciviousness. Her opinion of him is not very high. As the daughter of a physician and a teacher, she is part of a well-educated and respectable black family for whom Ortiz's drumming, dancing sorcerers had been an embarrassment. She has read the work of his teacher Cesare Lombroso, the famous criminologist, and attended workshops on the "social ills" putatively related to Abakuá, which have referred to his studies.

Fernando Coronil, in his introduction to the new edition of *Cuban Counterpoint* (1995), as well as in his *The Magical State* (1997), recuperates Ortiz's notion of transculturation—a theoretic improvement on the anthropological concept of acculturation—as a subaltern critique of occidentalism. There is no doubt that Ortiz includes Africans and their descendants as important constituents of Cuban culture; rather, what is at issue here is the characterization of the quality of that participation. Ortiz's preoccupation, if not racial and sexual essentialism, makes only a *slight* move, to *cultural* essentialism. Following Hortense Spillers's provocation in the epigraph to this chapter, my aim here is to begin a genealogical inquiry into the co-construction and interarticulation of race/sex/gender in Cuba. I begin by uncovering Fernando Ortiz's concept of transculturation, which finds expression in popular Cuban culture as well as in Latin Americanist scholarship. After a close look at the particular moves that Ortiz makes here, I compare related sleights of racial and sexual formation in Cuba and in other sites in the Americas. I analyze the material effects of mixing discourses on those who seem still insoluble in this alchemy practiced by civil society and by the state.

Ortiz's Manichean moves in the foundational Cuban studies text *Cuban Counterpoint: Tobacco and Sugar*, is expressed as follows: African is to European as male is to female as tobacco is to sugar. These metaphorical constructs have unexpected alignments that precisely do not, as Coronil claims, "destabilize," but rather reinforce notions of a fixed polarity. Here tobacco and sugar represent human actors as well as material things looked at in terms of a complex "fugue," according to Antonio Benitez-Rojo (1992), expressing a Cuban race/color, gender, and sexual *common sense*. Ortiz points out that this *contrapunteo*, or counterpoint, is appropriate and quintessentially Cuban, and he gives examples of the "antiphonal liturgies, erotic controversy . . . and versified counterpoint" in Cuban folk culture—mostly performed by African-descended Cubans—by sexing, racing, and assigning class characteristics to sugarcane and tobacco. Although this allegory that prefaces his more clearly functionalist text is relatively short, it provides the logic through which his explanation of the history, culture, and political economy of Cuba emerges. Ortiz seems here to valorize Afro-Cuban culture, yet he reifies the vision of black Cubans themselves as indolent, superstitious, and sensual producers of music and dance, which Cuba must transform to assert its singularity among other nations. A normative, or more precisely, naturalizing discourse is deployed here, in which (tobacco) blackness is the counterpoint against which whiteness is defined, and femininity is the counterpoint to masculinity. Ortiz begins his allegory with a litany of "amazing contrasts" between "dark tobacco and high yellow sugar," which I quote here at length to give a sense of the breadth of his allegory:

> Sugar cane and tobacco are all contrast. It would seem that they were moved by a rivalry that separates them from their very origins . . . one is white, the other dark. Sugar is sweet and odorless, tobacco bitter and aromatic. Always in contrast! Food and poison, waking and drowsing, energy and dream, delight of the flesh and delight of the spirit, sensuality and thought, the satisfaction of an appetite and the contemplation of a moment's illusion, calories of nourishment and puffs of fantasy, undifferentiated and commonplace anonymity from the cradle and aristocratic individuality wherever it goes, medicine and magic, reality and deception, virtue and vice. Sugar is she; tobacco is he. Sugar cane was a gift of the gods, tobacco of the devils; she is the daughter of Apollo, he is the offspring of Persephone. (1995b: xix–xx)

At the same time that Ortiz presents these contrasts, he recuperates machista notions of women as flighty and consumerist and he casts the mulata in the role: "Tobacco is dark, ranging from black to mulato; sugar is light, ranging from mulato to white. Tobacco does not change its color. It is born dark and dies the color of its race" (1995b: 9). Here again, blackness is a stable sign in a universe of hybridity: "Sugar changes its coloring; it is born brown and whitens itself; at first it is a syrupy mulata and in this state pleases the common taste; then it is bleached and refined until it can pass for white, travel all over the world, reach all mouths, and bring a better price, climbing to the top of the social ladder." Sugar—cast as any light-skinned mulata/o or Cuban/ Spanish Creole is seen as a social climber. She has high-class aspirations, though she is born of humble origins. Here is a retelling of Celia Valdez and the often-repeated tragic story of the social-climbing mulata. The mulata who, as much as she whitens, can only meet with tragedy in the end if she seeks to be something she is not. Ortiz tells us that "sugar is assimilated in its entirety." He avers that like women, sugar is constitutive of "sensible pragmatism and social integration," and there is "no rebellion or challenge in sugar, nor resentment, nor brooding suspicion, but humble pleasure" (16). Tobacco, on the other hand, is the "noble" child of the devil, which seduces with the promise of intoxication and danger. Satisfied with its position, it does not seek to "climb" and is not nourishing or medicinal, but nonetheless comes to represent Cuba outside of the island.

The effect of these moves can be read on various levels, which speaks to the complexity of this contrapunteo. One level of abstraction finds that, so objectified, tobacco (blackness) and sugar (feminine/feminized) can easily and rightly be consumed and enjoyed. The consumer—Ortiz himself, but also other elite subjects within and outside of Cuba—may enjoy the fruits of both, mostly from offstage. On another level, we must engage and critique the Creole or otherwise Hispano–Latin American intellectual project here. While Fernando Coronil is certainly correct in his critique of Western (read northern) imperial alchemy, we cannot allow to go by the magical sleight of hand, which seeks to decenter occidentalist discourses in order to re-recover the European inheritance of *real* whiteness, for Hispano-latin Americans. Coronil avers that "*Cuban Counterpoint* was the product of a career that sought, from multiple angles, to interpret Cuban society, analyze the sources of its 'backwardness,' and valorize the distinctive aspects of its culture" (F. Ortiz 1995b: xvii). And the civilization that Cubans needed, according to Ortiz, was European. Coronil notes that "against the imperial alchemy that turns a Western particularity into a model of universality, *Cuban Counterpoint* calls attention to the play of globally interconnected particularities" (xiv). The play, or process by which particularities are globally interconnected, is transculturation, which is thus a civilizing project. Ortiz cannot valorize African culture in Cuba for its music and languages and religions without, in the same fell swoop, preferring European refinement and reason. His alternative conception of Latin American development revalorizes popular and regional cultures but maintains an evolutionary framework that finds African cultures backward and Western European cultures the height of civilization.

The process of transculturation takes two phases: one is deculturation, or the loss of culture, and the other is neoculturation. The former is the loss of a group's original culture(s), and the latter is the adoption of a new culture that is born of contact with other culture(s). Rather than seeing transculturation in terms of a value-free cultural process, therefore, I want to consider it as another sort of imperial or (neo)colonial project. Although it takes place in the margins of the Caribbean and Latin America, this recasting of *mestizaje*,[4] seeking as it does the production and maintenance of more "whitenesses" at the same time that it reserves the privileges of masculinity, is no less a (neo)colonial project. Decentering provides Latin America—and, not unrelated, also the elite subjects that produce it[5]—with another form of whitening. Indigenous, African-descended and Asian people are, as in Eurocentric discourses, retrenched to the margins in this decentered vision that allows mestizos or Euro-Creoles to garner the colonial privileges of whiteness, among which is identifying a center. Reimagining Cuba as the mulata/criolla who has fallen by way of her mixture yet also is climbing upward (northward and westward) is a sort of decentering discourse, but for more reasons than Coronil asserts. He would take exception to this reading. As he presents it, decentering, which follows Ortiz's transculturation, is about the ways in which Latin America(ns) have been made marginal to rhetorics of modernity that see that process and movement flowing out of the European center, and only eventually and weakly finding the far reaches of the southern parts of the Americas. But the Americas, constituted as a place of "new world" discovery and conquest, is always already modern. Modernity begins with the invasion and conquest of indigenous Americans and the invasion and forced immigration of Africans. The very foundations of modernity were first perfected in *ingenios* (sugar plantations and refineries) driven by the labor of enslaved Africans. As Sidney Mintz's classic work *Sweetness and Power* (1985) details, the ingenios were pre-Fordist factories of a sort, and were therefore a model of things to come in industrialization in the Americas. Whitening discourses too often have the effect of the aestheticizing or eliding of these violent histories of contact between Europeans and Africans, and Europeans and Native Americans, throughout history. Our concern here is with those recipients of "clash," "disarticulation," and very real "violence of conquest and colonization" (xiii) that Guillén hauntingly tells us lose blood on (cane) fields in which whitenesses are reproduced:

> El negro
> Junto el cañaveral
> El yanqui
> Sobre el cañaveral
> La tierra
> Bajo el cañaveral
> !Sangre que se nos va!
> [The black next to the cane field;
> the Yankee over the canefield;
> the land under the canefield.
> How our blood is lost!] (1967: 15)

It is not enough to merely point out that Western Europe produces hegemonic power knowledges, in order to create different ones. Gesturing toward a history of violence and the horrors of historic slavery while rescuing the privileges of whiteness for elite Latin Americans without acknowledgment of the continuing effects of this particular brand of modernity and modern racisms created and perpetrated in the region does not constitute a subaltern theory. Decentering is not useful for a progressive project unless the ways in which the signs and status of whiteness are *recentered* in the Americas is acknowledged. The celebration of mestizáje is a celebration of black holocaust. As Ortiz writes: "There was the transculturation of a steady stream of African Negroes coming from all the coastal regions of Africa . . . all of them snatched . . . their own cultures destroyed and crushed under the *weight of the cultures in existence here*, like sugar cane ground in the rollers of the mill" (1995b: xxv).

The story of tobacco and sugar takes a more clearly functionalist turn with a discussion of the ways each crop is nurtured, harvested, and prepared. Ortiz compares the production conditions of tobacco and sugar, respectively, as relating to the immigration of whites on one hand, the slave trade on the other; liberty and slavery; delicacy versus brute force. Later on, the seeming inconsistency of white or "high yellow" sugar being associated with brute force becomes clearer. In an interesting inversion of the trope of the feminine as needing constant attention, here it is tobacco that "requires delicate care" by white specialists recruited from Spain to raise it, while sugar, the large cash crop "can look after itself," notwithstanding, of course, the enormous efforts of the enslaved Africans who cultivated, harvested, and processed it for European and North American tables.

In this section of *Cuban Counterpoint,* sugar becomes associated with brute force because it must be crushed and eviscerated in order to whiten and become saleable. Likewise, Africans had to have their cultures "crushed." Women, to return to the originally gendered "sugar is she," must in this scheme be crushed enough to yield consumable *sweetness. Sweet* men and boys threaten incoherence, and women deemed *too* dark for recognition of femininity, or those who refuse to "yield their sweetness" are cast as other or elided because of, finally, illegibility within this peculiar grammar. Ortiz insists throughout on the maleness and virility of dark tobacco. Tobacco is to Ortiz a "boastful and swaggering thing, like an oath of defiance springing erect from the lips" (1995b: 15). What is racialized as black is also virility, sexual power, and sexual aggression. Tobacco is a *guapo,* the tough guy who represents, following Nadine Fernandez, a completely Cuban invention and style (1996a) that is also resonant with so-called cool pose or the aesthetics of flossin' and swagger. To wit, Ortiz contends, "One might even say that tobacco affords satisfaction to the touch and the sight," unlike sugar: "What smoker has not passed his hands caressingly over the rich brevas or regalias, held delicately between lips and fingers . . . titillating" (1995b: 9).

This homophilia reminds me of a heterosexual-identified respondent who confided in me, "No me gusta los hombres. Yo soy heterosexual, pero . . . [I do not like men. I am a heterosexual, but . . .]." Months later, I returned to this theme, and this man revealed that during his compulsory military training "as a youth," he had sex with—that is, had been penetrated and had penetrated, orally and anally—one or two of his comrades. "For the sight," writes Ortiz, "is not a cigar in the hands of youth, a foretaste of manhood?" Considering the preoccupation among (Cuban) men with penis size and function, and its relationship to one's masculinity, one can hardly resist reference to Ortiz's challenge to "tell me what *vitola* (size and shape of cigar) you smoke and I will tell you who you are," as he compares long, thin esplendido cigars to short fat brevas in relation to power and personality. What is more, at the end of smoking, Ortiz tells us, there is a "rapt ecstasy that comes over them . . . leaving in the air . . . signs like ineffable promises of redemption" (1995b: 9).

Ortiz's elegy to the "pristine simplicity" of the cigar—"naked, unadorned, without the adulterations, mixtures, wrappings, perfume, and refinements of a decadent civilization" betrays his obsession: "natural," unadorned, and un-civilized African masculinity. In another sign, even in this homosocial fantasy the notion of "macho" or hypermasculinity is held up as preferred to "per-verted" sweet and perfumed *mariconeria* (faggotry). Women, he says, "smoke more perhaps than their hardy mates . . . but limit themselves to cigarettes, the babies of cigars . . . all wrapped in rice paper, and with gold tips, even perfumed, sweetened and perverted like effeminate youths" (15).[6] Predictably, in the last instance comes the marriage of tobacco and sugar, "in which there have never been any conflicts between them . . . Just a bit of friendly bick-ering, which should end, like the fairy tales, in living happily ever after" in heterosexual marriage (xxiv). And through their coupling, alcohol (rum) is conceived, in the womb of wanton sugar. Like all fairytales, this one too is didactic.

Why indeed should this fairytale not end happily ever after? This resolu-tion through the nation-making strategy of heterosexual coupling and pro-creation within marriage is an illustration of bell hooks's contention that not only have dominators often used sexuality as a domain in which to enact their domination, but "sexuality does not just provide gendered metaphors for col-onization, it is a process of colonization (and national construction) in itself" (1990: 57). That this is imagined as the heterosexual coupling of masculinized blackness to feminized whiteness reveals the obsessive fantasy/fear of Pen-insulares and white Creoles. This flight of the imagination is of course his-torically unfounded. While white women's bodies were carefully "protected" from just these scenarios, the bodies of black women and men—constituted as chattel—were offered to be "sold" by white men to other white men and their families, including white women. Ninety pages of Ortiz's book, repre-senting oppositions from the herbological to the industrial to the aesthetic to the ethical, economic, and political, are, as if by magic, disappeared as tobacco "takes" sugar as a wife and alchemically begets the mulata/o: rum. Ortiz sug-gests, in his historical-allegorical-theoretical treatise, a future for Cuba that is akin to his support for whitening schemes favoring European immigration, during his tenure as a member of the Cuban legislature (1995b: xvii). Beyond this, the notion of naturalized mestizáje/mulatáje is also a meta-archipelagic (Benítez-Rojo 1992) prophetic hope for the entire Caribbean, whose history of sugar and tobacco (i.e., European Creole and African) is similar to Cuba's own, and is aestheticized, celebrated, or rendered innocuous or serendipitous by various scholars.

The "future" for Coronil and the "unknown . . . differential equation" is transculturation, which is a process of alchemy, mapping almost seamlessly as mestizáje—always already the ethos of Caribbean culture. This sleight of hand (transculturation/mulatáje) "marries" industry to geography to culture to history to nature to society in a way which, although falling short of the biological determinism and positivism that Ortiz had originally espoused, nevertheless presents an argument so resonant with the prevailing hegemonic discourse that it seems to have the force of truth. The effect is, in fact, to take the oppositions of tobacco and sugar as natural, and the "marriage" of the two as the happy resolution. In this marriage there is no real discord because the fundamental issues are seen to neatly exist in a heterosexually productive union of opposites. This is implicitly one in which the female (feminized) subject is believed to have her greatest expression as a caretaker of the masculine(ized) and the children. In this case, the children represent the Cuban nation. In any case, the magic ingredient for this "resolution" is active, obsessive forgetting. The fundamental differences between men and women and between white and black are "gradually ironed out," Ortiz says, by "machines and capitalism . . . [which] dehumanized their economy, and made their problems more and more similar" (1995b: 93). Here is the rub of the discord between tobacco and sugar (i.e., between men and women; black and white; macho, maricón, and marimacha) in Cuba today. Currently, black Cubans find themselves not simply consumed by a new alchemy post–Special Period; instead, ironed out by the "new and improved" machine of global capitalism, they create their own subaltern alchemy, or black magic. In the next section, I want to examine some resistance to the logic of the contrapunteo and myths of mestizaje in Cuba before the 1959 Revolution and its consequences, at the moment of its triumph, and in other places in the Americas.

Our Americas / Our "Race Problem"

José Martí, the intellectual hero of Cuban independence, invoked the biological truth that there is no such thing as "race" in order to present a "colorblind" vision in his Our Americas. While this vision is often uncritically embraced as antiracist, so-called colorblindness must be examined more thoroughly. Martí's vision elides historical differences and sets up formidable barriers against claims of racism or colorism. As he wrote, "There can be no racial animosity, because there are no races" (1891: 93). Thus the denial of "race" and conditional inclusion was one of the rhetorical linchpins of the Cuba Libre (Cuban independence) movement. In Cuba, mestizáje (more appropriately, whitening) became the established ideology of nationalists because it could accrue to Afro-Cubans a measure of belonging—that is, recognizing their crucial role in winning the war to end Spanish colonialism, while maintaining the status quo of European Creole (structurally white) control. As Aline Helg (1995), Alejandro de la Fuente (2001), Ada Ferrer (1999a), and others have already shown, for black and other Cuban patriots of color who had fought hard for their own emancipation and the independence of Cuba, the terms of the past were certainly not acceptable. But in lieu of liberation and full equality, they were offered José Martí's vision of a "raceless" (i.e., "mestizo") Cuba. For people of color, equality was tied to questions of merit, virtue, patriotism, and education, while value was assumed a priori for Peninsulares and Creoles. Yet, even in the absence of equality, Cuban nationalism held that blacks "should be grateful for the abolition of slavery and recognize the great sacrifices that whites . . . had made to 'liberate' them" (de la Fuente 2001: 29). This is prescient perhaps of current race debates in the United States, Brazil, and other places on the appropriateness of measures like affirmative action that are meant as reparative gestures for the effects of slavery and systematic racism. Following the social Darwinism and positivism then in vogue, the "race problem" was a problem of the person of color who, the reasoning goes, had been liberated from slavery by the altruism of wealthy white people. Thus, race and racism could not be talked about as a social issue but rather a cultural one—namely, a problem of innate "ethnic instincts" and aesthetic perceptions that time would correct through "indirect" and "gradual" means of mestizáje.[7] That is, in order to work, whitening must involve the (at least) social death of blackness. The massacre of 1912 that resulted in somewhere between five to six thousand actual deaths during a racial siege at the hands of Cuban soldiers, is evidence that the death of black(ness) is not merely a metaphor.[8] Having gained little ground with a national government that offered only token inclusion, the Partido Independiente de Color (People of Color Party) and other groups of blacks advocated supporting separate institutions and movements that would ensure a "rightful share" for Cubans of color, and sought to end United States intervention in Cuba. Helg demonstrates that this "Afro-Cuban consciousness and autonomous challenge incited the white elite to make more explicit the ideology of white supremacy" (1995: 16), which was expressed through various means including this heinous crime. In order to prevent the Partido Independiente de Color from participating in elections and thereby forcing recognition of their issues, black supporters were massacred. This bears repetition. Organized people of color who dared challenge the prevailing racial hegemony were killed. Helg provides exhaustive historical context and detail, for this issue; my aim here is merely to place black Cubans' continued consumption of pre-revolutionary rhetorics of inclusion in the context of racial terror and racial trauma. Helg quotes the daily newspaper *El día*'s account of the massacre from May 26, 1912:

> This [demonstration by Independísta supporters] is a racist uprising, an uprising of blacks, in other words, an enormous and a common danger. . . . conceived as black as hatred. . . . They do not have any purpose. . . . Driven by atavistic, brutal instincts and passions: they devote themselves to robbery, pillage, murder, and rape. These are, in all parts and latitudes of the world, the characteristics of race struggles. . . . Cuban society . . . with its . . . Spanish civilization . . . prospects of wonderful, splendid civilization is getting ready to defend itself against barbarism . . . this is the free and beautiful America defending herself against a clawing scratch from Africa. (Quoted in Helg 1995: 196)

The trauma visited upon black Cubans does not diminish. Racial terror does not end with the abolition of slavery or throughout the pre-revolutionary period. Racial terror is extended through symbolic violence. As Helg states:

> If the myth of racial equality helped to keep Afro-Cubans in check, it was not sufficient to stir the white population into active repression of nonconformist Afro-Cubans. Racism needs the support of caricatures and distortions . . . therefore, efficient icons of fear are drawn from deeply rooted racial and sexual stereotypes [including] . . . the Haitian Revolution . . . [and the] caricature of the black brujo and ñañigo . . . [which] embodied in the male image of the black beast and the black rapist of white women and in the image of a black mulata seductress. (1995: 18)

Sadly, the legacies of slavery and the pre-revolutionary era are evident in the contemporary lived experiences of the entire population. It is extant in the rhetorics of so-called inclusion that find blacks to be bestial, insolent, hypersexual objects who, if not already sufficiently mixed, are eminently expendable. Cuba seems to have been struck not only (color) blind but also dumb—silencing race and thereby reinscribing racial terror. Cuba has been loath to address "the race question" and is therefore currently ill equipped to deal with the particular material and psychic trauma in lived black experience. If we are going to talk about moving beyond or ameliorating racial inequality or "improving race relations" in the Americas, then transatlantic chattel slavery, postemancipation racial terror, and continued racial trauma and material disenfranchisement must form a large part of the background against which we take up these issues. Otherwise, mestizáje and other ideologies of mixing are rendered as innocuous, or worse, utopic, visions of *Our Americas* and beyond: *free and beautiful America defending herself against a clawing scratch from Africa.*

Gender, racial, and sexual hegemonies are constituted by national elites and disseminated to the masses as innocuous and stable "Cuban culture" that carries the force of "nature." The shift from severely controlled and ordered difference to the revolution's attempt at erasure of difference was in fact discursively sleight in Cuba—that is, shifting political ideologies while leaving racial and sexual ideologies firmly in place. Of course, the ideologies through which these hegemonies are announced are found throughout the Americas; for example, as evidenced in current debates on racial pluralism or multiculturalism in Brazil and Nicaragua. According to Peter Wade (2001), there is a tendency to look at twentieth-century history in Latin America as a move from nationalist modernist homogeneity that erased or severely controlled difference to a sort of postmodern multicultural heterogeneity; a move that he rightly asserts is forced in large part by the counterhegemonic tactics of oppressed minorities, particularly racial and ethnic minorities.

Premature calls to universalism, official multiculturalism, and discourses on diversity and multiculturalism in the Americas most often cloak within their high-sounding platitudes of cooperation the erasure of blackness itself, or at least the rights, citizenship, or autonomy claims of those who are less mixed than others. *Oh, how our blood is lost.* This has by now been well elaborated in a number of works, including Abdias do Nascimento's *Brazil: Mixture or Massacre?* (1989). Thus, we do not aspire to render yet another exposé of the fact that "racial mixture," mestizáje (or *mestiçagem*, in Portuguese), does not preclude racism in Latin America, or perhaps more controversial, that there are not or have not historically been synchronous whitening projects in the United States. But a short review is in order because these myths continue to persist.

João Costa Vargas in his essay "Hyperconsciousness of Race and Its Negation" (2004) explores the similar sleight of hand by which the dialectics of white supremacy work in Brazil. He argues that more-contemporaneous practices of representation of race in Brazil at once vehemently negate race at the same time that they are compulsively hyperconscious of it. This is certainly also true of Cuban independence–era rhetorics that have been rehabilitated in revolutionary discourses. In Cuba, the "party line" is, as I was told at first by a few respondents during my initial research foray to Cuba, that "race does not exist." I came to realize, however, that these individuals meant that the brand of state and institutional racial violence of the United States reported in Cuba does not exist there. But the common racial ideologies that have structured the political economy of the Americas do not merely slip off quietly into the dustbin of history.

In 1987, Nicaraguans finally confronted their racial and ethnic diversity (formerly understood as mestizo) by recognizing blacks and indigenous people of the Atlantic Coast (*costeños*), as both different from the mestizo majority and legitimately part of the nation. Nicaragua was among the first of the Latin American countries to adopt multicultural citizenship reforms. Juliet Hooker writes, however, that even with the special collective rights of costeño autonomy guaranteed in the constitution, not only do discourses of multicultural citizenship still carry the resonances of mestizo nationalism in which the nation was represented as mestizo and costeños as marginal interlopers, but also that multicultural citizenship has led to "the emergence of a new variant of this discourse, mestizo multiculturalism" (2005: 17). That is, after some sixty years of literary production, on the ground activism on the Atlantic coast, and politicking in the National Assembly, "many non-costeño legislators, understand collective rights whose intent was to recognize the specific entities of black and indigenous costeños as an acknowledgment of mestizaje" (19). Here we see a similar logic to the one in Cuba that insists that Cubans are at once "mixed" and therefore include all elements of African, indigenous, and Iberian elements while at the same time are exceptionally raceless—*color Cubano*. Hooker cites a Miskitu song, sung by artists from the Pacific coast, that she says repeats the phrase "Somos mestizos, con un gran diversidad cultural. Somos un país multingüe y multiracial" (2005: 39), which translated states, "We are mestizo [mixed Indigenous and European, but also precisely nonblack], with a great cultural diversity. We are a multilingual and multiracial nation." The hegemonic logic of mestizáje thereby overwrites attempts by those on the margins of nationalist discourse to claim space within the nation—even if that space, as in the Nicaraguan case, is alongside and figured within regional autonomy.

Despite the historical and contemporary realities of antiblack racism and racial terror in Latin America, scholars and politicos in the United States have long drawn simplistic comparisons between race relations in the United States, Cuba, and especially Brazil. By the 1990s, this turns to notions of "diversity" and "multiculturalism." The argument by Americanist scholars and popular pundits usually begins with the mistaken assumption or historical lie that race making in the United States is so peculiar that it has made for a singular binodal racial formation of blacks and whites. While this is certainly a dominant view, it has never been the view from below. It is not the practice in "ethnic white" communities and among immigrants to the United States who have successively whitened. It is not reflected in black communities wherein in many instances, one's proximity to whiteness is sometimes as important as "the real thing," when proximity—*Creole, high yellow, quadroon, biracial,* or in fact *passe blanc* (passing as white)—are all that one could hope for. That is, access to further whitening, through intermarriage, class climbing, and educational attainment, for example, was conditioned by one's ability to pass from the blackest of the black to versions of hybridity that can be appreciated in phenotype. These are, of course, not merely symbolic gestures but attempts at managing the material effects of racism. Shirley Thompson's historical reading of United States Creole (and) black *"lieu de mémoire,* a site where 'memory crystallizes and secretes itself'" (2001: 233) not only methodologically opens up the usual archives and standard ways of reading race and imbrications of citizenship, nation, gender, and sexuality in the United States, but also reveals, germane to the current case of the death of blackness, the deep historical ambivalences and struggles on the ground, around so-called mixed race, hybrid, black (and) Creole of color subjects. Thompson's subject, Toucoutou, "sued her neighbor for slander. The neighbor had committed the insufferable offense of calling Toucoutou a woman of color." This "slander" threatened to render her marriage to a moneyed white man *plaçage*—that is, precisely not marriage, but nonetheless socially recognized institutionalized "concubinage" practiced by French Creole men and "outside" women of color.[9] Read from below—the black and avowedly Creole of color perspective on the affair—the case of this "climbing," and now certainly "tragic mulatta," adjudged by the Louisiana court to indeed be of African descent, became a *cause célèbre* of the day and was immortalized in a Creole song, a situation reminiscent of the cautionary Celia Valdez stories by Villaverde.

Gary Nash, the former American Historical Association president, echoing the multiculturalism ethos of Klor de Alva, opines that "what is needed is a 'pan-ethnic, pan-racial, anti-racist sensibility.' . . . Only through hybridity—not only in *physical race crossing* but in our minds as a shared pride in and identity with hybridity—can our nation break the 'stranglehold that racialist hermeneutics has over cultural identity'" (1995: 962; emphasis mine). Nash and others see mestizáje as the enemy of racial absolutism and hold that "racial blending" undermines the master idea that race is an irreducible marker (1995: 60). Even reading this generously, it betrays a naive racial analysis. While on the surface, advocating nonessentialist "mixing," this reasoning actually works to reify biological or otherwise essential notions of race. Despite the various moves back and forth, the rumbas, the antiphonies, and the transitions between unlike elements, the underlying logic at work here and in the Cuban contrapunteo, or transcultural counterpoint, is thus what Carole Boyce Davies refers to as "unicentricity" (1999). Boyce Davies is precisely not arguing, as Coronil does, for a recentering in which a new Latin American center is constructed. In fact, she critiques Ngũgĩ wa Thiong'o, for what she finds is his wish to "relocate the center" (1999: 92). Neither does she suggest a sort of reimagination, following what I will call here ludic or "Benetton ad" multiculturalists who merely want a representation of multihued, polysexual, and multiple-gendered harmony without all the messiness of actual individuals and their issues—quite the contrary in fact. Boyce Davies's definition, she writes, emerges out of her observations of the relational operations of

Eurocentrism and Afrocentrism, both of which, she avers, share a logic that "legitimizes its gains, seeking and expanding the set of peripheries that it gradually pulls into its orbit. . . . thus, inevitably . . . becom(ing) a colonialist project . . . the basis for domination and control" (96).

BioPower / GenderFuck

As Michel Foucault famously averred, "We . . . are in a society of 'sex,' or rather a society 'with a sexuality': the mechanisms of power are addressed to the body, to life, to what causes it to proliferate, to what reinforces the species, its stamina, its ability to dominate, or its capacity for being used. Through the themes of health, progeny, race, the future of the species, the vitality of the social body, power spoke *of* sexuality and *to* sexuality; the latter was not a mark or a symbol, it was an object and target. Power delineated it, aroused it, and employed it as the proliferating meaning that always had to be taken over again, less it escape; it was an effect with a meaning value" (1980: 148). Sexuality stands at the nexus of ideas of culture, nationhood, and race in Cuba. After all, it is the "mixing" of Africans, Iberians, indigenous people, and Asians—in cases consensual, coerced, and violently imposed—that has produced the majority population today. In high and low cultural representations, the nation is constructed as a people with various inheritances, including sensual and erotic power. This has its roots in the slave system in which black bodies were the express "property" of white men, and white women their implicit property. While sexuality and sex itself is certainly not "determined" by biology in the simplistic ways averred by sociobiology and newly biologically deterministic projects; it is articulated to the social and cultural lived experience of race and racism through historical processes and cultural production. Sexuality is much more inclusive a concept than the limited reading of sexuality as "sexual orientation," or the conflation of the concept of sexuality with homosexuality. These limited conceptions of sexuality are heterosexist, just as rendering women the problem category in gender is based upon sexist assumptions of manhood as an unmarked or empty category. My respondents and friends joked that sex is as necessary as sugar is to the Cuban diet, and as plentiful. Additionally, to talk about sexuality is to talk not only about the everyday lived experience of the sexual(ualized) body and its reproduction, but also about the cultures, histories, and political-economic realities of the nation (region, diaspora, globe), and the historicity, imagination, desires, and intentions of the sexual(ualized) subject.

Before 1959, Cuban sexual ideology was characterized by an uneasy concordance of Iberian and African cultural and religious values that both upheld hierarchy and patriarchy, although in substantially different ways. Roman Catholic teaching held masculine sexuality as wanton and therefore requiring particular controls. While the most important of these controls are marriage and self-denial, for the expression of desires deemed inappropriate under the rubric of "sacred" and socially sanctioned marriage within the racial/class group: sexual encounters with lower-class or darker women and men provide crucial outlets and loopholes in this logic. This rationalization steeped in Roman Catholic and colonial rhetorics provided a foundation for the access of white men who required sating of "baser desires" not only through structural rape in the slave system but also through sexual coercion or some measure of consent, after the abolition of slavery at least legally freed black bodies from a system in which they could neither decline nor consent to sex with their "master." To justify this, Africans were cast as always already debauched. According to Ortiz, for example, the sexual practices of African descendents were "corrupt." Ortiz's claim that the "African psyche" is prone to "uncontrollable sensuality," including practices of oral and anal sex and sex outside of marriage (1913), contributed to the imagination of sensationalistic popular novelists who stereotyped black sexuality as pathological. Sexualities of Africans and African descendents were, of course, no more uncontrolled or debauched than those of Europeans. Africans had come from cultures in which polyamory and various levels of female autonomy in particular areas outside of their homes were acceptable. Additionally, at least in Yoruba or Lucumí culture, contextual transgender practice and performance was also accepted—the gods themselves crossed gender and sexual grounds, just as they crossed lines of living and dead, spiritual and corporeal. Family and social formations of sexuality and gender were different from those of Europeans, which Foucault has famously revealed as characterized not by "repression" as such, but more precisely by an obsession with the known and imagined practices of intimate others—the colonial subjects—as objects of fear, desire, and curiosity.

Women's Bodies as Battlegrounds
of Honor and Shame

Hortense Spillers offers that "sexuality is the locus of great drama—perhaps the fundamental one—and, as we know, wherever there are actors, there are scripts, scenes, gestures and reenactments, both enunciated and tacit" (1984: 153). She convincingly argues that the black woman—invisible and unspoken (*for*) in public discourse on sexuality, yet everywhere commented on, vilified and central to the way the social is constituted, "became the principal point of passage between the human and the non-human world . . . At this level of radical discontinuity in the 'great chain of being,' black is vestibular to culture" (155). Witness, then, the work that Ortiz did as a statesman to increase immigration of Spaniards to Cuba so as to ensure a *thinning* of the darkest hues of color Cubano. If black, following Spillers, is vestibular to culture, the womb of the black woman must, therefore, be policed (at least, but also "used") in order to render a *civilized "mixed" Cuban nation*.

The hegemonic vision of Latin American womanhood has at its center the chaste and morally superior figure of Mary, Mother of Jesus—the archetype of marianismo or hembrismo. In this political economy of gender, spheres of interest are divided in machista/hembrista agreement, finding women in the home (*casa*, "house") and men in the public sphere (*calle*, "street"). Long-suffering wives stay home with children and pray for their men, who are out earning money and cavorting in the public sphere; virgins await men who can financially support such wives revered as spiritually superior and morally clean, while men retain social dominance. To mark a woman black, especially *negra*, is thus to introduce incoherence to the—again ironic, or "magical"—logic of whitening. To call on black womanhood is to signify the non-Christian African woman whose body was bought and sold—constituted as sexual chattel. She suckled white people's children, and bore children conceived with men to whom she was not (necessarily) married and who could not financially support her or protect her from harm (ironically, other than her so-called owner). This image is antithetical to that of chastity, modesty, and fragility, putatively deserving of "respect" as the "weaker" or the "fairer" sex. She certainly cannot therefore bring "honor." These ideologies are variably *lived through* and *as* class, which can whiten or blacken, make invisible or visible, feminize or masculinize.

Throughout the Americas, sex/race ideology holds that proper white sexuality is the opposite of savage and debauched black sexuality, and the cultural mythology of mestizáje claims for itself variable elements of both at the same time—as long as the latter is appropriately suppressed. In Cuba and elsewhere, difference appears subtly colored by celebration of the mulata as an intervening character with less honor than the white woman but more than the dark-skinned negra. The mulata enjoys a complex flexibility that should not, however, be read as freedom. Her image is one of a bastard child born of an unsanctioned and often violent union—poised for ruination and tragedy because she is hopelessly between two worlds. The position and representation of the mulata in Cuban literature and culture has already been well elaborated by Verena Martinez-Alier (1974), Nadine Fernandez (1996a), and Vera Kutzinski (1993), among others. As the consummate liminal figure, the mulata is desired by white and black suitors alike, who seek to exploit what is posited as the mixture of respectable European femininity and beauty with unbridled African sexuality.[10] She can never be "respectable" in the white world. In the black world, putatively, she can never be trusted.

Dancing with Fidel, but to the Same Old Tune

Prerevolutionary discourses on blackness, gender, and sexuality and their relationship to the nation have been "'recovered,' modified, 'encased' and 'encrusted' in new forms" (Stoler 1995: 61) in revolutionary Cuba. To understand the seeming intransigence of racial and sexual ideologies in state and cultural institutions and practices demands an analysis of both what is currently happening on the ground, and what Gramsci would call the *long view* of history. The black Cuban scholar, Carlos Moore, is mostly correct in his assessment that "the Cuban Revolution was . . . a victory of the anti-imperialist segment of the white Cuban middle class" (1988: 5). Still, though Moore casts Fidel Castro and the revolutionary vanguard as callous racist elites, Peter Wade warns us that "the maintenance of a racial hegemony happens through the complex articulation of projects which are not necessarily coherently or intentionally racist" (2001: 847). Moreover, the revolution inarguably improved the relative position of black Cubans. Recently, Moore himself has clearly stated this (2008). And barring none, whatever their opinion of the contemporary political and economic situation, each of my black Cuban respondents refers to "before the Revolution" as a time of widespread corruption; control of the Cuban economy and government by the United States and its corporate interests (including organized crime); legal barriers to recourse for disenfranchised women and sexual minorities; wholesale political violence against anyone who opposed the order; and perennial targeting of poor blacks. Their vision is illustrated by the remarks of one of my respondents, Leudís Ferrer: "When they came down from the mountains . . . at the triumph of the Revolution, we were very happy. My cousins were there with them. I was too young, but there were many black men there . . . No more stepping in the street to move out of the way when a white person walks by . . . Now we can have some dignity. The Revolution gave all Cubans dignity, but especially Afro-Cubans who had been so despised. We could be men. Not that we were not men before, but we could be so in the eyes of the world." Ferrer's words betray the fact that the project of the Revolution was profoundly gendered as a masculine one, but also focus on the fact that it provided a space of dignity for black Cubans. Also inarguable, however, is that *even a revolution* has yet to undo the centuries of racist and sexist hegemony that have shaped the nation. As Fidel Castro, Raúl Castro, and others have admitted, "errors" were made. Still unacknowledged, however, are the ways in which racism and sexism undergird rhetorics and policies of racelessness, thereby leading to their hyperconscious negation.

Black intellectuals pushed the revolution to recognize the contributions of their communities and the fact that unlike the war of Independence, this revolution must acknowledge the contributions and particular difficulties of people of color. The black Cuban sociologist Juan René Betancourt Bencomo, writing in the popular Cuban magazine *Bohemia*, made explicit what had been circulating in middle-class Afro-Cuba since the unlikely qualified success of Fidel Castro and the revolutionary fighters at the Moncada Barracks in Santiago: there had been little reference to the revolution's program for racial reform other than rehashed rhetorics of racelessness. As Betancourt wrote, diplomatically but assertively:

It is impossible that anyone should believe, seriously and in good faith, that by ceasing to refer to "blacks" and "whites" the people will forget their existence, and racial discrimination will thus be liquidated by this miraculous method . . . For only a social force, supported by a government of the generosity and prestige of the present one, can realize the task of unleashing a new socioeconomic force . . . national integration . . . We harbor no fear that Fidel Castro may forget his black brothers. (Quoted in Moore 1988: 16)

Carlos Moore suggests that Castro's speech of March 22, 1959, was forced by comments by Bentancourt and potential unrest among black Cubans more than it was a commitment to racial justice. On March 22, 1959, Señor Ferrer listened to the speech in which Fidel Castro laid out the "party line" on race and racism in Cuba. Forty years later, he told me that "Fidel created a new universe for the man of color, for the black people in Cuba." Indeed, Castro's candor in breaking the silence about antiblack racism in Cuba was seen as "revolutionary." This speech, just a few months following the triumph of his July 26th Movement, announced important new policies based on the principle that continuation of segregation and lack of equal access would cripple national unity. Therefore, both access to jobs and educational facilities and access to recreational centers would be immediately open and available to all Cubans. These measures promised to eventually undo historical inequalities. Racism, and race, was to disappear. President Castro's actions did indeed open up a new world, which stood in stark contrast to legal racial segregation in the United States and the apartheid system of South Africa, where segregationists were using coercion, terror, and the law to fight education, accommodation, and housing desegregation and to enforce racist spatial practices. With this speech, the revolutionary's rhetoric on land reform, education, housing, and wealth distribution was articulated to institutional racism and racial discrimination that held the notion *juntos pero no revueltos*—together, but not mixed. Even if one regards this as another sleight of hand, its profound significance was not lost on anxious Cuban elites. According to René Depestre, the very next day after the speech in which Castro, by fiat, effectively removed legal barriers against blacks, the old motto linking communism and pro-black policies and sentiments recurred. Signs reading "Neither black nor red" appeared. As Depestre writes:

All the white petty bourgeois elements . . . became panic stricken . . . [that] Fidel Castro has invited Black men to invade the country's aristocratic sanctuaries to dance and revel with the vestal virgins who, until then, had managed to preserve themselves from the terrible radiations which emanate from black skin . . . (due to) negrophobia. . . . Very respectable white ladies left the country, stating that since Fidel's speech, Blacks had become impossible. (Quoted in Casal 1979: 6; emphasis mine)

The image of those vestal virgins (who seemingly magically and through much skill had somehow avoided black masculine "emanations") leaving forlornly and temporarily for Miami provides an irresistible and colorful retelling of Cuban "exile" narratives. Days later, Castro responded in a televised interview. This was addressed as much to the international community (read United States and Soviet Union) that he had been engaging since the days in the Sierra Maestra, as it was to the "white petty bourgeois elements" that Depestre cites and Moore counts Castro among. Fidel said, "I have dealt with this problem not to open old wounds, but rather to heal the deep wounds which have existed, since centuries ago, in the core of our nation" (quoted in C. Moore 1988: 7). In the interview, he attempted to quiet the "negrophobia" without being seen to backpedal too much. Substantiating Depestre's claims, Castro answered rumors that black men could, under this new racial regime, go into dance clubs expressly to dance with white women: "People ought to dance or stroll about with anyone they please. They must mingle with anyone they like. Who will force anyone here to dance with someone they dislike?" On the question of the red peril, however, Castro holds his ground: "In Cuba the only thing that everyone will be forced to dance with is this revolution!" He then goes on to state that "in Cuba, the exploitation of man by man has disappeared, and racial discrimination has disappeared too." And with that, as if by magic, discussion of the issue officially ended—for at least a generation.

The conjunctures of intentions of revolutionary leaders, black intellectuals, and the Hispanic Cuban elite in Cuba, as well as the cold war politics of the United States and Soviet Union, conditioned the choices of the revolutionary government at the triumph of the Revolution. They promised a people's revolution, but they were also strictly constrained by old hegemonies and new political exigencies. Foucault points out in *The Archeology of Knowledge* (1972) that discourses are constantly recuperated and reformed in various ways. In this instance, racialized and sexualized hegemonies that reckon the root of racist segregation as the behavior of Afro-Cubans, which would be gradually improved by the progressive force of European culture and "European genes," is now posed, in a lightning-quick sleight, as a superstructural effect of the base of capitalist oppression, which following Marxist reasoning would be cut off with the establishment of a socialist society.

The triumph of the Cuban Revolution of 1959 cannot be said to have completely ruptured the old racial order, due to its recuperation—even *sleight*—of the same racist tropes that hold, as the common Cuban aphorism states, *está en la pinta*, or "it [that African element that makes black people behave in *a certain way*] is in the blood." It did bring the promise of a new "raceless" society in which black and other Cubans of color could rise from the ranks of the permanent underclass—only if in fact they were willing to make themselves into *proper* Cuban subjects. The anti-imperialist radical wing of the middle class, following Marxist principles, cast the historical interpellations of blacks as lazy, insolent, hypersexual, and superstitious as negative tendencies that socialism would cure. In analysis and discursive affect, this is not qualitatively different from Ortiz's moves or motivations. Here there is a revolutionary sleight of hand—or a *handing off* of partners in the rumba. Their policies and pronouncements did not challenge the bases of racial and sexual ideology, but rather uncritically accepted and reified them. The revolution read race, gender, and sexuality, as extrinsic effects of capital, not as co-constructed and interarticulated through political economy, history, culture, and individual agency. Thus, the revolutionary government and official intellectuals sought to change behaviors that were observable among the poor, uneducated masses in general yet thought to stem from Cuba's African inheritance. The new regime immediately set out to create policies to combat "negative tendencies," which they framed as a result of poverty and disaffection from the mainstream of prerevolutionary Cuba, in which the labor and human potential of the masses were alienated and suppressed.

Moore points out that "with Castro's victory, the radical nationalist wing of the Hispanic Cuban middle class, which had been frustrated in the war for Independence, ostracized in the early decades of the Republic, and thwarted again in 1933, came into its own" (1988: 5). It was after the triumph of the military campaign that they were then faced with turning their July 26th Movement into a "revolution." This happened in an atmosphere of the height of the cold war—in which the Soviet Union and the United States were paying close attention (not to say that both sides were seized with paranoia). The revolutionary government grafted Marxism-Leninism onto Cuban nationalism, which had had a long history of struggle against United States imperialism and Spanish colonialism. This vanguard of radical Cuban nationalists and Latin American internationalists like Che Guevara saw itself as a catalyst for "the sleeping masses" that would need to be awakened to develop a revolutionary consciousness. The movement had realized through earlier efforts the futility of expecting a "spontaneous revolution" to spring up from the masses. As Tzvi Medin states, "Even at this early stage the guerrillas realized that revolutionary consciousness could not be developed merely by means of propaganda or indoctrination, but must arise fundamentally from revolutionary praxis: armed struggle and the restructuring of the land tenure system, participation in military action, and change in the living conditions of the peasantry" (1990: 68). At this point there was, as Medin notes, not a "superstructural reflection of economic conditions or the automatic reproduction of a consciousness that already predominated," but rather an explicit and conscious molding of revolutionary consciousness from above (69). Among other things, the restructuring of the conceptual and axiological world of the Cuban shifted the center of evil from the former Cuban dictators who were puppets of the United States to the United States itself. That the United States was engaged in a renegotiation of its own racial politics through the civil rights movement of the 1960s and that the concomitant violent resistance to it was broadcast on international television, provided myriad opportunities to point out the moral superiority of the socialist system, which won Cuba friends among antiracism activists and other leftists. In the 1960s, while police dogs attacked orderly United States citizens and local government turned the other way as churches were firebombed and children killed, Cuba claimed to have solved the race problem, ninety miles away from the shores of the United States South.

As the old Cuban regime was deposed, the new government that sought to unite Cuba as one nation silenced, in the public sphere, what had become a polemical racial discourse that impelled separate black political and social organizations before the Revolution. In the early days of the Revolution, Fidel Castro and the Cuban leadership responded to various inputs, including the Soviets, the United States, and potential unrest among blacks on one hand, and the potential emigration "brain drain" of even more white professionals on the other. Old prejudices within the vanguard and in the populace were left unchecked in a naive Marxist formula that the end of capitalism meant the end of racism and sexism, without equal participation of women or blacks in the vanguard of the Revolution. At the same time, discourse around the proper conduct of men and women, formerly left to the cultural realm, was made explicit.

The revolutionary project is (still) characterized by the *babbling on* (de Certeau 1984) of ideology, even as the structuring hegemonies are left uninterrogated—bracketed as they are in a less-than-sophisticated materialist analysis, wherein race is seen as located to the north of their own shores and where feminism and queer liberation are (even if for understandable historical reasons) eschewed as a liberal invention of the same. Like all nation-states, revolutionary Cuba set out to codify a narrative of cultural practice and ideology and to engender particular forms of consciousness that would be most appropriate to the socialist national project. Sadly, revolutionary ideology did not include the liberation of all Cubans from pernicious limits on their freedom and expression. The revolutionary Cuban government has marshaled an expressly raced, sexed, and ideologically singular sex/gender system, putatively in order to constitute and defend the socialist nation-state. The "New Man and "New Woman" would have to be in a position to be seamlessly stitched into the fabric of international socialism led by the Soviets. The New Man and New Woman that the Cuban Revolution sought to create is recognized as a man *or* a woman. He or she is ideologically and politically Marxist, sexually "straight," religiously atheist or agnostic, and racially "mixed."

Disciplining Unruly Subjects

The early Revolution certainly did ask that people "dance" with others that they did not "like"—it legislated compulsory heteronormativity. But heteronormativity and heterosexism did not suddenly appear with the 1959 Revolution. Heterosexism and homophobia, like misogyny, racism, and colorism, are dynamic and reiterative processes. The Cuban historian of sexuality Abel Sierra Madero (2003) points out that official heterosexism existed in the Spanish colonial period, at least since the denunciation of "sodomites" in the seventeenth century, during which the barbarism of the Crusades was locally reflected in the form of burning executions of effeminate men. Moreover, he holds that "one of the first documents expressing incipient nationalist sentiment . . . A critical letter about the man-woman," printed in *Papel Periódico de La Habana* on April 10, 1791, was "possibly the first document to refer to effeminate men as the counterpoint to masculine men, who were exalted as appropriate representations of the nation" (2004: n.p.). The literary scholar Emilio Bejel likewise argues in his landmark work *Gay Cuban Nation* that "the notion of homosexuality and homoeroticism is inscribed, by negation, in the prescriptive models of the national Cuban narrative" (2003: xiv). Incipient articulations of Cuban nationhood figured the "failed" effeminate homosexual as a dire threat to national consolidation, protection, and flourishing.

Revolutionary understandings of the New Man were diametrically opposed to the prevailing attitudes about male homosexuals, who were thought to be rapacious and flighty—concerned only with their own pleasure and unwilling to make sacrifices. Women who have sex with women seemed not to be talked about at all. Lesbians are effectively disappeared. As Allen Young writes, "While prejudice against homosexuals coexisted with the sexual openness of pre-revolutionary Havana, that prejudice was institutionalized and reinforced in post-revolutionary Cuba as part of the political program of the nation" (1981: 14). At the triumph of the revolution, male homosexuality—defined as effeminacy and evidence of weakness, pleasure seeking, and penetrability[11]—was seen as an artifact of capitalist bourgeois decadence. Not only is the *maricón*, or homosexual, said to be effeminate and unmanly, but also a coward and untrustworthy. A maricón, therefore, cannot be a revolutionary. Homosexual men were not thought of as "healthy" or robust, physically or mentally. The following comments by Fidel Castro point us back to the (pathological) heteropatriarchal obsession of the former colonial or newly independent state to discipline certain bodies toward particular projects of legitimation and consolidation:

> Nothing prevents a homosexual from exhibiting a correct political position. In this case he should not be considered politically negative. And yet we would never come to believe that a homosexual could embody the conditions and requirements of conduct that would enable us to consider him a true revolutionary, a true Communist militant. . . . A deviation of that nature clashes with the concept we have of what a militant Communist should be . . . In the conditions under which we live, because of the problems which our country is facing, we must inculcate our children with the spirit of discipline, of struggle, of work. . . . This attitude may not be correct, but it is our honest feeling. It may be in some cases that a person

is homosexual because of pathological reasons. (Quoted in Lockwood 1967: 124)

Castro's comments on homosexuality and revolution here illustrate revolutionary society's profound ambivalence around male homosexuality. Homo-*sociality* is both culturally accepted and built into militarization techniques to build the New Man. Although Castro holds that a "homosexual" can (with proper training or abnegation) exhibit the correct position, there is the assertion that a homosexual could never be a "true Communist militant" because of the antinomy between preconditions of communist militancy and the "nature" of male homosexuality, which Castro suggests here is an illness or otherwise the result of "pathology." Militant communism as defined by the repressive Stalinism of the Soviet Union—and therefore, especially conflated with Cuban notions of masculinity—had no room for what was seen in both as inherently untrustworthy, weak, and effeminate. Still, in these comments Castro holds out the possibility—facing tremendous scrutiny from the North and criticism from radicals and progressives in the United States and elsewhere who might have been allies—that discrimination against homosexuals might in fact be wrong. Fidel's ambivalence is palpable here. He equivocates, once again, to assert that Cuba's development under siege required a sort of sacrifice on the side of caution. That is, his argument seems to be that *open male homosexuality is certainly dangerous to the development of Cuba, if not also—possibly—morally corrupt and unnatural.* Thus, "the homosexual" is not merely a person who has sex with someone of the same gender, but also a sign. If *not just anybody can be a citizen*, then some would-be citizens must be reeducated and some re-cast to become eligible. Others, found too unruly and contagious, were to be contained, in the interest of nation building.

In 1965 the Unidades Militares para Ayudar Producción (UMAP) work camps were set up, putatively to politically reeducate religious dissidents such as Jehovah's Witnesses, men who "refused to work" or go to school, disaffected youth with long hair and hippie dress styles, and homosexuals and those who were thought or rumored to be homosexuals. The UMAP camps remained open until about 1967, when they apparently ceased to be forced labor camps (Salas 1979). Soon after opening, it became clear that the motto of the repressive camps, with the command "Work will make you men" reportedly inscribed on the gate, did not pertain to all inmates. Indeed, (purported) homosexuals were segregated from the general population in order to "separate the men from the girls" as Young (1981) quotes General Escalona uttering, thereby marking them as uneducable and irredeemable to national manhood—oddities to be interned and contained (but occasionally used too).

My respondent Jaime was taken to the camp in 1966 after he was arrested on La Rampa dressed in "tight embroidered jeans."[12] He is very handsome and fit, but in his fifties at the time of our interview, he is now more conventional looking—he wears a polo shirt from the Rose Hall Sheraton Hotel in Jamaica, where his nephew once worked. He smiles widely as he describes his 1960s glory: "And [I had] long hair too, believe me. Not *good hair*, but long, almost an afro. They [the police] did not know quite what to make of me." If the police initially did not know, other men at the train station, East Havana beaches, and late-night baseball fields did. He was a hit in these dark corners and meeting places, where he tells me he met many men who found his "dark skin and young, exotic body irresistible."[13] When he was picked up on La Rampa one afternoon, walking to meet his cousin, he protested to the police that he was not in fact a maricón. He did not have the swishy gait of the other men, and other than his adventures in furtive sex he "did not hang around maricones" and thus did not have the *queer* affect that many perform. Confused, the police nearly released him, admitting that his tight jeans and "long bad hair"—an afro—had thrown them. Jaime had just dropped out of the university where he was enrolled, against his wishes, as an agronomy student, to informally study literature. This could be read as an aggravating factor rather than a mitigating one, considering the number of members of the Union Nacional de Escritores y Artistas Cubana (UNEAC, Cuba's Union of Artists and Writers) who had already been harassed or rounded up by 1967—including, very briefly, Virgilio Piñera, among the nation's most revolutionary and artistically distinguished playwrights—signaling that no member of the literati was safe. Jaime went to the general population in the camp, but he was promptly transferred to the special section for homosexuals and transvestites when he was caught having sex with an older man also interned at the camp. Here is his account:

JAFARI: So the camps, I have read, were to be "reeducation." What was taught there? Was there a particular curriculum, like those given to campesinos to make them fit for city dwelling?

JAIME: Nothing. . . . Well we were forced to be agricultural workers. . . . The guards would make comments about manhood. . . . There was sometimes a psychiatrist or something who asked question, but I do not know why . . . as I have said . . . I do not talk about these things . . .

JAFARI: [pause] . . . So what did you do there?

JAIME: Well . . . some agriculture. . . . The maricones were treated very badly. . . . Well, not beaten, but hit a lot. Teased. I was young so it was not so bad for me, and there was attention . . . people knew internationally. Sometimes there were games and always talking . . . black humor really. Laughing at the absurd . . .

JAFARI: Were there people who were especially targeted?

JAIME: . . . On the street? . . . Well, yes, people like me [black—*indicates the skin on his hand*] were always picked up.

JAFARI: How did you get out?

JAIME: . . . It was never run to be profitable, and they say that Fidel was regretful when it was revealed how bad [inmates] were treated. I was just told one day, after several weeks there, that I should go back home, which was not far from the camp [near Camaguey] . . . but I had no interest. . . . I went back to Havana, and stopped wearing those clothes, did not hang out with scandalous fags, but still remained in contact with some friends and had many lovers before "getting married" [monogamous coupling].

JAFARI: What happened after? What were the lasting effects?

JAIME: It was easier for me since I can be *entendido por no dicho*, not like many queens. It was very repressive during the seventies and eighties, but it did not stop parties and gays and lots of sex. . . . According to the Third Resolution,[14] I should not have this job [at a cultural institution] since I have that on my record . . . a threat to youth. . . . But if you behave well no one cares, really. . . . I have many arguments with Fidel, but I have a good life here . . . things are improving for the young homosexuals—"gays" [He chuckles at "gay," which he claims is "a new term" for him].

The UMAP camps were an inexcusable violation of the human rights of free expression and free movement. At the same time, to equate these with "concentration camps" or work camps of the African Middle Passage, the European Jewish Holocaust, or even the Russian Stalinist gulag, as does the documentary *Improper Conduct*, is a sensationalistic overstatement of "as bad as [Cuban state] propaganda," according to Jaime. While Jaime was pursuing a less flamboyant life in La Lisa, at the National Congress of Education and Culture in 1971, amid plans to incorporate sex education and coeducational classes and teaching, the National Assembly also resolved that all "manifestations of homosexual deviations are to be firmly rejected and prevented from spreading." This was undone by the 1978 labor law, which found it discriminatory, but the rhetorics of homosexuality as contagion had already become part of the unofficial official policy. The 1979 Penal Code, while decriminalizing homosexuality and homosexual sex, extended the metaphor of containing a contagion by proscribing perhaps the most "dangerous" part of homosexuality—effeminate or transgender performance in the street and male sexual affection. Laws against "scandalous conduct" targeted "public ostentation and homosexual acts in public where it might be seen by others (Salas 1979). The 1980s were a time of increased vigilance against male homosex, experienced in waves of repression, but there was nothing as concerted as the UMAP. Respondents that experienced this period seem to agree with the novelist Reinaldo Arenas that this was also a time of increased sexual activity and widespread public sex between men, especially in Havana. As Arenas writes, "Perhaps as a protest against the regime, homosexuality began to flourish with ever-increasing defiance . . . I honestly believe that [the repression] actually resulted in the promotion of homosexual activities" (1994: 192). The arbitrary and capricious Ley de peligrosidad (Law of dangerousness), which is still on the books and variously interpreted or ignored by police on the street, provides a sentence of up to four years of psychiatric therapy or prison for the sort of (mostly uninterrupted) campiness and *mariconeria* I witnessed and participated in on the streets of Havana and Santiago, between 1998 and 2005.

Twenty or so years later, in 1988, Fidel Castro returned to the speech in which he seemed to equivocate so uncharacteristically. In 1988, in an interview on Spanish television, Fidel Castro noted that "a certain rigidity" had governed "attitudes toward homosexuality and [the effectively banning of public practice of] religion." While "God needed seven days to make the world," he averred, "you must understand . . . Our society, our party, our government [now] have ideas that are clearer, wiser, and more intelligent about many of these problems" (quoted in Lockwood 1990: 71). Fidel amplified his mea culpa in 2010, admitting that the UMAP was a "great injustice" that arose from the island's history of discrimination against homosexuals. He said he was not prejudiced against gays, but "if anyone is responsible [for the persecution], it's [him]."[15] Currently, Fidel Castro's niece, the daughter of the president Raúl Castro, Mariela Castro Espín, who heads the country's sex education institute, CENESEX, seems to be moving the country forward from this past that continues to have deleterious effects.

3 The Erotics and Politics of Self-making

Just as technologies of control run the gamut from overt coercion to implicit persuasion, so modes of resistance may extend across a similarly wide spectrum. At one end is organized protest, explicit moments and movements of dissent that are easily recognizable as "political" by western lights. At the other are gestures of tacit refusal and iconoclasm, gestures that sullenly and silently contest the forms of an existing hegemony. And far from being a mere reflection—or a reflex expression—of historical consciousness, these acts are a practical means of *producing* it.
—JEAN COMAROFF AND JOHN COMAROFF, *Of Revelation and Revolution*

Much in Negro life remains a mystery; perhaps the zoot suit conceals profound political meaning; perhaps the symmetrical frenzy of the Lindy Hop conceals clues to great potential power—if only Negro leaders would solve this riddle.
—RALPH ELLISON, quoted in Robin D. G. Kelley, *Race Rebels: Culture, Politics, and the Black Working Class*

ONE AFTERNOON IN CENTRAL HAVANA, while talking with men playing dominoes and gossiping, I witnessed a rare occasion. Across the street Lili was leaving home in the brightest part of the day. The men's conversation about the upcoming baseball championships and the appearance of red beans at the local food distribution center ended abruptly. Lili walked out of her apartment wearing bright-orange capri pants, flat sandals, and a floral shirt tied just below her ample breasts. Some residents of the neighborhood had suspected Lili's avocation for some time. The brightly colored spandex and lycra dresses and fancy hose hanging out to dry on the apartment balcony at the back of the building suggested to them that the young man they knew as thirty-three-year-old Octavio, whom they suspected to be a *pájaro* (sissy, literally "bird") because of his effeminate gait and public shyness, was actually a *transformista* (transvestite or "drag queen").

Instead of cowering in the darkened doorways of streets where she would be less likely to be recognized, or quickly getting into a tourist taxi, Lili slowly sauntered down Calle Romay to the Malecón—Havana's famous sea-walled boulevard—where she flagged a *colectivo* (collective taxi) for the ride to Playa. Lili was traveling to attend a party for a friend, La India, who had returned home from Montreal to visit Cuba. The moment Lili turned from her doorway, she was greeted by stunned silence, grumblings of disdain, then laughter. One of the men around me commented that Octavio was a "sick faggot who ought to be put away" for the disgrace.

Then, an old woman from my apartment building, two doors down from Octavio's, threw a mango peel from her window. A litany of epithets was thrown as well: *maricón!* (faggot), *puta* (whore, feminine form), *sucio* (dirty, masculine form), and *loca* (crazy, feminine form, also sissy). Lili ignored the comments, at first seeming slightly bemused. Walking deliberately, with more than a bit of rhythmic twist of her hips and shoulders, finally, before reaching the corner to cross the Malecón to catch her colectivo, and as the comments grew uglier, Lili turned and replied directly to one of the insulters: "Go ask your father how good a whore I am . . . I still have bigger balls than you!"

Later that afternoon, as laughter and stories gave way, I asked a few of the dominoes players what they thought of the scene. I told them about the violence often visited on transsexuals and other transgender people in the United States and other places. I was concerned that Lili, now "out," would become a target for this type of attack. Although no one knew personally of a case where a homosexual or transformista had been physically abused "by anyone other than their own family . . . or a *bugarrón* [male insertive sexual partner]," they agreed that this midday walk had been a risky gauntlet. Later, I asked Octavio why he did not merely travel with clothing to change at the party, the way he normally had. Lili told me that she was "just so tired." Lili explained to me that La India's return visit home after many years in North America reminded her how she had allowed custom to keep her from fully expressing herself *en la calle* ("in the street" or in public) and in daylight. From now on, Octavio would saunter out in whatever attire suited him—as Lili, or a young man with a swishy gait. Although Lili confided that she will always be a *vampirosa*—a creature of the night who sucks men dry—she said she would spend no more of her meager earnings to hire neighborhood children to fetch her bread and fruit in the morning. Octavio receives a share of his parent's household monthly allotment of sugar, rice, and other necessities, as well as tickets for fresh bread, which he gets during his several visits per month to their home, just outside of Havana. Octavio brings them things like cooking oil, imported cookies, and whiskey, which are only available in stores that trade in U.S. dollars, and sundry items he had received as gifts. These are goods paid for not by Octavio's state job, which he only attends part-time, but rather Lili's highly unofficial jobs of entertainer, party hostess, and occasional sex laborer.[1] No one in the family asks the source of these goodies or question how it is Octavio can afford to pay rent to his absentee *dueña* (apartment owner) with only two roommates, including one cousin and a few transient friends who share the small cot or old sofa.

Lili reports being undeterred by her street corner detractors, insisting, "I too can walk the streets of my country." After a while, Lili becomes "bored with politics" and begins telling me stories of sexual adventure with some of the neighborhood men—a couple of whom were present on the street corner days before. I attempt to steer the conversation back to the subject:

JAFARI: In the United States we have a motto that is shouted during gay demonstrations: "We're here. We're queer. Get used to it." This seemed like your attitude that day on Romay . . .

LILI: [laughing] . . . I know . . . "we're fabulous" . . .

JAFARI: [laughing] . . . Yes, "we're not going shopping!" . . . So, where did you hear that . . . ?

LILI: [laughing] Oh yes, I have heard that . . . I have faith that they will get used to it. . . . It has been a long time, but one must have faith. I am not religious . . . we always say here *no es fácil* [it is not easy] but we must have faith. The boys in the street [who were abusive to Lili] will get used to me being here. They will think, maybe, "he must be serious about this to take such abuse," and it will no longer be fun for them. . . .

JAFARI: [joking] . . . So are you saying that eventually Fidel will make room for transformistas and maricones in the Communist Party?

LILI: . . . *Machito negrito* [precious black boy[2] (snap!)], they are already there, darling!

For Lili, no one is more embattled and struggling for the full expression of humanity—as Cuba portrays itself—than the black worker and transgender transformista. Octavio's outlook on the value of the Revolution is informed by his experiences of feeling privileged to attend boarding schools in the provinces where he experienced greater freedom than he did in the city and where he metaphorically and literally could "breathe easier." Octavio remembers how hard his parents worked to become educated later in life, and how they encouraged him to continue his formal studies and to pursue the arts, with the support of state training. Octavio holds that Cubans owe him respect because of his contributions to mass organizations, his job, and family.

At the end of a casual conversation with Lili, I asked her to respond to some of the differences between her and Octavio. I insist on drawing distinctions between the two because, unlike transgender individuals who are forging permanent new gender and often sexual identities that may have been formerly repressed,[3] Octavio insists on Lili as a part of himself that he helps to come out through *accentuation*, not as a substitute that is more truthful or that will one day subsume Octavio. While on the surface this may appear to be dissemblance, this evaluation must be taken further. There is no untruth being perpetrated, but rather it is a deeper truth of existence as both man and woman—negro and mulata, a thirty-something technician from a "good family" and a coquettish twenty-something occasional performer and consort of mysterious origins. While Octavio is playful about Lili's genealogy, it seemed clear to me that the complexity of Lili's identity is a reflection of Cuban gender and race common sense. The woman that Octavio presents as part of himself is an idealized feminine type borne of his acculturated imagination of what a woman is. According to Octavio, women are certainly "strong," but most "essentially" are sensuous and simple. Yet they are not without guile—the image of the sexy and coquettish mulata. His imagination reflects sex/race/gender ideology promulgated through popular culture over three hundred years. I pushed Lili one day: asking how it could be that Lili is twenty-three years old when Octavio's *carnet* (official Cuban identification card) says that he is thirty-three. To this, Lili replied: "What carnet? I do not know what you are talking about, my heart . . . And you must have learned by now that a lady's age is a state secret. Not even the CDR [Committee for the Defense of the Revolution] captain knows that!"

I realized that I would get only more puns and playful flirtation from interviewing Lili, since the core of her performance is mystery and lightheartedness. Still, there are gnawing questions about the disconnections between Octavio the man and Lili the woman that he has created using his own body. So, several days later, I asked Octavio about the differences again: Why did he identify Lili as mulata when he identifies and is identified as negro himself? "Are you sure that is what I said?" he asked. When I assured him that he had, he began again: "Well. It is a problem of *guíon* [direction, as in a film or play, but also "script"] . . . We are obsessed with the mulata here [in Cuba]." For Octavio, the common sense represented by Fernando Ortiz's *Cuban Counterpoint* (1995b) is inescapable. The woman he imagined for or *as* himself, even as negro, with negro parents, is mulata. To be "successful," if not completely believable, Lili must practice, perform, and *wear* culturally uncontested signs and symbols of attractiveness and desirability. One's drag must index for the viewer the apex of cultural understanding of feminine desirability, which in Cuba is La Mulata.[4] Though he and his mother share a rich brown skin color, Octavio cannot even imagine being a tobacco-colored woman. Thus, Octavio's transformation from man to woman is attenuated by *color drag* from negro to mulata.

Octavio must extend the suspension of disbelief that a man can be(come) a woman, to a tobacco-colored man be(come)ing a mulata. First, liquid foundation makeup and powder two or three shades lighter than Octavio's skin color is applied. Lili draws lips covering only two-thirds of Octavio's actual lips and brushes on—"never draws on"—eyebrows that accentuate eyes that are "*poco* China" (a little "Chinese looking"). A straight wig, or "wet-and-wild" hair extensions, braided at the base then combed out and spritzed with water for the appearance of natural curls, *bring out* the phenotypical features that suggest mulatáje.

Watching Lili emerge through the application of makeup made me think not of the drag queens I have seen perform in the United States and in various parts of Latin America, but more pointedly brought to mind a few very respectable black ladies and Latinas of my parent's cohort in the United States, now in their sixties and seventies. They also contour(ed) their lips—drawing them on thin perhaps in an effort to hide a mark of putatively disreputable black female sexuality. Eye shadow expertly "reshapes" and "sharpens" with subtle color Octavio's already aquiline nose. Then hip padding is added under a sort of leotard to make curves where there were once angles. What Octavio has proudly reported is a generous endowment is, "for safe keeping," pulled and tucked between shaved, moisturized thighs, thereby completing the transformation. Lili's choice of songs to lip-synch, from Beyoncé, Mariah Carey, and the now ultrawhitened Colombian Shakira, replete with hair tossing and shoulder shaking, is as essential to the illusion as are high heels and *feminine bravada*. This suggests a form of *passing* or whitening that is not, of course, completely believable to all audiences, but which is convincing enough to some individuals for it to have similar effects of lessening perceived and real difficulties associated with blackness, and increasing one's possibilities. That Lili has begun taking this performance beyond the bounds of fiestas and carnivals where temporary Bakhtinian reversals are allowed and enjoyed by everyone is a significant overstep. Perhaps, Octavio thought, Lili could do shows abroad like La India, and save money to build an extension on Octavio's parents' small house. Lili has moved from the private sphere, under the cover of night in which movements between liminal or illicit spaces are mitigated by the use of private taxis, to *the streets* of everyday Cuba. Here, folks may curse and deride rather than tip and applaud.

THE CONSTRUCTION, OR MAKING, of the self has historicity, with important material effects. Judith Butler argues that the gendered self—a consumer of a certain historicized view of "womanhood," for example, *makes* herself into a woman, hoping that the performance is convincingly attuned to cultural norms. That is, the putative facticity of womanhood is meaningless until understood in terms of a strategy of fashioning oneself within appropriate historically delimiting possibilities of womanhood (Butler 1990). Octavio's erotic "transvestic" practices not only transgress the boundaries of gender, but also pointedly question the potent symbolism and power associated with the trope of the mulata.

Doubtless, Lili's actions instantiate a critical locus of enunciation and transgressive articulation. Still, while on one hand Octavio/Lili's story is an example of erotic transgression, on the other it may also illustrate the ways in which individuals may take on or endorse meanings associated with received categories. Octavio's loyalty to old race/color tropes—scripts that he *plays out*—in some ways makes him an agent of his and Lili's own oppression. But who can blame those who, like Octavio/Lili, use infrapolitical gestures, mimicry, or other coping mechanisms to protect themselves from daily insult; to earn a comfortable ride home in a tourist taxi, or two months of rent. Most folks are merely looking for this private moment of personal respite from the daily onslaught.

Making Subjects, Building Resistance

In this chapter I will consider innovative and historically recurrent productions of self and community as an opening toward considering how to make sense of oppositional (and alternative) everyday expressive practices. These and other gestures must be read closely for their impulse toward personal freedom, which when thought through and redeployed collectively may instantiate moves toward liberation, or a larger freedom. Here, I begin to argue for the recuperation of quotidian spaces and practices of personal agency as political. These disparate contemporary scenes illustrate self-making— from expressing gender fluidity and lessening the sting of racial terror to attempts to embody the "New Man" gestured toward earlier. Here I follow Gina Ulysse (2007) and especially Saidiya Hartman (1997) who argue for a nuanced theorization of self-making, and who insist that such self-making necessarily embraces contradiction and contingency. Whatever our vision for progressive or revolutionary politics, counterhegemony rests on the recognition of one's own self, intentions, and desires. In order for there to be resistance—whether in the form of a planned strategy or improvised tactic—we must have a thinking, desiring, decision-making subject. Michel Foucault offers that "all these struggles revolve around the question: who are we? They are refusals of the abstractions of economic and ideological state violence which ignores who we are individually, and also a refusal of a scientific and administrative inquisition which determines who one is" (1983: 212). Beyond this grounding in experience, however, there are more steps toward transformation. After all, as Audre Lorde states, "without community, there is no liberation, only the most vulnerable and temporary armistice between an individual and her oppression" (1984: 26).

Whereas "resistance" is a useful concept to describe challenges to abstractions and rationalities of power structures, it must nevertheless be teased out and pushed further. In Cuba, infrapolitical moves are not necessarily "oppositional," and are certainly not seamless and noncontradictory. Octavio/Lili's story demonstrates limited and contradictory agency and contingent self-making, motivated by embodied desire. It shows that while "the weak" are almost never completely dominated, and have tremendous faculties of creativity and resiliency, they are also not always the savvy architects of counterhegemony or change agents that theorists have imagined.

In Cuba, the government privileges economic (human) rights over sociopolitical (human) rights,[5] and any organized public demonstration or gathering not sanctioned by the government is illegal. The public transcript or "party line" is not only well rehearsed, but also (still) deeply felt by many. It reflects loyalty to the nation (*patria*) and is an expression of shared resistance to global capital and imperialism (understood as headquartered in the United States), which pushes significantly in another direction from Scott's understanding of division between the public sphere in which an official transcript is performed and insistence that the theorist's task is to unveil the hidden transcripts of the powerless. Though many studies of resistance feature a dominant oppressive state, a large corporation, or a feudal lord seeking to lessen the "dignity and self-assertion" (James Scott 1990: 137) of less powerful groups and individuals, the case of contemporary Cuba requires a more capacious analysis. The 1959 Revolution not only advertised itself as the champion against such dominance but also has proven to be sort of a champion of the poor, in terms of its redistributive policies. The Revolution is the author of black Cuban discourses of dignity and self-assertion. Although their loyalty is constantly stretched, individuals work to resolve the increasing dissonance between, on one hand, the lofty aspirations of the Revolution and its important early successes and, on the other, everyday experience of most Cubans on the ground. The Cuban Revolution lifted masses of (black and) poor

Cubans out of deplorable material circumstances and provided the promise of a new society to which they could contribute and benefit—under very particular conditions. Moreover, Cubans are aware that overt political protest would not only contravene Cuban law, but also embolden efforts by the United States government and activist anti-Castro members of the Miami Cuban exile community to cast their expressions of frustration into a wholesale indictment of the revolutionary project. It is difficult, perhaps impossible, therefore, to oppose the "revolutionary state" without being cast as "counterrevolutionary." My respondents are aware of prerevolutionary conditions. They believe that open protest would risk a return to the bad old days of United States control and racialized capitalism, rather than the modified or more socially open social(ist) welfare state that the majority of my respondents, and in my experience most Cubans, imagine and advocate. Thus, gestures and actions like those analyzed here are of the utmost importance. Moreover, these forms resist or cannot be absorbed into state projects or transnational "NGOization" that might limit their creativity and autonomy (see Incite! Women of Color Against Violence 2007).

FOR BLACK FOLKS, resistance always takes place in a field already constrained by the lingering question of black abjection with respect to subjecthood. Frank Wilderson in his fine polemic "Gramsci's Black Marx: Whither the Slave in Civil Society?" (2003) argues that blacks "impose a radical incoherence" upon the assumptive logic of a subject constructed through its relation to labor exploitation.[6] Wilderson's thesis that "the Black subject reveals Marxism's inability to think White supremacy as the base" (n.p.) resonates with Cedrick Robinson's *Black Marxism* (2000), which carefully details historical and philosophical (dis)articulations of black(ness and) Marxism. Wilderson points out that if we follow Antonio Gramsci's expansion of Marx, depending on civil society as the site of struggle (i.e., "war of position") we reify racial terror, since for black subjects civil society is the site of recurrent racial terror. Where I have to depart from Wilderson is in his contention that the black subject is thus in a position of *"total objectification . . .* in contradistinction to human possibility, however slim," required for a war of position (2003: n.p.; emphasis mine). Wilderson finds the black subject in a "structurally impossible position." I must argue, following bell hooks's use of Paolo Freire, however, that "we cannot enter the struggle as objects in order to later become subjects" (1989: 29). Part of my friendly disagreement with Wilderson is ontological, or, I readily admit, spiritual. Unlike positions that deny notions of a deep psychic self, I want to affirm the inherence of inalienable innate human dignity, and what I might gloss here as "spirit," which is offended not only by force but by any extrinsic practice that threatens the individual's sense of personhood.[7] On another score, Wilderson's "stress on objective contradictions, 'impersonal structures' and processes that work 'behind men's backs,'" as Stuart Hall describes the conventional culture and discourses of the left, "disable[s] us from confronting the subjective dimension in politics in any coherent way" (Hall, Morley, and Chen 1996: 226). Thus, in some ways Wilderson takes us back to the "old" Marx that Gramsci, Hall, and others attempted to rethink apropos of our new times, even as he points out the limits of Gramsci to contend with these social and historical facts of blackness. This orientation leaves no air for black transgression or resistance outside of "the final solution." In the interim, however, what will condition, reeducate and raise consciousness toward revolution?

In her "Deviance as Resistance: A New Research Agenda for the Study of Black Politics," Cathy J. Cohen calls on us to draft the architecture of collective black resistance, and she challenges theorists to employ more "analytical precision to our efforts to identify and understand the political potential contained in deviant behavior" (2004: 39). In order to take Cohen's challenge seriously, we must first affirm her position that *not all agency is resistance and not all deviance is intentional.* Still, it is crucial to avoid throwing out the personal value and political potential of often tacit or virtually unnoticed actions that constitute what James Scott would call "infra-politics." Scott, followed by Robin D. G. Kelley and others, theorized everyday action of indentured servants and formerly enslaved marginal subjects, which can be oppositional but are much more often merely alternative, or a counterpoint to the hegemony under which they labor. Cohen's account reads constraint more prominently, holding that transgression is not necessarily *resistant*, while Kelley tends to read resistance in historical sites that may fail Cohen's test of intentionality. Still, I am persuaded by Kelley's work in *Race Rebels* in which he writes that his black historical subjects were:

> neither total victims of routinization, exploitation, sexism, and racism, nor were they the "rational" economic beings driven by the most utilitarian

concerns. Their lives and struggles were so much more complicated. . . .
We must begin to dig beneath the surface . . . into the daily lives, cultures,
and communities . . . [and] step into the complicated maze of experience
that renders "ordinary" folks so extraordinarily multifaceted, diverse, and
complicated . . . We must not only redefine what is "political" but question
a lot of common ideas about what are "authentic" movements and strategies of resistance. (1994: 3)

I accent agency here—however limited and contradictory—not because I
believe this to be more important than markedness, regulation, the power
of global capital, or the state, but following Stuart Hall (Hall and Jefferson
1990), Paul Gilroy (1993a, 1993b), and Kelley (1994, 1997, 2002), in order
to understand political potential, we must be able to sensitively and incisively
read what Gilroy—brilliantly riffing on Bob Marley's metaphor of the "small
ax" chopping down the big tree—theorizes as "small acts." We make no claim
that all of the action described here is intended to be oppositional in the sense
of a formal political movement. Some of these acts are, in fact, following Raymond Williams's construction, merely "'alternative' . . . attempts to create
autonomy over one's life, to pursue desire, or to make the best of very limited
life options" (quoted in Cohen 2004: 40). Perhaps Audre Lorde's "temporary
armistice." Still, considering the pace with which technologies of global capital, the state, and powerful cultural institutions dehumanize by at once atom-
izing and aggregating individuals throughout the globe, these are significant
epistemological, spiritual, and cultural transgressions.

Following Cohen, here we are primarily concerned with showing "people
living with limited resources . . . us[ing] the restricted agency available to them
to create autonomous spaces absent the constant stream of power from outside authorities or normative structures" (2004: 40). In subsequent chapters
I want also to endeavor to meet her challenge of "intention to resist" (which
she charges is missing in recent work on black resistance) by showing the outlines of work in Cuba that is "mobilized in a conscious fashion" (2004: 29).
To wit, these two modes of agency—improvised quotidian action to make
one's life easier to manage and (organized and intentional) resistance—are
not diametrically opposed but are interrelated, with the former often but not
always following the latter. Moreover, even organized and intentional action
is not always effective or radical.

Thus, although it seems contradictory insofar as Cohen's project asks for delimitation rather than a proliferation of *resistances*, here I take up her charge by highlighting lives that "are indicative of the intersection of marked identities and regulatory processes, relative powerlessness and limited and contradictory agency" (2004: 29). Before I can lay the foundation of the architecture of black resistance, I begin here by digging beneath the surface in an archaeology of everyday action.

Tengo: Coleridge Santiago Is the Man

As a Cuban who had immigrated from Barbados in the 1950s, Coleridge (Cole) Brathwaite Santiago's father, Peter, was thankful for the opportunities presented to him by the Revolution. He wasted no time, helping to build the new Revolutionary society by volunteering to teach literacy in the interior provinces. Peter met Cole's mother, Marisol, while they were students at a special institute for advanced studies in agriculture. His father and Cuban-born mother became decorated veterans of Cuba's Internationalista movement of technical assistance and ideological training of Africans and Latin Americans. Cole remembers his father repeating many times that he should follow his own example and resolve to show that Antillanos (black Caribbean people) would contribute much to the Revolution if given a chance. Cole, who does not identify as Antillano, has taken this a step further: Cole sees himself as Cuban. To put a fine point on this, he adds "¡Ya!" (that is all), accompanied by the Cuban gesture of one hand chopping the other. The chopping gesture seemed to me to mark a certain cutting off of history.

Coleridge is twenty-five years old and a student of philosophy at the university, where he is a member of the Federación de Estudentíl Universitario (FEU, or the University Students' Union). We met at a conference between North American and Cuban scholars at the university, in which for several days philosophers from North America—mostly from the United States—talked about the problems and prospects of the continuing Cuban Revolution with their Cuban counterparts. During a meeting between North American student conference attendees, Cuban members of FEU and the Young Communists Union (UJC), and a few North American students who had been studying abroad in Cuba, the atmosphere became surprisingly tense. Unlike the conference delegates, the students from the United States had spent much of their time on the streets of Havana, meeting young people for whom communism seemed less of a pressing everyday concern than collecting good music and exciting experiences. They were unprepared for the political convictions of the FEU members and communist youth whose ideological struggles are central to their studies, and also for whom relative success at practicing these principles and putting across "correct" viewpoints and analyses condition their chances to become part of the leadership in the future. Coleridge was the only (visibly) African-descended Cuban present.

Acia, an undergraduate from California who is about twenty-two years old and considered mulata in Cuba, much to her chagrin as a self-identified black woman of biracial (white and black) parentage, pressed the question of "participation of black Cubans in the government." Acia directed her statements directly to the FEU official chairing the meeting and fielding most questions. Intermittently, she would glance pleadingly in Cole's direction. The chair, frustrated with her probing for the number of black students at Cuban institutions of higher education and the numbers of black comrades in FEU, announced in what I had come to expect as the typical Cuban response: "We do not have 'racism' in Cuba like you do in the United States. It would be a mistake to call this racism." Coleridge now seemed obliged to break his loud silence. In official discourse mode—quoting and invoking Antonio Maceo, Fidel Castro, and Che Guevara—he held forth on the contributions of "the mulato general" and that of Internationalistas like his parents, who had tried to repay the Revolution for what it had done for all Cubans. As Coleridge continued to speechify, I recognized the words of Nicolás Guillén's famous poem "Tengo" (I have) (1967). But, far from the irony with which I had been used to hearing this cited, or the righteous indignation that the rap group Hermanos de Causa expresses in their composition of the same title, cleverly charging, "I have what I have without getting what I've had"—Cole's elocution was not ironic but pedagogical. He wanted to teach Acia something about (black) Cuba that she might not learn at popular dancehalls like La Pampa or La Tropical. And he meant no irony. He passionately and sincerely believes himself to be a beneficiary of the struggles and triumphs of revolutionaries before him.

Like Nicolás Guillén, Cuba's revolutionary poet laureate, Coleridge is a brilliant black man who has benefited from his position as one of a few chosen as *exemplary* blacks. Guillén was a member of the Communist Party for some twenty years before the Revolution, and he had been a political prisoner of the Machado regime before becoming famous for his genius literary exploration of *color cubano*, which also happened to be politically useful in terms of constituting Cuba as one people beyond racial description in celebration of a rich national ethnicity. Cole emphasized the beginning lines of the poem, "I had nothing yesterday and today, I have everything," and then recited the line that explains that one of the things the common person has gained through the Revolution is "a modest room. Not a huge one—a room where I can rest," "respectfully," in his words, suggesting that Acia ought to be more concerned with the class inequality in her own country than the appearance of racial nonparity in his. He agreed with his comrade, and when pressed further by Acia he became visibly uncomfortable. Clearly, she had placed him in a very awkward position—or rather, she made his already awkward, precarious position evident. He went on to say that "the problem [or issue] of many people . . . inclusive of many Afro-Cubans . . . is not a problem of race or racism, but a problem of history . . . and lack of education and morals . . . which begins in the family." That is, the problems lay in the homes of those who could stand to benefit most from the full realization of the Revolution.

After this event, our paths crossed at university events and around the city. Coleridge was always polite, even charming. He worked the room, being attentive to his female colleagues without overtly flirting, and he seemed to assert himself as among the smartest and most charismatic men among his comrades, but did so with great nuance—neither self-aggrandizing nor typically "macho" or aggressive enough to elicit a backlash from the threat he would therefore pose. While denying that the double standard he was subject to was sine qua non of "racist" treatment, he admitted a sort of racialized reaction—that because of his color the predictable backlash for not suppressing what was putatively *in his blood* would be severe. He could not risk being too aggressive or loud, like many of his nonblack male classmates, as he was sure that even the suggestion would have him cast immediately as lurid and evoking *chavacanería*—an accusation launched against blacks as uneducated and socially backward—evidenced by inappropriate ribald behavior and speech. Much later, I asked about the flowery language he used during his speech at the meeting. Cole explained that his parents insisted that he master Castillian Spanish as well as Cuban Spanish so that he could never be accused of using the "broken" Spanish speech of enslaved Africans, *bozalonzón*. This rhetoric and practice of respectability emerges out of the contradictory position of the "uplift class" among black societies, diasporically. It holds (often quite tenuously and contradictorily) that work by middle-class blacks—"ten times harder than whites"—is rewarded with position, status, and respect. Perhaps this is truer in Cuba than in other sites in the African diaspora. However, this hope reflects a strategy of denial of pernicious structural, ideological, and "cultural" racism. The playing field is anything but level. Nonetheless, this strategy can sometimes facilitate successful navigation of treacherous systems. Here, engagement with the singular critique of Carlos Moore is key, although Moore has faced criticism for his highly polemical work. In *Castro, the Blacks, and Africa* (1988), Moore criticized what he saw as "racial overcompensation" among his Cuban contemporaries. Following Frantz Fanon, he argued that this attitude leads to what he called the "Gracias Fidel" syndrome (1988: 44). That is, he found that blacks in Cuba, abused and locked out for so long before the Revolution, "overreacted" to small gestures and basic human consideration by uncritically pledging their unswerving loyalty to the Revolution.

When Coleridge and I finally met alone for the first time—very discreetly, since he was initially cautious about being associated with a foreign researcher—his positions on blacks, women, and homosexuals in the Revolution, and the efficacy of black identity for Afro-Cubans and other contemporary social issues, struck me as "textbook." Coleridge's comments reflected the most centrist points of view. He took seriously the anecdotal evidence of a preponderance of black Cubans in jail, the numbers disproportionately living in poverty, and other measures of marginalization. Still, Cole continued to hold that this was evidence of the failing of individual Afro-Cubans and not a failure of the state to enact affirmatively acting policies to remediate several generations of slavery and legalized oppression that found the children of the margins still excluded from the center of Cuban power. He confessed to at once not understanding male homosexuality and having a fascination with lesbians. On the economic future of Cuba, he opined equidistant between those who advocate rapid transition to a mixed economy and favor a massive increase in tourism and market liberalization and the hardliner's demands for vigilant defense of the socialist economy. Coleridge's ability to articulate the middle of the road while still appearing passionate and resolute is a formidable and profitable skill for a young man in his position. As I wrote in my notes: *Here, finally, is the elusive example! Coleridge Santiago is the Man—the New Man.* Although it is Che Guevara who is cited as the exemplar par excellence of the New Man, Cole reflected more pragmatism than the wide-eyed optimism of El Che. Instead, he sounded more like a young Fidel Castro—serious and erudite, yet popular and profoundly affecting.

In the course of my next field stay in Cuba, during the Havana Carnival, I happened upon Coleridge again, walking with my friend Yaineris. Nearly one year had passed since I had talked to Cole or Yaineris. After many trips to and from Havana, I was no longer surprised by the connections between my various respondents from different "scenes" around town, but this one intrigued me. Yaineris had described herself to me as a free spirit who, while "socialist at heart," personally wished for liberties that her foreign colleagues and acquaintances seemed to enjoy, like travel and "free expression" that she felt were denied to her by the socialist government. During the previous year, she and Cole had met at a party and rekindled a childhood friendship that they had lost many years ago. While Yaineris says that they are just "very close friends," Cole merely smiled when I asked him to confirm this.[8] Yaineris identifies as lesbian, and she has a female lover in another country who is working on getting her an invitation to work and perhaps emigrate there. Whatever their relationship, it is evident that Yaineris and Cole are each a *friend of the other's mind*, as Toni Morrison might put it and that this relationship and the circles in which Cole was now traveling had profoundly affected him.

One year earlier I thought that, finally, I had found in Cole an example of the Cuban New Man—or New Cuban Man of color. Since I had for the most part been interested in those at the margins, and I ran with an eclectic mix of folks in Havana—young hip-hop hangers on, sex workers, gay men and lesbians, black and New Afrikan political exiles from the United States, artists, and intellectuals—I rarely encountered folks aspiring to and practicing "the party line." Coleridge's revolutionary lineage, political aspirations, and status as a literal "card carrying" (Young) Communist, made him fascinating and probably attractive as a sort of straw man. Yet he insisted on showing sinew and heart during our conversations. Now, having been *turned out* by Yaineris and her cohort of *new* radicals, Cole dared to ask questions and to interrogate received knowledge. He could admit the ways in which his "New Man" masculinity was conditioned by his race and color. At a party at the Art School—a place he would have avoided a year before for fear of being associated with artists because of the putative preponderance of gay men—he and I talked about his new interest in Barbadian culture and Cuba's historical and symbolic place within the Caribbean and its contradictory formal status outside of the Caribbean economic community (CARICOM). Cole had found a new appreciation, for example, for the racial and cultural dimensions of African and Caribbean anticolonial struggles and their own precarious relationships with the United States, which conditioned their formal ties to Cuba while the affective ties might have been much different. He had begun to reread Walter Rodney and other Caribbean revolutionary icons, but this time as scholars and visionaries and not symbols to be selectively quoted. I confided in Cole that I wished I had brought to Cuba the notes and tapes from our conversations of a year ago, in order to play them back and have him listen to the "party lines" he delivered so convincingly. Now, Cole talked excitedly about how he recognized he had covered counterrevolutionary machista and homophobic perspectives in centrist language. He admitted to parroting the party lines but also insisted that it was no insincere performance. He reminded me that true intellectuals are not dogmatic but adapt and integrate new information. Just over one year before, he had seemed to me *insodable* (unreasonable) and *enigmatico* (aloof)—that is, impenetrable. Now he was espousing ideas that bordered on the heretical for his FEU comrades and the center of Cuban politics.

The new information on black consciousness, gender formation, and to a lesser extent, queer theory that Cole learned from Yaineris, Delores, and their friends and close colleagues was shared in a unique space within contemporary Cuba, which is characterized by a confluence of United States black nationalist discourse, Cuban rap music, and progressive gender and sexual politics. Far from a movement of dissension, this informal network is made up of supporters of the Revolution. The newness of the information, however, was only a part of this. Through informal gatherings with individuals associated with a collection of intellectuals, artists, blacks and other people of color including black and Latina and Latino feminists, gays, and lesbians, and others from Cuba and abroad, Cole had begun a new form of education.

This transformation did not take place instantly (or completely), but instead through intimate friendship with Yaineris, which inspired in Cole a suspension of disbelief that, for example, those who hang out with foreigners are, per force, jineteros or jineteras and (therefore) counterrevolutionary. He began to consider that there could be an ethical imperative for revolutionary Cubans like himself to support the struggles of Cuban sexual minorities and to pay more than rhetorical lip service to women's critiques of revolutionary policies. It was not the rhetorical or intellectual force or reasoned arguments that *moved* him—though the discussions were characteristically rigorous. Instead, it was the personal connections with individuals who drew on examples from their (re)interpretations of literature, art, and theory—that with which he was familiar and those he had never heard of—that gave him pause. He came to recognize that the successes of the Cuban Revolution, along with other ruptures of the last fifty or so years both inside Cuba and abroad, had changed the terms of the debate apropos of the meaning and flow of capital—pointing to dense matrices of articulation rather than simplistic *economistic* formulas. Cole argued with critical race feminisms. He refused, at first, to accept that any "identity" or experience could be as meaningful or deterministic as economic class, despite his own experience and that of his family. Although he sometimes frustrated a room of folks who tried to be patient with his "old" ideas, Cole quietly observed women who regarded him as a brother and demanded that he treat them as sisters and not as sexual objects. The women—some, but not all, lesbians—"do not count on him for affirmation like most women," as Delores once said. They do not see him as a potential partner, and therefore feel the freedom to contradict and "school" him, as well as to generously invest time, love, and care in close relationships with him. Cole says that his university classmates also often supported each other but kept close watch on those who might outshine them. In his barrio, his *socios* (friendly acquaintances) included him in street games and preadolescent intrigues. Still, he tells me, there was always a subtext of competition that extended beyond games of *cuartro esquinas* and *guerrilla*. There was competition for the affection of the most desired (and therefore, in adolescent logic, desirable) women, for credibility in the street, and as they grew older, for selection to the training or higher education most coveted. Since his late adolescence corresponded with the onset of the Special Period, this was especially acute. While previously it seemed that there would be a place for everyone and that the place hardly mattered because of tightly controlled and meager salaries for nearly everyone, supported by a healthy state system of provision, this has changed. Each wanted and sought a way to make ends meet, or a way out—out of their current conditions, through jobs that would garner hard currency, or out of Cuba itself. Where once boys exchanged their dreams, young men learned to stay mum, inscrutable. The young men of his neighborhood chat, boast, and bullshit on and on, but they are careful to say nothing at all. "No one talks here," Cole said. "It is too dangerous . . . for anyone to know what you're thinking." He was very surprised and uncomfortable then, sitting in YaYa's apartment after a lively discussion on sexism in Cuba and elsewhere, listening to people "open up" about their wishes for individual freedom within a communist Cuba and for a worldwide socialist movement in which political prisoners in the United States would be free and where the voices of the people—syncopated to hip-hop beats and bata drums—would be heard. We can certainly see connections between the informal discussions at YaYa's and black and Third World feminist praxis that insists on expressing one's position and engaging the work of epistemic training. In this process, quite to the contrary of detractors, one does not concretize a fixed "identity" but in fact examines standpoints that are always dynamic and contingent, and, in the context of a group project between friends, all of this is open to interrogation and reformation.

Hegemonic structures that restrict free thinking and religiously limit erotic possibilities cannot offer the intellectual challenge and close personal connection that can be provided by the sort of "friendship of the mind" that Yaineris extended to Cole. Here there is an erotic sense of attraction in which intimate connection and interexchange—intercourse, if you like—impels each person to grow. Cole's transition was impelled not only by exposure to the unique mix of black nationalist ideology, progressive gender and sexuality politics, and liberal/progressive rhetorics of Yaineris's set. It was, moreover, impelled by an erotic attraction to Yaineris, and more broadly to possibilities he had not imagined and for which the orthodoxy certainly had not prefigured for him. This inspired him to become open, and thus *penetrable*, in a way. Cole listened. It has inspired him to be a more committed Cuban socialist, *with a difference*—to uphold the Revolutionary project yet demand substantive changes. Now, Cole would have to consider how to bring these ideas to his companeros at the university without inciting suspicion that his revolutionary resolve had been compromised. This was especially important to him because he felt, and I agree, that what he had experienced was key to the flourishing of Cuban socialism.

As I talked with Delores about her *identidad social,* or "social identity," one night, she ran through a litany of negations of the expectations attached to the cultural, political, and national identities interpellated for her:

I am not the Revolutionary woman who goes to FMC meetings and dresses the children for Pioneros camp. . . . I am not the Afro-Cuban who wears *colares* [Yoruba necklaces representing gods to whom the wearer is consecrated], goes to *toques* [sacred drumming rituals], or does folkloric anything. . . . I am not a stunning mulata or a selfless negrita, nor the only occasional lesbian who performs for men.

This practice of *disidentification* (Muñoz 1999) is a crucial first step in order to first demystify then strategically rearticulate parts of the knowledges that each so-called identity position brings. For Delores, this process began in weekly discussion groups at YaYa's, then expanded through her participation in Oremi, which I address in the last chapter. We are not arguing that Delores learned to become black, or a woman, or an "out" lesbian in these spaces. What needs to be underscored here is that through evaluating her own experience and those of others around her, Delores reasoned a cogent and supportable critique of dynamic interlocking structures of state, cultural, and global power that find her multiply oppressed but at the same time offer her a variety of roadmaps toward liberation (or at least moments of "liberty"). It was through conversations with others—whether raucous discussions among Cuban rappers about black nationalism and feminism at YaYa's, impromptu social gatherings, or meetings held at CENESEX (Centro Nacional de Educación Sexual), Cuba's center for sexual education, Delores was able to compare what she formerly thought of as her own singular and nonrelatable story of disidentification to that of others who were similarly situated. As we observed in Cole's case, institutions like schools, heteropatriarchal families, and especially states cannot complete their totalizing project in the face of these processes through which we engender democratic collective practices and proliferate intense erotic friendships. After all, as Jacqui Alexander reminds us, "no one comes to consciousness alone, in isolation, only for herself, or passively. It is here we need a verb, the verb *conscientize,* which Paolo Freire used to underscore the fact that shifts in consciousness happen through active processes of practice and reflection . . . The fact of the matter is that there is no other work but the work of creating and re-creating ourselves within the context of community" (2005: 283).[9]

In Cuba, state apparatus attempts to construct particular types of revolutionary practices through political education or indoctrination. But whereas political education asks individuals to memorize, rote, from established texts, consciousness raising, or *to conscientize*, is to interrogate the living texts of individuals' lives. Patricia Hill Collins uses the nineteenth-century reformer and mystic Sojourner Truth to illustrate a related position. In pointing out that Truth constantly traveled—migrating across geographic, racial, religious, and other borders—Collins writes that "no truth was possible without a variety of perspectives on any given particularity" (1998: 23). Delores's practice of radical becoming begins at disidentification but is only enabled or operationalized by the constitution of a space of critical enunciation, in which competing narratives, standpoints, and knowledges are debated and performed publicly.[10] That is, while the process of erotic self-making is understood to be deeply personal and "private" in many ways, it is precisely not individualistic in its politics, motivations, and intentions. Individual desire is honored and at the same time understood to flourish only in the context of a community-building enterprise.

Transcendent Erotics and Politics

Toni Morrison's character Baby Suggs from *Beloved* is audacious in her insistence that former slaves claim their own bodies and bodily pleasure as their own. Black Cubans in late socialist Cuba are no less transgressive. They assert their bodies and minds not only as instruments of pleasure and conduits to joy and perhaps transcendent connection to a beloved community but also for mundane purposes that may merely make it easier for an individual to live day to day. Morrison writes of Baby Suggs's sermon in a forest clearing:

> "Here," she said, "in this here place, we flesh; flesh that weeps, laughs; flesh that dances on bare feet in grass. Love it. Love it hard. Yonder they do not love your flesh. They despise it. . . . Love your hands! Love them! Raise them up and kiss them. Touch others with them, pat them together, stroke them on your face 'cause they don't love that either. . . . This is flesh I'm talking about here. Flesh that needs to be loved." (2004: 88–89)

Transcendent erotics and politics is a sensuous practice that includes the deployment of sexualities pitched and styled to play various games more effectively or to at least less painfully experience psychically or materially marginal circumstances. I am offering the practice here as a way of posing the relationship between individual infrapolitical gestures and the impulse (or intention) to build community. Transcendent erotics and politics insists on creation of a new space, which may become a political organization or a heretical theoretical paradigm, but also may be a new name that defies, reappropriates or refuses old labels, or a complex of acts beyond what is interpellated within prevailing ideologies. It is in this space, which bell hooks might call a *homeplace*, in which there is the creation of radical subjectivity and fertile ground for communitas. If not yet "community," certainly congregation. It is not new to suggest that there is power in moments of communitas through ritual or celebration. There is a profound and widespread bawdy/body tradition in black diaspora cultures, represented prominently in carnivals and festivals but also extant in house parties, *limes*, and other quotidian practices—in clearings of various kinds.

Transcendent erotics and politics preserves two senses of the word "transcendence." One is the sense of the spiritual or psychic, which is especially appropriate since many of these practices are explicitly spiritual or sensuous/spiritual. This is of course grounded in a principle of a universal human endowment of positive rights and a set of human intentions to exercise those rights to things like bodily integrity, freedom from harm, freedom to fantasize, and so on. The second sense goes to the actual exercise of this agency, which is a process of making intentional interventions in a potentially malleable world. To transcend is to surpass (expectations), overstep (boundaries), go beyond (limits), outstrip (the maximum allowable quantity or quality), transgress (rules and hegemony), and encroach (on the ideological or real territory of others), for example. I do not wish to suggest that racial and sexual identities are ignored or erased "here, in this place" of transcendent erotics and politics but rather are reformed in a way that perhaps more closely resembles deeper subjective realities. These transcendent erotics and politics serve to break down parts of the scaffolding of oppression, although the state of their communitas is not some perduring political-cum-metaphysical movement. This personal experience of communitas instantiates "antistructure," but not in the sense of a "structural reversal." As antistructure there is an imagination and therefore a lived experience of alternatives to the prevailing order. This may be for only a moment. It is in this space that one who suffers as subaltern in normative structure, or various games within the structure, may *be*—that is feel, experience being, imagine herself or himself—detached from the social structure and bond with others who are similarly situated. Liminal states, according to Victor Turner, are "defined by the surrounding social statuses which it abrogates, inverts, and invalidates—as the sacred is defined by its relation to the profane. Liminality provides a propitious setting for the direct, immediate and total confrontation with human identities." He then goes on to say that "this way of experiencing oneself and one's fellows can be portrayed, grasped, and sometimes realized." If nothing else, Turner tells us, what has been achieved is "a loving union of the structurally damned pronouncing judgment on normative structure and providing alternative models for structure" (1982: 50). The current moment demands the fashioning of new tools and the use, as tools, of that which is ordinarily ignored. The transcendent erotics and politics of communitas not only addresses and critiques pernicious structural issues but also points to ways in which these structures can be made more malleable, permeable, workable, and transgressable—toward their destruction. This, with no guarantees.

The politics of erotic transcendence is in fact a three-part movement. It goes from momentary transcendence experienced in flashes of self-awareness, communitas, love relationships, or "Heiligeweg,"[11] to transgression of the hegemonic rules of a particular public, to actual transformation of the standard practices of the public. This hermeneutic of eros follows Audre Lorde's "Uses of the Erotic," which is not only about the power of one's own sexual energy but also, more profoundly, the erotic includes and goes well beyond associations with sensuality, sex, and sexuality to Lorde's "deep longing within," a site of knowledge production and energy, which is alternative to regimes of the state and received culture. For Lorde, the erotic is the deep subjective, which she recognizes as "a lens through which we scrutinize all aspects of our existence, forcing us to evaluate those aspects honestly in terms of their relative meaning within our lives . . . not to settle for the convenient, the shoddy, the conventionally expected, nor the merely safe" (1984: 57).

The erotic realms of life often elicit the most surveillance and disciplinary rigor by the state and the long arm of cultural hegemony. Each act of erotic self-making—that is, exercises of individual agency toward developing *who we are* in changing worlds, despite who we are told we are or *ought to be*—is thus *political* because it challenges the status quo allocation of social and material capital, moving the individual toward improving her or his own felt/lived experience by critically reading one's own experiences and objective relations to the world.

Erotic subjectivity—deeper understandings and compulsions of the body and soul—simultaneously embodying and invoking sex and death—works toward not only transgressing but transcending and finally transforming hegemonies of global capital, the state, and of bourgeois, limited, and limiting notions of gender, sexuality, or blackness, for example. That is, the erotic can be a catalyst for the creation of community. Moreover, the erotic can be used, as I attempt here, to push us toward a more holistic understanding of subjective agency. I employ erotic subjectivity as a way of posing the relationship between a number of individual "infrapolitical" actions (James Scott 1990), which Hanchard might refer to as "contextual micropolitics with macropolitical implications" (2006: 41), and the intention to build political communities or foment movement. My formulation owes a great debt to M. Jacqui Alexander. Following Lorde's formulation of the erotic, Alexander's notion of "erotic autonomy" (1997) suggests a belonging to oneself, which is beyond state interpellations, inscriptions, and exclusions.

Through the use of erotic subjectivity, we may create a counterpublic in which new forms of art, affective and erotic relations, and rules of public and private engagement not only inform all of our choices, as Lorde suggests, but in fact condition new choices and new politics. This is an alternate way of knowing, which looks to one's own lived experiences and one's own intentions and desires that are certainly complexly made but also more "authentic" than ways of knowing that are imposed or imbued by others. Still, this is not "individual" in the sense that it is unconnected to the intentions and desires of others. Experience is thus "raw material," as Satya Mohanty has offered.

Mohanty's important intervention, "The Epistemic Status of Cultural Identity: On *Beloved* and the Postcolonial Condition," offers that (women's) experience can be a "significant repository of oppositional knowledge," but this does not mean that experience alone, outside of an active and collective politics, "serves to ground feminist knowledge" (1993: 51).[12] This seems to echo the entreaties of Audre Lorde and Barbara Smith, among others, who stressed the crucial element of critical community formation and convincingly argue that submerged, discredited, or "alternative" knowledges expose a wider horizon of political possibilities than had been imagined previously.[13] In black feminist theorization, art, and praxis, the unique positionality of black women to self-define and self-valuate their own lived experiences (Collins 1990; Davis 1981; Guy-Sheftall 1995) is a preliminary step toward *radical becoming* (hooks 1994). But experience does not take us nearly far enough toward radical or revolutionary practices. Individual experience, or private standpoints unconnected to a movement or community project, is especially susceptible to be uninterrogated, leading to what Joy James might call "neoradical feminism" in which the radical or revolutionary intentions of black feminisms are "blotted out" (2002: 248) and in which one's own position and the political climate of the times are the only metric for one's politics.

Chela Sandoval correctly points out that oppositional consciousness is an important element of the logic at work in United States–Third World feminist social movements, and she cites the notions of "the outsider within" (Patricia Hill Collins 1998), "inappropriate otherness" (Trinh T. Minh-ha 1989), "the house of difference" (Audre Lorde 1984), and "strategic essentialism" (Gayatri Spivak 1987). She could have added concepts articulated by black gay feminists such as Essex Hemphill ("invisible son," 1991) and Joseph Beam ("brother to brother," 1986), along with James Baldwin's *Another Country* (1948), which is only one title and concept in his grand oeuvre that has greatly contributed to our understanding of living with and within difference. Of course, W. E. B. Du Bois (1903) coined the term "double-consciousness" to describe the in-between, cosmopolitan, hybrid, "schizophrenic" character of blackness in the Americas. While Sandoval also energetically follows and enlarges Gloria Anzaldúa's (1999) "consciencia de la mestiza," which is an excellent example of differential consciousness, it bears repeating, so as not to be taken to fall into an uncritical trap of ludic understanding of "hybridity" and "mestizáje," that this difference or in-betweeness should not be posed as if a happy partnership or an articulated tension between two equally valued constituents. It is more often characterized by a violent clash.

We must not sit easily after we have dug to the messy level of erotics where we find "opposition" and "transgression." How do we understand, then, our own experience relative to others' experiences, extrinsic power structures, and our own deep erotic subjectivities? The everyday erotic is gravid with transformational potential in Cuba, not only for Lili/Octavio, Cole, or Delores but also within realms of expressive culture and political praxis that seek to "open up" individuals and "tap into" spaces previously closed so as to work toward interventions in political and cultural doctrine previously unimagined. Group "epistemic training"—whether animated group conversations over coffee and guava pastels, rum, cold beer, and unfiltered cigarettes, or smaller settings with a new love interest or longer-term partner—helped Delores give voice to formerly inchoate feelings. Whether in an "official" state-sponsored focus group, music blaring at a friend's party, or with children screaming for attention in the background, no longer did Delores feel that she might be "crazy" for having feelings that were unreflected in the public transcript. The mystifications of identities of the "New Woman," "strong black woman," "global queer," or "hot mulata" are not simplistically undone through this process. Rather, they are rigorously contested and often gradually supplanted—Delores's anger and desire is theorized and validated in common union. Each of these stories illustrates differential consciousness at work and *in play*. In the chapters following, I suggest crucial distinctions between them—even as the ethnographic vignettes necessarily "spill over" the analysis offered.

4 De Cierta Manera . . . Hasta Cierto Punto

(One Way or Another . . . Up to a Certain Point)

DOMINGO GREW UP IN REGLA, just on the other side of the bay from his current haunt, Old Havana, in an apartment building built by a microbrigade—one of the self-help projects of the Revolution wherein local volunteer workers built homes for fellow workers. He nostalgically recalls helping to pull weeds and move small stones from the walkway while his parents and the comrades who were to become their neighbors laid cinderblocks that would become the home he now visits only on occasion (and not without *candela* [drama and conflict]). During the height of the Revolution, when prices and salaries were carefully planned and subsidized, and when incentives for good work came in the form of family vacations, theater tickets, and household items, Domingo's family enjoyed a "comfortable but not luxurious" lifestyle. By the middle of the 1980s, however, difficulties increased. Now, Domingo tells me, "everyone is struggling . . . We [he and his wife Mercedes] do what we can . . . We have always had a high level of culture . . . and survive, thanks to my ancestors, and to Ogun for providing guidance . . . [and help us to] yield good things in the struggle." The good things that have come include a CD "boom box," a few new articles of clothing, several small household appliances, and costly eyedrops for his daughter that he is able to purchase with the money he receives from foreign friends and clients. Mercedes does not ask where he goes at night, or what sorts of friendships he engenders to warrant these gifts. They are kind to each other, although at times they seem to be acting out ill-cast scripts of domesticity. She unquestionably runs the household. His work on the street—not the profession the state prepared him for, but *luchando* (fighting or struggling) *en la calle* (in the street)—is his concern. Her friends envy her new rice cooker—not the state-sponsored one but a new model that actually works well—and her hand-me-down clothes washer. And because Domingo is charming, handsome, and impeccably *hombre hombre*—the thin walls between apartments reveal the story of their passion—his standing among their friends remains high.

Still, the blond, green-eyed neighbors who live two flights above them raise suspicious eyebrows. They receive monthly remittances from family members living abroad that vastly outstrip what they could earn in Cuba, and they regard Domingo's forays into the streets as evidence of what they believe to be always already the case. To them, criminality and licentiousness is *en la tinta* (in the blood) of black Cubans. This neighbor interrogated me outside of their building one day—he was in disbelief that I could be from the United States "and be so black." While Mercedes, Domingo, their two children, and a cousin crowd into their tiny apartment, this couple's twenty-something son, who "officially" lives with them, actually resides several blocks away in the two-bedroom apartment left by family members who return to Cuba very infrequently (always bearing the spoils of imperialism that one can buy at the Walmart Supercenter in Hialeah). These family members manage to regularly remit funds for their kin to live comfortably without working. To Domingo's family, luchando en la calle is a necessary solution for survival. The everyday challenges of Mercedes and Domingo, who do better than many others in Havana, is emblematic of the difficulties and opportunities emerging from multiple ruptures: the Revolution of 1959; the Rectification period of the early 1980s; the Special Period, which arrived on the heels of the Rectification in 1989 and lasted until about 1994; and the current transition period.[1]

In this chapter, I will examine the multiple effects of revolutionary gender, sexual, and race rhetorics (and silences), as well as family hygiene policies, on contemporary subjects. "Proper" sexuality and gender performance have become closely conflated with one's status as a revolutionary. The Revolution demanded very particular gender rhetorics and practices of identification and disidentification that required cultural and racial renegotiations on the part of all Cubans, but most especially blacks, sexual minorities, and women. In this chapter I will therefore consider the ways in which the project of building the revolutionary family betrays its intentions to curtail the erotic autonomy of all women by completely eliding the experiences of lesbians and punishing men thought to be too effeminate, or homosexual, while at the same time pathologizing black families and individuals as "deviant."

De Cierta Manera

The classic film *De cierta manera* (One way or another), produced in 1974 by the Instituto Cubano del Arte y Industria Cinematográficos (ICAIC), is one important illustration of the way Cubans have attempted to deal with the changes that the Revolution demanded. While *De cierta manera* illustrates the tensions of the early revolution, the Special Period that Domingo and Mercedes live in constitutes another rupture, which impelled still more renegotiations. Some of these are dramatically out of step with the state's visions of progress and revolution. During the Special Period, and in its wake, the state is no longer able to enforce a number of its disciplines, as the nation has turned its attention to survival. In this light, Domingo reconsiders not only his career choice and loyalty to the ideals of socialist deportment espoused by his parents, but also tradition, family, and sexuality. After a description of revolutionary policy, and before taking a look at how this plays out on the ground, I will describe the daily conundrum that *De cierta manera* depicts and with which contemporary Cubans like Mercedes and Domingo struggle.

In many ways, Domingo and Mercedes's contemporary reality can be seen as a sort of sequel to *De cierta manera*, which was directed by the black Cuban filmmaker Sara Gómez. *De cierta manera* is a revolutionary film "about real people and fictitious ones" (González 1993: 128) in the real Miraflores neighborhood being built on the footprint of the infamous "marginal" pre-revolutionary slum, Las Yaguas. Here, Cubans struggle with the moral and political demands placed on them by the 1959 Revolution, which held a number of gender, racial, and cultural implications. In his moving personal remembrance of his close friend Sara Gómez, the screenwriter and playwright Tomás González writes that "she didn't sing to revolution, she sang from within, bringing out the anonymous good and bad. She homed in on the revolution, but with a vocation for truth" (130). He writes that when Gómez first invited him to collaborate on the film she told him, "'We'll do a film about a real screwed-up couple. . . . He has to be real marginal, from *el ambiente* ["underworld" scene]. He'll have a gold tooth,' she laughed. 'And she has to be all screwed up because of her middle-class background. A white woman with a *jabao* ["redbone," or light-skinned man with "African features"].' 'Why not black [negro]?' I asked. 'It'd be too much,' she replied, 'and we want this film to get shown, right?'" (135).[2]

As a journalist, artist, and intellectual with educated parents, Gómez was poised to take advantage of the opportunities presented by the triumph of the Revolution. She remains the only Cuban woman to have directed a feature-length film produced by ICAIC, and she is one of three blacks and the only black woman to be a part of the prestigious institute. Reportedly also the first woman to wear an afro in Cuba, Sara Gómez is exceptional in a number of ways, not only because of her native and cultivated talents that find expression in her films but also in terms of her position—her moment in time. In the film, race/color and gender in the new society is central, but it is rarely made explicit—exemplifying the complexity of her thinking as a revolutionary black Cuban intellectual, and the tensions of the moment. *De cierta manera* departs in some ways from the heavy-handed didactic style of many early socialist films, and yet in other moments it seamlessly reproduces revolutionary propaganda. As such it allows for multiple understandings of gender, revolution, race/color, and African religion, via a single complexly intersectional point of view. The contemporary black Cuban filmmaker Gloria Rolando's work continues this tradition. Rolando, an independent filmmaker, has taken on more expressly black critique and cultural and historical issues, such as her film dramatizing the 1912 massacre.[3]

The protagonists of *De cierta manera*, based loosely on friends of Gómez and González, are unlikely heroes. The male lead, Mario, is torn between the "man's code" of the street and his collective at work. En la calle he is expected to continue to uphold the machista[4] values and cultural styles of his friends, who, unlike him, "took the pledge" to become Ñañigo, or members of Abakuá, the African-derived male mutual-aid society. Mario, however, had thought himself "saved" from this life by his conscription into military service. Now as a laborer at a state-owned factory, his worksite organization, led by his stalwart revolutionary father, demands a very different code of behavior and ideology. The film opens on a documentary-like scene in which Mario's coworker, who was once a close friend, pleads his case to the work tribunal. He has been brought up on charges of repeatedly evading work—the most recent being an extended weekend absence, for which he could be sentenced to a work camp. The strapping mulato worker tearfully claims that he was called away to Santiago to the bedside of his dying mother. Mario knows the truth—that the coworker, who serves as a kind of foil to his character and therefore likewise an exemplar of black masculinity, was vacationing there with a woman, while the rest of the workers took up his slack under tremendous production demands. Yolanda (apparently white by Gómez's reckoning) is Mario's love interest—the other half of the "screwed-up couple." Raised in a relatively privileged household of professionals, the young divorced teacher must learn to take the criticism of her senior colleagues at her new school in Miraflores, where Mario was raised. Her challenge is to quiet her bourgeois penchant for judgment and condescension toward her mostly black and poor pupils and their parents. The film suggests that she must also learn to trust in her relationship with Mario. In a tense discussion with a parent about a child failing in school, Yolanda chastises the black woman, telling her, "I know you are a good worker, but . . ." *you have to take better care of your children*, citing their attitudes and behavior, to which the woman tersely replies, "es la calle!"—that it is the element of el ambiente that negatively affects her son, not her parenting skills. Here we begin to see the complexity of the argument that Gómez is building in the film. The woman, who appears poised and well put together, takes umbrage with the accusation that she and her family are at fault—at once begging the question of her victimhood and her culpability. In another scene a frail blanquita, by way of explaining her son's poor behavior in school, tells Yolanda that all of her children have different fathers, none of whom live with her and the children. Gómez wants to show the dignity and strength of these characters and the real women like them, but she also wants to indict the "backwardness" that she and other revolutionaries judge as a consequence of the "lifestyle" in places like Las Yaguas. Yolanda, whom Gómez invites the viewer to identify with, must deal compassionately with those she has committed to help *uplift*.

Voiceovers from a narrator explain that underemployment and unemployment, low education levels, "antisocial attitudes," "marital instability," crime, and drugs had plagued these "marginal" neighborhoods of individuals from "oral cultures" (of Africa and Andalusia)—as if we are to understand, a priori, the relationship between these things. Actual footage from Miraflores in 1962 shows the razing of pre-revolutionary slums and building of new housing. The repeating imagery of the wrecking ball destroying old, nearly uninhabitable structures expresses dramatically, but not stridently, the structure of feeling in early 1960s Cuba, during which a new society was being built, as I will argue here, without excavating the deep foundation of racism and misogyny. Throughout the black-and-white film, Gómez expertly intersperses "documentary" footage of conversations with workers at the real jobsites where her fictional characters work, and scenes of the demolition of the solares and slums of Las Yaguas—seamlessly interweaving these stories of profound change taking place literally *on the ground* and within individuals. This combination of fictional narrative with documentary "evidence" elevates the work beyond other cinema vérité or social reality filmmaking. In addition, there are two very different inserts that expand and deepen the documentary and fictional narrative. One is an "ethnographic" explanation of Abakuá, the male mutual-aid society of Ñañigos; the other is a sort of biography of the black guitarist and songwriter Guillermo, whose voiced-over personal narrative includes serving time in prison for a murder he committed in self-defense to protect the honor of his fiancée and the writing of his song "Véndele" (Leave him). Both of these threads provide more layers to the fictional narrative of the romance of Yolanda and Mario, which we are offered as political instruction. We'll return to these later.

De cierta manera not only reveals that an old political economy characterized by unemployment, lack of education and healthcare, and poor housing existed prior to the triumph of the Revolution, but more pointedly, *One way or another* betrays the assumptions of revolutionary ideology that see African descendents as morally deficient. I have analyzed Fernando Ortiz's elaboration and naturalization of race/color and gender differences and revolutionary reinterpretation of these themes, and here we revisit this, briefly, as another example of the "culture of poverty" thesis.

Most infamously espoused in his highly influential (if not also by now discredited) "The Negro Family: The Case for National Action," and the Senate "Moynihan Report" excerpted from it, Moynihan's logic of black families as "a tangle of pathology" (1995: 12) goes something like this: United States blacks had been deracinated of culture and family structure due to the slave system. As a result, black men, "emasculated" by their lack of opportunities to be the sole family breadwinner and decision maker, drop out, or are forced out of heteronormative gender hierarchies in families and in sexual relations, by out-of-control black females. This situation constructs various iterations of deviance and criminality in black families and black communities, which constitute the Negro problem. According to Moynihan and innumerable acolytes and uncritical apologists, the problem here is not the enduring racialization of political economic structures, or the lack of forthright intersectional analysis, but the Negroes themselves. The "cycle" of unwed pregnancies, criminality, and poverty, this mythology holds, cannot be ameliorated until African Americans are disciplined by particular moral gender and sexual hygienic practices. This "just so" story has indeed become "common sense" in the Gramscian connotation. It is acceptable to United States liberals and Cuban revolutionaries alike because it absolves both of any responsibility in favor of an indictment of long-dead slaveholders and an irresponsible, damaged black underclass. Another sleight of hand. In this one, there is a washing of the hands of the state, corporate interests, and others who continue to benefit from the multiple political and economic legacies of slavery.

In Cuba, blacks (or Afro-Cubans) are likewise seen as sexually prolific, deviant, criminal, with unruly gender practices.[5] The Cuban difference is that it is precisely (African-descended Cuban) culture—understood to be rich, deep, and highly elaborated—that is at fault. In both cases, gender inappropriateness is charged. This brand of the "culture of poverty" thesis is deeply entrenched and ubiquitous in the United States and Cuba partially because it seems to concede an axiomatic fact—that slavery damaged black people. Yet it obfuscates much more than it pretends to reveal. Rather than qualify, quantitatively account, or hold accountable for the material and psychic damage of slavery, one will hear, as I did on innumerable occasions, moral arguments coming from dyed-in-the-wool materialists. For example, the response to this question, *If the Revolution liberated all Cubans, why are blacks still overrepresented in sports, music, the margins, and el ambiente, while underrepresented in the government, academe, and the professions?*, nearly always was that "they" (often still disidentificatory *they* when talking to blacks) had low levels of education and "culture" (understood here, equivocally, as European culture) and were always already "predisposed" or prone to music, sports, fucking, and stealing. That is, while these material conditions emerge from capitalist structures, they remain due to personal failures *en la tinta*, or in the black family. "Not determined . . ." one well-educated woman told me, "but predisposed."

Thus, despite their antimony, there are in fact profound and wide links between Cuban Marxist-Leninist ideology and United States (neo)liberalism. Each identifies variously "savage" populations and finds them all wanting in social advancement relative to Europeans. Each depends on a single social trajectory (most productively thought of as white supremacist heteropatriarchy). Liberalism claims to be the savior of the individual, while socialism claims to situate the individual within ethical communal structures. Here, "culture," "family," "man," and "woman" are deployed as if natural rather than supremely interarticulated through the multilayered and interpenetrating projects of imperialism, racism, and patriarchy—each of which emerge through the exploitation of the integrity of the individual. These are the apparitions of the past that confront Domingo as he sets out at night—or more so, when he returns two or three days later with dollars in his pocket and a new table fan. Mercedes does not speak of it during her friendly chats with the eyebrow-raising neighbor who receives phone calls from foreigners asking after her husband (as one of only two or three families in the building with a telephone, they accept a few dollars every month or so for the service).

The contemporary conundrum of the real-life Domingo and Mercedes—building a household out of the detritus of cultural expectations, religious obligations, and revolutionary ideology—seems synchronous with the real and imagined subjects of *De cierta manera*. Domingo, a mulato from Regla, met Mercedes, a jaba from the famous Alamar high-rise apartments in East Havana, while they both were attending technical school. As noted above, they live in a small apartment with their two children and, occasionally, Mercedes's cousin. A small sleeping loft sits above the kitchen where two people can barely fit at the same time. They have a small two-burner propane stove; a compact refrigerator, which Mercedes has elaborately rigged to squeeze more use out of the thirty-year-old appliance; and a small sink, next to which

Domingo one day proudly placed a compact Korean-made clothes washer. Their cramped quarters are in no way unusual. In fact, many households have two or three generations of family members living in one small space—a situation that necessitates elaborate sleeping arrangements and profound patience, and that makes the notion of personal privacy, as many have come to know it in North America, laughable. Mercedes and Domingo were fortunate to get this efficiency-style apartment, even in its state of disrepair, while they worked at one of the local clinics after completing their training, but now after two children and no building upgrades they must find a way to move. Over more than a year of occasionally accompanying Domingo to the Cuban Council of State offices, and later a local cooperative housing agency recently sanctioned by the state, to ask after possibilities for a larger place, I have seen him be at turn plaintive, demanding, and even argumentative, but also always profoundly savvy about the official processes one has to follow. Emerging alternatives to the old, slow bureaucracy, like the new cooperative, provide a glimmer of hope that things will change, but this too is highly variable and has its own logics and rituals.[6] Domingo's official letters to the Cuban Council of State are regularly sent every six weeks or so, and they are worded excruciatingly "correct." At once beseeching and entitled, Domingo cites the problems in his building and how it endangers his children. He does not say, however, that he is rarely at home but instead more often at the home of a European friend. He underscores the fact that he and his wife are professionally credentialed and are members of the appropriate mass organizations. He does not say, of course, that he has been on indefinite leave from work for nearly two years, at the same time that he faithfully attends every religious ceremony at the home of his *padrino* (religious godfather) and dutifully works the informal markets of *la calle*. Domingo expresses both his fidelity to the Revolution and his patience—his knowledge that, as he writes, "this is a moment of great difficulty for all" in which everyone must "stand unified and work hard to make tomorrow better." These rhetorical skills, dictated to a European expatriate friend who lends him both typewriting and help with grammatical phrasing, has been honed through his experience in the youth brigades and in other mass organizations in which his parents insisted he participate. At the same time that he has faith that his letter will be answered affirmatively one day, he dare not wait, as his father counsels him to do. He has faith in the state only inasmuch as he can ask his ancestors and Orisha

FIGURE I. René Peña, *Untitled*. From the series White Things, 2002. © René Peña.

to intervene. And he has faith in his own ability *pa' resolver*, the difficulties he and his family face, in the street.

Making New Men and New Women

With the Revolution of 1959 the personal became more political than ever as blackness, male homosexuality, and women's autonomy (not to be conflated with "equality") were each increasingly posed as threats to the Revolution's bedrock discourse of national consolidation. The Revolutionary government set out to construct socialist subjects who could rectify the position of Cuba as civilized and sovereign, as well as protect the new nation from (real and imagined) threats from the United States. The Revolution challenged Mercedes and Domingo, their fictitious forbearers Yolanda and Mario, and all Cubans, to become "new" men and "new" women. They were given examples of Che Guevara and Mariana Grajales (the long-suffering mother of General Antonio Maceo). Some were given new homes and earned new opportunities. For many the price of revolutionary Cuban citizenship would be costly. As I demonstrated in the previous chapter, for some, putative unruliness would preclude it.

M. Jacqui Alexander reminds us that while all states attempt to regulate particular bodies in ways they see fit, there is in fact an additional burden placed on postcolonial nations. We must be mindful of whether some bodies (women's bodies, sex workers' bodies, queer men's bodies, putatively excessively or inappropriately ethnic bodies) "are offered up . . . in an internal struggle for legitimation . . . Not just (any) *body* can be a citizen any more" (1994: 6). She asserts in a related work (2005) that *some* bodies, like that of the lesbian and the "prostitute," cannot be included as citizens in former colonies of the Caribbean because they embody a sexual agency and eroticism that is radically out of step with the aspirations of the nation to advertise itself not only as independent but also as developed, disciplined, and poised to join in the number of "civilized" states.[7] This is resonant with Roderick Ferguson's queer-of-color critique in which he carefully disidentifies with historical materialism due to its silences and assumptions vis-à-vis the non-heteronormative subject of color, holding that "both bourgeois and revolutionary practices were conceived through heteropatriarchy" (2004: 10). These related insights—that heteropatriarchy is *left in place* in Marxist and otherwise revolutionary societies and that the state (all states) depends upon racialized heteropatriarchy to constitute and maintain itself in the global hierarchy of states—are crucial to understanding the current situation and theorizing spaces beyond it. Moreover, Kamala Kempadoo (2004) has advanced our understanding of the ways that "notions of essential native sexuality" in the region enervate moves toward national and individual liberation. Here, by attending to the ways that heteropatriarchy is also antiblack, we hope to push these key contributions further.

In sturdy *common sense* in Cuba and throughout the Americas, proper families and civilized nations are run by white(ned) men and supported by selfless white(ned) women. Departure from this—single-female-headed households, for example, "cultural blackness" or adherence to African or black stylistic practices—causes great anxiety. Beyond this, radical transgression—"public" homosexuality, "prostitution," transgenderism, for example—precipitates state crisis.

In one of its earliest and most visible moves, the new revolutionary Cuban government immediately began to sanitize Havana of the "counterrevolutionary" element—namely, el ambiente of sex laborers and sex enthusiasts, including homosexuals, working in the cafés and casinos, which were largely under United States corporate (or) organized crime control. They also unleashed, and then later rescinded, harsh disciplines of male style and sexuality while attempting to reeducate female sex laborers and situate them in new occupations—such as mothers, teachers, and seamstresses—in the service of the Revolution. Cast in this central role, as a mother who would nurture future generations of the nation, the policing of the moral hygiene of the revolutionary woman—*the ground* in which the new society would grow—was a central enterprise. That is, the revolution begins at home. This, of course, dovetails quite well with "traditional" expectations, pre-1959, of close family affiliation with women organizing the daily, affective relations that nurture those bonds. It uncritically reified the old casa (home) and calle (street) distinctions that seek to keep the woman's place in the home or private sphere, although this would seem at first blush to directly counter socialist rhetorics. If the revolutionary nation is to be built first at home by "new" women—and tangentially, "new" men—why have such fidelity to narrow bourgeois structures of heterosexual coupling and nuclear families? It seems in fact that there is not enough newness here. Has the model of the heterosexually reproduced nuclear family not already been exposed as an instrumental invention of capital? Has this model not also by now been revealed to be nearly unsustainable without the exploitation of racialized labor and the elision of female autonomy? Certainly, large socialist societies, like China, have found that nuclear families are less efficient in terms of production than are extended and extended-stem arrangements. Did Frederick Engels not write that class antagonism's advent "coincides with the development of the antagonism between man and woman in the monogamous marriage, and the first class oppression was that of the female sex by the male" (1968: 76)? Why, then, as prerevolutionary structures were to be brushed toward the dustbin of history, are so-called traditional understandings of masculinity, femininity, marriage, and family so assiduously codified? Put less polemically, and perhaps more pragmatically: what anxieties underlie the racial, gender, and sexual hygienic projects of the (early revolutionary Cuban) state? How have these been undergoing change, or forced to contend with perhaps unimagined realities today?

Women's status in socialist revolution is in fact a site of ambivalence, on the ground. The Revolution, following Marx and Engels, saw women's subordinate social position as a historical effect of the advent of private property, in which women's potential biological role in reproduction was uncritically conflated with a social role of caretaking and domestic obligation. It was thus posed as "natural" for women to be excluded from other forms of production outside of the household. Engels wrote that women's emancipation is only possible when women participate in large-scale production, do not have to depend on men, and have only minor domestic obligations. When socialism was officially embraced by the revolutionary government in 1961, they also seemed to embrace the socialist ideal of marriage, in which, as Engels wrote, women and men were to be equal partners, and not with "the woman as the proletariat and the husband as the bourgeoisie" (1968: 77). Still, there was no analysis beyond this, little attention was paid to reeducating men to take up the slack at home, and an examination of "the woman question" as discrete and not conflated with "family" was refused. That is, as the new ideology loudly announced itself on and on in other arenas, the lack of radical analysis of gender and sexuality (*the silence* that no doubt was more comfortable for those whose privilege would be threatened) inevitably resulted in the intransigence of heteropatriarchy. The assumption was, naively (or perhaps, instrumentally), that as private property diminished and institutional arrangements that barred women from productive occupations outside the home were lifted, "the woman question" would be solved. But this of course is predicated on a "woman question" posed by patriarchs who saw their domestic arrangements as "natural." Like the silence in revolutionary policy around race and color even after the issue was forced by black intellectuals, the July 26th Movement's program manifesto did not include a specific critique or analysis of women's oppression under capitalism. And it certainly did not include any notion of positive sexual rights.

As we have observed, gender hierarchies were instituted not to construct individual persons or bodies—"not just *any* body"—but rather *some* bodies that would be constituents of closely prescribed revolutionary collectives. Far from families being a "private" place where one may retreat from work or the state, communism begins in the home and is an extension of the public sphere. Socialist theory holds that the goal to build a new and just society is first practiced in the home. Membership in mass organizations like the Federación Mujeres Cubanas (FMC), the largest among Cuban mass organizations, which at its height counted 80 percent of Cuban women as members, and especially the Comites por la Defensa de la Revolución (CDR), whose motto is "revolution in every neighborhood" and which earned its reputation as the front line of state surveillance, are examples of the ways in which ordinary citizens are expected to integrate into the collective. This happens through participation in groups of one's immediate neighbors (CDR); classmates, from primary school through postgraduate education (e.g., Union Jovenes Comunista, FEU, Pioneros); and gender (FMC). The family is therefore only the smallest unit of this mass organization scheme—disciplining persons as proper Cuban communists through the proper communist family.

Women, "the Family," and Revolution

The experiences of women and families I have come to know show that the policies of the revolutionary government have dramatically improved the lives and life chances of most Cuban women and families—extending this well beyond the class privilege that the wealthy alone enjoyed before the revolution. Still, fear of the dissolution of gender and sexual privilege has stymied the leadership, thereby resulting in incremental change as opposed to a gender/sexual revolution. From this perspective, the Family Code, and the work of the FMC on behalf of heterosexual Cuban families, represents a failure of political imagination. A revolutionary change would constitute a set of rhetorics and practices that rather than reencase old hegemonies would address current (and future) human needs and sexual rights. Minimally, this includes equal recognition of the erotic subjectivities and agency of men and women, protection from impediments to consensual private expression of sexuality, and freedom to identify with and express gender in whatever way the individual chooses. Finally, rather than state sanction of the choices of (heterosexual) individuals to cohabitate and commit to the person(s) of their choice, would not a gender/sex revolution mandate the abolition of "marriage" as a function of the state? It would support the composition of families through which individuals may associate, cohabitate, and raise children or not, in the way they choose. This may thus prove to be more *communist*—that is, cooperative and more centrally devoted to collective endeavors beneficial to the nation. Whether or not one agrees with this radical view of sexual citizenship, it seems apparent that the Revolution has been laboring under outmoded and in some cases patently racist and sexist assumptions, which in other contexts it vehemently rejects.

The First Party Congress of the Cuban Communist Party (PCC) stipulated the Family Code in 1975. It is constitutive of a litany of important changes to official Cuban gender ideology and policy, such as "equal rights and responsibilities for both (heterosexual) partners in marriage," including that of nurturing and educating children; joint responsibility for upkeep of the household when both partners work outside of the home; and affirming the right of each partner to practice his or her profession or skill with the support of his or her partner. The right to birth control and abortion was affirmed under the condition of medical counseling. Heterosexual marriage, formerly a privilege of those who could financially afford this state recognition, was made widely accessible. Divorce laws were also codified, and for the first time required a judicial decree. In cases of births outside of marriage, under the Family Code mothers would now be able to list the father's name on the child's birth certificate with or without his permission, and fathers were mandated to provide material and other support. These changes dealt a formidable blow to traditional prerevolutionary practices that gave exclusive custody of children (and wives) to married fathers and no rights to families outside of marriage, thereby reserving economic power for men who were often the only breadwinners, and giving control of women's reproductive health and sexual practice to husbands, fathers, male doctors, and judges. Clearly, the Revolution made headway on some issues of women's status more quickly than was the case in nonsocialist nations. At the same time, women's status is collapsed within discourses of the family rather than the individual.

Some consideration of the meanings and practices of family, motherhood, and matrimony, and the ways in which they effect compulsory heteronormativity and patriarchal control, must be undertaken here. Although Cuba's Family Code codifies a number of important gender policies, women and gender transgressives still face tremendous limitations in the private sphere, which can be traced to the limits of these policies to attend to individual women, as opposed to the number of gender roles they are asked to play. The late Vilma Espín, FMC president and, not incidentally, the wife of Raúl Castro, asserted at an International Women's Year conference that contrary to the feminist movement in the North, which advocates freedom from the assumption of a biological imperative to be responsible for the nurturing of children and a husband, women's equality "is not a question of fostering antagonistic contradictions between men and women. It is a question of upholding the dignity of the couple, the family nucleus."[8] For many radical feminists, whose politics in other areas may resonate with Cuban communists, the putative "traditional" nuclear family is the foundation of the reproduction of male privilege, supported by the state.

The Cuban Constitution, however, protects the family, motherhood, and matrimony (Dominguez 1978), and not women as agents who may or may not participate in those roles or who may perform them in ways Espín and the FMC would not recognize. The Cuban state, mostly through the FMC, has launched projects designed to address what they recognize as the cultural and political-economic heritage of male chauvinism, which they rightly claim is a major impediment to equality in the home. The vast majority of people I talked with agreed that women should be paid equal pay for equal work, and generally should be as free as men are to make their own decisions about work, sex, relationships, and other important determinations. The FMC has also succeeded in popularizing language for confronting forms of gender inequality like the double duty of working women. However, these measures have not yet gone far enough, precisely because of the enduring analytic frame that finds gender ideology a mere superstructural reflection rather than a productive relation, and the belief that gender can be read in isolation from the complexly constituted matrix of race/class/gender/sexuality.

The meanings and practices of "family," "motherhood," and "matrimony" are certainly no less contradictory in nonsocialist contexts, as two generations of feminist scholars have shown. In Cuba and other socialist nations, the hand of the state is much more openly seen doing its magic. However, in nonsocialist contexts, civil society putatively functions independently of the state. Misogyny, for example, thus seems to recur only in civil society—for example, in religious institutions or cultural beliefs—and the state is cast as disinterested protector of individual rights. This of course flies in the face of critical race feminism that sees the (neo)liberal state as one element of a closely articulated apparatus of heteropatriarchal control.

It is difficult to qualify the notion of a "Cuban feminism." Although there are certainly a number of feminist-thinking individuals and group projects, what one will hear more often is women who, like poet Georgina Herrera, describe their work as "feminine, not feminist" (quoted in Sarduy and Stubbs 2000: 119). Herrera and others hold that their analysis comes out of very particular standpoints conditioned by their status as Cuban women. As Conrad James explains, "what emerges quite powerfully [from her work] is the image of a woman whose vocation is the empowerment of women" (2003: 475). Espín herself had reportedly also used this formulation of *feminine, not feminist* often. Sujatha Fernandes's work on Magín, the would-be competing Cuban women's organization, shows that this group of women media professionals were eager to join the global network of women's NGOs, but were ultimately thwarted in their attempts by state bureaucracies (2006). Magín, which counted prominent black Cubans such as Georgina Herrera and the national poet laureate and essayist Nancy Morejón as founding members, according to Fernandes, had begun to articulate positions on issues that departed from those of the FMC, which was attractive to many women who increasingly think of the FMC as irrelevant. For example, Magín weighed in a critique of what they thought of as the FMC's bourgeois understandings of female sex labor by asserting that the young women sex laborers should be recognized for their resourcefulness and self-esteem, rather than denounced as counterrevolutionary. Nancy Morejón's insistence on affirming her Cubanness, womanhood, and blackness without preference or exclusion (certainly with a Guillén-like nuance that is pitched to Cuban *realpolitik*) can be read as a pro-black feminist position. The work of the filmmakers Sara Gómez and Gloria Rolando likewise represents black Cuban culture, history, and life with a special interest in gender. The hip-hop performer Magia, who explicitly refers to her lyrics as feminist, has elevated the level of gender discourse in popular culture; Las Krudas, and Oremi, the erstwhile gathering of lesbian and bisexual women—both of whom we will hear from—have pushed the boundaries of (black) Cuban women's representation and artistic expression well beyond the boundaries of what the state or elite cultural institutions in Cuba currently admit to the public discourse. Still, explicitly feminist identification in Cuba has been enfeebled by a false dichotomy. This finds, on one side of the Florida Straits, the tendency to conflate large and diverse feminist theories, discourses, and practices with the bourgeois values of United States liberal feminism; and on the other side, the charge that the work in Cuba, including especially the FMC, is per force not feminist because of its insistence on Marxist or integrative analysis and its close relationship with the state. Cuban women's resistance to taking up the language of "feminism" is not only conditioned by the antagonisms between Cuba and the United States state but also is resonant with the experiences of some black and women of color in the United States and in the Third World who regard the term as belonging to a movement of middle-class white women whose political interests are often opposed to their own.[9] While a number of black women and other women of color have historically participated in the larger feminist movement in the United States and other places (and continue to do so), many women of color have also articulated and organized their own movements and discourses, which draw on their own experiences and analyses. The term "black feminism" can be traced to the 1970s in response to the larger movement's refusal to incorporate the lessons of black liberation and include intersectional analysis and personal politics.[10] At the same time, as Barbara Smith reminds us, "Black women were never fools, we could never afford to be" (1998: xxvii). That is, black women's participation, from the abolition and suffrage movements to anti-lynching activism, civil rights efforts, and HIV prevention, for example, has had long and deep engagement in intersectional analysis and action. The same is true for Cuban women, whether or not they use the term "feminist." In "A Black Feminist Statement" the Combahee River Collective, including Smith, connects socialist political activism in transnational communities of black women with the most intimate and personal political areas of everyday life. Moving precipitously beyond the sort of feminism that Espín and others eschew, this speaks directly to the current struggles and triumphs of my Cuban respondents and friends:

> We realize that the liberation of all oppressed peoples necessitates the destruction of the political-economic systems of capitalism and imperialism, as well as patriarchy. . . . We are not convinced, however, that a socialist revolution that is not also a feminist and antiracist revolution will guarantee our liberation. . . . Although we are in essential agreement with Marx's theory as it applied to the very specific economic relationships he analyzed, we know that this analysis must be extended further in order for us to understand our specific economic situation as Black women. (Combahee River Collective 1983: 268)

Hasta Cierto Punto

Sara Gómez begins a conversation on masculinity and respectability in *De cierta manera* that Tomás Gutiérrez Alea, the most celebrated of Cuban directors, amplifies in his film *Hasta cierta punto* (Up to a certain point) in 1983. The title makes fun of the qualified acceptance by Cubans of revolutionary gender policy only "up to a certain point" and it exposes the limits of revolutionary society's interrogation of the notions of exploitation and domination. Perhaps in homage to his former student and collaborator Sara Gómez, Gutiérrez uses similar techniques of documentary within the feature film as a meditation on where the Revolution had progressed by 1983. While the Special Period has begun to receive deserved scholarly attention,[11] this moment in Cuba's history should also be more thoroughly investigated.

During the 1970s under the SDPE, or System of Direction and Planning of the Economy, Cuba had begun market reforms that more closely resembled a pragmatic market orientation. To ameliorate social and economic problems thought to be caused by the SDPE, the Third Party Congress of the Cuban Communist Party announced the Rectification program in 1986. While the external threat of reforms in the Soviet Union was, of course, a major impetus for the Rectification campaign, the 1980 Mariel flotilla and the unprecedented Afro-Cuban protests of 1984 reported by Alejandro de la Fuente (1998) certainly must have also figured substantially. It has been reported widely that blacks, homosexuals, and practitioners of African religions—alienated by labor and social practices carried out in the name of the Revolution—were disproportionately represented in the Mariel "boatlift" and the subsequent demonstrations of unease in the predominantly black neighborhood of Central Havana. Farmers markets and other openings of nongovernment planned production were closed, and production of consumer goods was reduced. The Rectification's reform of "errors and negative tendencies" returned Cuba to a more centralized decision-making apparatus and to mobilization techniques that had been very successful in the 1960s. However, the by-now hackneyed practice of mass mobilizations and voluntary work were met with skepticism. Moreover, the Rectification period allowed for a film like Gutiérrez's that laid bare some of the contradictions of the revolutionary society. The film within the film of *Hasta cierta punto* is ostensibly about the machista attitudes of dockworkers, so the director, a progressive revolutionary and well-known screenwriter (who might be thought of as Gutiérrez himself), goes to the docks to interview laborers about their gender attitudes as research for his screenplay. *Hasta cierta punto* is a poignant comment not on gender politics among workers but on the machista sensibilities of the Cuban revolutionary screenwriter. Even though throughout the film, black dockworkers are represented as spokesmen for machista ideas—silencing their female companions, posing, and spouting machista rhetorics—the screenwriter's behavior toward his wife and his new lover, one of only a few female dockworkers, reveals to the critical viewer the profound levels of gender privilege unconsciously enjoyed by those whose compound identity includes white, male, and middle class.

The Rectification program did not have the economic effects intended by its makers. By the late 1980s, when Soviet President Gorbachev announced his policies of Glasnost and Perestroika (restructuring), which led to the dissolution of favorable trade relations between the two countries, the social and political debates over the revolution's "errors" and missteps seemed to be secondary.

The Cuban economic crisis known as the Período Especial en Tiempo de Paz (Special Period in Times of Peace) was brought on by the dissolution of the Soviet Union and Cuban state inefficiency, and worsened by a tightening of the United States blockade. This period of more than ten years of structural adjustment, economic depression, and social upheaval has forced a reappraisal of the revolutionary project, as Hernandez-Reguant points out in her comprehensive introduction (2009). The Special Period reached its height in 1993 as the island's economic crisis broadened to a one-third drop in gross domestic product. The government sought a way to prevent the economy from collapsing by attracting hard currency within this "special period for the capitalist model of development throughout the Caribbean and elsewhere" (Klak 1998: 207). The Special Period necessitated *maquinando* ("machinations," or as a friend told me, "making things work"), *pa' resolver* (in order to resolve) material problems through creative home economics, as this period of internal structural adjustment, like other internal crises, brought the interrelatedness of race and color with gender and class into relief. More than any other time, the Special Period brought the reality of the global public sphere to the doors, beds, and dinner tables of Cuban families.[12] At the same time that the Special Period damaged the economy, it also forced an increase in informal individual production and trade, and concomitantly, new or renewed avenues of intellectual, ideological, artistic, erotic, and stylistic practice. Cuban people—especially blacks and queers who had been shut out of other avenues—were likewise opened up to greater varieties of expression. This was due to a conjuncture of a greater array of choices, changes in the capacity of the impaired state to repress those expressions, and powerful global forces exerting their own hegemonies on local ones—making the position and potential politics of deviance of black (and) queer subjects especially problematic and promising.

Exclusion of dark-skinned Cubans from the center of Cuban life (and therefore access to hard currency)—whether de jure before the Revolution or de facto today, as the nation recovers from the Special Period—finds many eking out a living in "unofficial" spaces titled with little irony the mercado negro (black market) and in entertainment, where access is less restricted to black Cubans. In fact, the working, dancing, smiling, sexing black body is essential to the nation's resurgent tourist sector. Not only, and certainly not all black Cubans are engaged in this. Further, as Nadine Fernandez has observed, most Cubans, who have been exposed to foreigners, have engaged in some form of *jineteando*, or hustling, if what we mean by this is the extraction of dollars from foreigners (1999: 85). *Luchando en la calle* (struggling in the street), has many facets, and can mean anything that earns money, consumer goods, or even the promise of migration. While the public spectacle of sex work by young women became a cause célèbre in the 1990s, women are effectively locked out of most other forms of informal tourism and street economies. Men have much wider access to life en la calle, and therefore to foreigners.

Employment, productivity, and middle-class consumption patterns are essential components in the construction of a respectable identity in Cuba. But in order to earn the markers of respectability—a livelihood and middle-class consumption and styling—many black Cubans must depend on areas thought by the larger society to be less than respectable. The Revolution unwittingly concretized this. At the onset of the Special Period, dollar remittances (primarily sent from the United States) to family members in Cuba were the largest infusion of capital to a nation then effectively isolated from the capitalist world by the United States blockade and dependent on aid from the suddenly defunct Soviet Union. Access to the U.S. dollar was limited to only some 50 percent of Cubans—many of whom are structurally white family members of those who left the country at the triumph of the Revolution, and who are now able to remit funds to their families on the island. U.S. dollars coming to Cuba this way are therefore *raced* at entry. Even after official and unofficial tourist income had surpassed remittances as the largest percentage of income among Cubans in the late 1990s, the limited circulation of remittances and under-representation of blacks in official tourist occupations in which one earns tips (which can be relatively lucrative), continues to exacerbate the historical color/racial class inequities that the Revolution had begun to address.

In order to prevent profiteering and other crimes related to the exchange of U.S. dollars, as well as to provide state access to hard currency that could be used for purchases on the international market, the Cuban government made the U.S. dollar legal tender in Cuba in 1993—setting up a system of three circulating currencies—until 2004 when it reversed this decision. The Cuban peso could be used to buy fresh food items, basic home and personal provisions, and nontourist transportation. A much greater variety of processed food, clothing, and other commodities could be purchased using the "convertible" peso, which was minted in Cuba, accepted in place of the U.S. dollar, and tenable only in Cuba. Finally, the U.S. dollar (*divisa*, or hard currency) was required in all tourist shops, hotels, and specialized markets (*el shopping*) that sell a greater variety of goods, including clothing, electronics, and house wares.

By the middle of the 1990s, Cuba saw a doubling of hard currency debt and an increase in work absenteeism. Even Domingo's steadfastly revolutionary family changed. His mother Marta, like many women, stopped working altogether at the distribution center she had served for many years, and she began to depend more centrally on her work as a *santera* (Lucumí priest). For many years Marta's religious obligations had been curtailed and carried on out of the sight of her husband—Domingo's father, Compañereo Lozano—as a way to pay respect to her avowed atheist husband and to keep up appearances of revolutionary comportment. Years before, her compañeros on the CDR would not have countenanced the drummings and consultations that by the mid-1990s she began hosting at her home. By then, they were also engaged in attempts to survive and grateful for the gifts of plantains and other food that she shared, as well as her spiritual advice to deal with material circumstances. One respondent, commenting on the religious practice of sacrificing (*ebo*) food and animals to the Orisha, told me that although priests must divine to find out from the Orisha how to dispose of the *ebo* after a ceremony, during the Special Period, "miraculously, [the Orisha] always wanted it to be cooked and eaten!" Compañereo Lozano, however, "disillusioned" by the "errors" of the Revolution and his own family, has become increasingly "negative," in Domingo's words.

Domingo's *luchando* earns him more than his state job—and because of both high-level mismanagement, which has led to recent (and more planned) massive layoffs, and the high level of education and training in Cuba, he is not missed in the formal workforce. His activities and those of folks like him gall his father, Señor Ferrer, and other steadfast revolutionaries and respectable black intellectuals, because it at once points out the failures of the Revolution to provide for its citizens, and seems to confirm old stereotypes that *esta en la tinta*. When I shared with Domingo some of the insights of my older respondents like Señor Ferrer and (unbeknownst to him) his father about "correctness" and respectability, he replied "that is the way it should be, but we are here now trying to find a solution for this present moment." At present, as access to currency is increasingly seen to trump education, "culture," and revolutionary usefulness, there is a fierce challenge to revolutionary understandings of a classless society in which artists, intellectuals, and certain professionals such as doctors and educators are accorded high status because of their contributions to the collective as opposed to the money that they earn. In 2001 (when U.S. currency was accepted in Cuba), a black Cuban woman professor once joked with me that she regretted being "too old to learn how to fix air-conditioning" instead of working at the university, because then she could earn U.S. dollars for her efforts.

Domingo's father must have heard the rumors that circulate around what his son does with foreigners—whether selling cigars, giving therapeutic massages, or having sex with foreign women and men. They have never discussed this, and Domingo expects that it will never come up. What his father does repeatedly remark on, however, is his dress, his hair, and his consumption of techno, hip-hop, and Cuban charanga and timba music. Much to his father's chagrin, Domingo wears his wavy hair very short and "faded" at the sides (as was the fashion among black men in the United States at the time) and he has a gold stud earring in his left ear. His favorite timba bands, Los Van Van, Bamboleo, and Charanga Habanera blast music with lyrics of lust, love, and contemporary hardships, with tongue firmly planted in cheek, rather than the more-subtle music of his father. The dancing, always suggestive in Cuba, is even more so than in the past. Although reggaetón had yet to hit Cuba as hard as it did in subsequent years, the *despelote* (all over the place) . . . *tembleque* (shake shudder) . . . and *subaste de la cintura* (waist auction) (Fairley 2006) had already begun to make appearances at clubs like La Tropical, El Joker, and Pekín where patrons danced to timba music, and La Pampa, the center of hip-hop for a few years in the late 1990s. So, when I asked Compañero Lozano if he would attend his son's Saint's Day celebration—promiscuously blurring the sacred and the secular, with bata drums giving way later to timba, charanga, and hip-hop beats, and rum and beer flowing continuously—he told me that it was "not to his tastes," referring both to the open practice of Lucumí and the music and dancing afterward, well into the night. Contemporary forms of black masculine fashioning—especially those identified as foreign—threaten respectable (black) masculinity for older black Cuban men like Señor Ferrer, whom I introduced in the first chapter, and Domingo's father, Compañero Lozano. Señor Ferrer delivered his pronouncements of the correct way for this and that with no apologies and no qualifications. For example, there should never be a need to raise one's voice to a woman, or even to be in disagreement, according to Señor Ferrer. The division of spheres of control and influence prevented this, he said. And if a man, as men do, decides that he wants to have extrarelationship sex, he must be prepared for the financial and other consequences as well as be discreet so as not to cause embarrassment to his primary woman. And although the Revolution has profoundly changed women's participation in the labor force by opening up for them educational and work opportunities that had been closed previously, male responsibility for providing financially still remains, at least in the imaginations of older men like Señor Ferrer and Compañero Lozano. As a widower with one child living in the United States, he himself had at least two women to whom he referred as "mi mujer." I never questioned the ambiguity in this term in Spanish, which means both *my woman* and *my wife*. His mujeres attended different grandparents clubs and lived in different parts of Havana—one who lived with only her middle-aged daughter in a nicely appointed carriage house off a large house, and the other in a crowded Old Havana solar (tenement).

Señor Ferrer said that he understood that young men no longer wear hats, and he could even excuse soft-soled shoes, but he insisted on clean, shined shoes and clean, well-pressed and creased trousers and shirts. As for the ragtag look of Fidel and Che—famously photographed in scraggly beards with unwashed faces and cigars dangling from their mouths at rakish angles—now enshrined as images of male bravado, he replied, "Well, that was in the Sierra Maestra. This is Havana."

Up until the late 1980s the road to revolutionary masculine respectability was a single trajectory through revolutionary schooling, military service, work, membership in mass organizations and unions, and, at the apex senior membership in the Communist Party. Señor Ferrer and Compañero Lozano's trajectories—coming of age in the 1960s and 1970s—typify this route in different ways. Compañero Lozano, a few years younger than Señor Ferrer, found his masculine reflection in Che Guevara, while Ferrer recalls identifying with the Cuban Independence hero Antonio Maceo, "The Bronze Titan." Historically, the respectable black male is an adult, strongly committed to family cohesion and continuity, racial mutual support, and the maintenance of individual personal dignity—even and especially in cases where this conflicts with the dehumanizing practices of the white majority (Gordon 1997). The Revolution of 1959 forever changed traditional black Cuban modes of respectability (and reputation) by closing all private clubs and effectively outlawing all *cabildos* (mutual-aid societies based on African cultural groups) as well as both the male-dominated practice of Central African Palo Monte religion and Regla de Ocha (Lucumí, or Santería), which although dominated by women holds privileged patriarchal positions for men. Beginning in the nineteenth century, the societies of color served as political associations that were more accommodating to white norms and preferences; indeed, they were not African based but aspired to models of Greek and Roman citizenship and high culture.[13] Ironically, however, it was from these groups, like the well-known Club Atenas (Athens Club), from which calls to political self-sufficiency for Cubans of color were launched, and not from the Ñañigo *potencias*, which were necessarily in cahoots with various police and other criminal elements in order to maintain their businesses and prominence en la calle. While the latter would most often be seen as "reputational" practice as opposed to "respectable" (in the language of P. J. Wilson and several generations of social scientists),[14] these disparate streams of respectability, which anchored patriarchal black society, posed formidable threats to the prevailing hegemony of white supremacy. Nonetheless, Abakuá and other African-based cabildos and mutual-aid societies gained their power among popular classes of blacks precisely because they stood in the gap where the state had failed, apropos of providing, for example, protection, insurance, burials, and space for leisure activities essential to the communities. Cuban social upheavals and ruptures seem to have diminished both of these aspects of the *cultural repertoire* of black masculinity in a manner similar to the way in the United States, in the words of Edmund Gordon, "respectability as an element of black male cultural repertoire was dealt a blow by the Great Depression and has been in retreat since the end of legal apartheid after the 1950s" (1997: 42). This denuding of exclusively black civil society was not only a result of economic hard times and material lack that challenged the authority of the black patriarch but also, concomitantly, state practices.[15]

"¿Yo soy macho?"

On one occasion, another foreign researcher working in Cuba asked me, "So, is Domingo gay?" This scholar had seen Domingo and I together on several occasions and perhaps assumed that he was *gay by association*. I did not answer, of course. But I was intrigued by the query. I had been so immersed in the complexities of masculine sexualities and men's gender performance that I found that I could not have given a completely satisfying answer, even if I had been invested in making Domingo's identification (or would it be his sexual behavior?) legible to my colleague. Perhaps Mercedes's cousin's formulation, remarked just out of earshot of Domingo and Mercedes one evening, can stand in as a provisional answer. As we celebrated the birthday of one of the family's children with two or three bottles of rum prior to Domingo showing up—bearing gifts, clean and well groomed but in last night's clothing—she and I both looked at Mercedes, then at Domingo, waiting. Mercedes silently challenged him with her eyes and stance, as the children clamored for their attention. He shrugged, then playfully grabbed Mercedes's ass and kissed her. When she smiled and returned his embrace, her cousin turned to me and said, "You must understand, in this moment . . . luchando en la calle must be done for the survival of the family."

Observers of Latin American masculinities tend to comment prolifically on what they appreciate as a contradiction between gender identity and sexual behavior. Rules of Latin American masculine sexuality that hold that being the insertive partner in male-to-male oral or anal sex does not necessarily equate to homosexuality; that often men who engage in homosex also engage in heterosex, and that a large proportion of those who engage in these activities do not necessarily identify as gay, bisexual, or homosexual, now circulate as truisms in academic literature. They have entered the popular imagination and some areas of public policy. However, too often the recognition that sexual behavior does not always signify sexual identity produces tremendous anxiety rather than confirming the fluidity of human sexual capacity and the constructedness of sexualities and sexual orientation or impelling us to make similar inquiries about female sexualities.[16] There is great demand in male-to-male romantic relationships, furtive nonpay sex, and tourism-related sex work for outwardly masculine, hombre hombre or "macho" men who will perform acts of *homosex*. More interesting and instructive, however, is that the declaration "yo soy macho" (I am macho), which Domingo claimed—in my estimation, like many *activos* to signify his emotional control, dominance, and masculine performance—is more of a discursive or rhetorical performance than social fact or experience—especially over time.[17] Although machos are appreciated by individuals in the community for their flawless masculine comportment, this does not always extend to sexual practices. The claim that "all machos are activo" is unsupported. As I have observed elsewhere (Allen 2000), sex between men in loving or trust-filled friendships sets the conditions for more flexibility in sexual behavior than has been previously reported.[18]

Hombría stresses sexuality in which the most powerful of men must dominate men and women in order to gain access to the widest expressions of his (sexual) desire. Hombría is among the most prized values in the society because it is always already constitutive of honor, dignity, strength, and bravery, and it is the "opposite" of homosexuality. Cuban heterosexism prizes manliness and eschews effeminacy—read as "homosexuality"—in all but comedic and carnivalesque representations. However, it is not the same as the "homophobia," that is, *fear and loathing* of homosexuals, that is experienced in the United States and elsewhere. Homosex, which is understood to be commonly practiced but very rarely discussed, is demystified—there is no fear of it. The contentious part is whether one can competently perform the strict masculine script, since masculine performance is a requirement for *respeto* (respect). Sexually satisfying a partner is a key feature of constructing and maintaining a masculine identity. Not only because the penetrated might move on to someone else but because it would mean a loss of face among the male cohort, which is unacceptable en la calle. There is thus a male homosocial foundation to every sexual encounter involving men. Even when the penetrated is a woman, the act is informed by a need to perform for the male cohort. *Chismoso* (gossip) among neighbors or friends that a man is not sexually satisfying can be a tremendous bane to one's standing in the community. Related to this, size matters—at least and especially to men. Phrases such as "a big dick is to be of use" and, among men who have sex with men, metaphors of larger animals eating smaller ones indicates an expectation that the partner with the bigger penis be the penetrator and thus is the manliest. Here, we can hear echoes of Fernando Ortiz's entreaty to "tell me what size vitola you smoke and I will tell you who you are."

In this way, sexual mixing among men runs parallel to mixing discourses of race in Latin American studies. I have avoided this well-worn path of race discourse because for my work in this book the point is not that there are any number of ways of describing particular phenotypical differences. What is more important here is the fact that these color and racial designations are nevertheless organized hierarchically in relation to superordinate whiteness—imagined, of course, as outside the nation, in Europe, but with white proxies nonetheless at the ready to vigorously take on the role. Likewise, while a few general comments follow, I will avoid an exhaustive account of how one can be a *man who has sex with men* without necessarily becoming a *maricón* ("faggot"). We have already witnessed one of these: transactional sex work, or what one "must understand," I was told, is done to support one's family. That is, as long as the family, like Domingo's, never discusses how much fun he is having.

While as a rule, figurative and literal penetrability is a threat to Latin virility, like the alchemy of mestizáje's ways of being nonblack, the privileges of heterosexuality, and even "macho" status may also be extended to the penetrated. The male body is allowed a fair amount of mixing and ambiguity, as long as the body performs the masculine gender script competently.[19] For example, homosex experienced in youthful relationships that bond young boys then passes is exempted from mariconísmo. Forty-two-year-old Roberto summarized the opinions of the vast majority of Cubans I talked to when he replied to my questions about his preteen homosex experience with no apparent shame or self-consciousness. He said, "You know, this is normal for boys to be curious."[20] *Hombres sin mujeres* (men without women), to borrow the title of Montenegro's famous novel, are also seen as deserving of an exclusion because of the absence of women in prison. However, routine penetration in consensual and noncommercial emotional relationships that others know about, or assume because of one's behavior, will render one a failed man—a "maricón," which is used to connote not only a homosexual but also one who is weak, cowardly, and ineffective. Emotional involvement is evidence of effeminacy, no matter which role one plays in homosex. However, as my respondent Juan reported, again expressing the opinion of most of my respondents and reflecting my own observations: "If you happen to have an accident when you are drunk, or want a little adventure . . . [fucking or sucking dick] is not a big problem. But, you don't do it again and you never talk about it." Many of the same gender-loving men and women I talked to reported that those friends and family who knew about their sexual behaviors or identities told them that they should not let anyone else find out because "it could cause you troubles." They should therefore adhere to the dicta *no dice nada, se hace todo* (say nothing—everything is done) and *entendido, por no dicho* (*in the know*, but not declared homosexual).

Friendship as a
Mode of Survival

5

What makes homosexuality "disturbing" [is] the homosexual mode of life, much more than the sexual act itself. To imagine a sexual act that doesn't conform to law or nature is not what disturbs people. But that individuals are beginning to love one another—there's the problem. The institution is caught in a contradiction; affective intensities traverse it which at one and the same time keep it going and shake it up.

——MICHEL FOUCAULT, "Friendship as a Way of Life"

Is it possible to explore the knowledge that is produced through Caribbean sexual praxis, and to ask whether sexual resistance offers a potential for a politics of decolonization or narratives of liberation?

——KAMALA KEMPADOO, *Sexing the Caribbean*

THE QUESTION IS THUS MUCH MORE COMPLEX than whether Cuba is or is not "oppressive" to homosexuals and gender nonconforming individuals. While Cuba is currently becoming freer and more open, in fits and starts, it also has quite a long way to go to fully realize the promise of the Revolution. Some official policies and practices have changed in Cuba, while the hegemonies on which they were based have proven to be sturdier. Today in Cuba, queer sociality is facilitating the start of long-silenced discussions. Cuban gender nonconforming individuals, women who have sex with women, and men who have sex with men are beginning to find air in public discourse, and perhaps also in state policy. But under what circumstances, if any, should those persons join together to address their marginalization—and how? As "citizens"? As lesbians, gays, bisexuals, transgenders, and "queers"?

In this chapter, I offer some notes toward the prospects for *sexual citizenship* and *erotic autonomy* for individuals whose sexual and affective relations with people of the same gender form an important part of their sense of self and connection to community. While sexual citizenship refers to notions of positive rights secured by states within an international human rights context, M. Jacqui Alexander's formulation of "erotic autonomy," which we discussed previously, is connected to Lorde's notion of deep longing or erotic subjectivity, which is at once self-possessed or "personal" and interdependent, connected, and committed to enlarging human capacity and social justice. Here, we ask, if an individual cannot be a citizen—whether in the socialist sense or the (neo)liberal sense—can he or she at least be (in one form or another) *free?* I query citizenship here not only because of the barriers black queers face when attempting to enjoy the full complement of citizenship—full "rights" within the political body of the nation—but more pointedly to ask whether the notion of citizenship, with its obvious rules of exclusion and exception, stands in for a wider range of assurances and freedoms. Is the larger freedom we seek more available outside of the purview of the state?

In Cuba, collectivity and cooperation are important and expected. Still, the collective has been organized centrally through state apparatus. The sites within Cuba that I visit in this chapter provide glimpses into a future communist Cuba that the leaders of the Revolution may not have conceived of before or readily recognize today. In this chapter I first consider the importance of *getting one's life*, and I engage friendship as a conduit to a new mode of life in black diaspora. I then move on to discuss responses to HIV/AIDS in order to show the complexity of the threats and opportunities in Cuba and beyond. Cuba's HIV prevention and care system had been a source of polemical debate based on what I will argue is a false dichotomy between liberal values of expression and privacy and socialist values of collectivity. This dichotomous thinking does not emerge from the antagonisms between the United States and Cuba alone, but instead is part of a hegemonic way of thinking that insists on approaching problems of society as "either/or" while people continue to live their lives as "and/both/but." Finally, I summarize with a discussion of lesbian organizing in Cuba that took place in an unlikely space, along with a lyrical hip-hop proposal to enjoin both sexual citizenship and erotic autonomy toward a larger freedom.

You Are My Friend

Here, I want to support the claim by Audre Lorde, Chela Sandoval, and others that the practice of loving friendship is a powerful tool (that we have now) that can be used to heal from the multiple and compounded traumas of race/sex terror. This constitutes what Kamala Kempadoo and others look for when they call for "sexual resistance." Further, it evidences Michel Foucault's "friendship as a way of life." This is what Joseph Beam longs for when he asserts "black men loving black men is the revolutionary act of the 1980s" (1986: 240), and what the vocalist Sylvester transmitted through his seamless soprano falsetto, crying, "You are my friend." Here, my aim is not solely to show restricted agency or particular tactics of self and world making, as I have done in the preceding chapters. I want to also take up Cohen's challenge of "intention to resist" by showing in the last section the outlines of work in Cuba that is, per Cohen, "mobilized in a conscious fashion" (2004: 27). A caveat must be raised here, however. Cultural, historical, political, and economic difference and pathos interrupt, exceed, and sully theorization. This is at once the risk and reward of ethnography. This bears repeating, for clarity and emphasis: these glimpses do not constitute political "organization" in Cuba but rather, like the preceding moves analyzed in this work, they are motivated by the erotic—this time consciously collective—as friendship.

Students of Foucault will recognize the reference to his "friendship as a way of life" in the epigraph above. Still, Foucault's intervention arrived late, and only after black feminist theorists and creative writers had imagined erotic friendship among black women, for example, as a way for them to know they were not crazy, stupid, or ugly, as Barbara Smith argues in "Toward a Black Feminist Criticism" (1998). It served also as a salve against the daily onslaught of racialized misogyny and gendered racism, and as a way to go about the work of personal and social transformation. They have written, for example, of breaking spells with the power of their screams in harmony; taking down a brick wall symbolizing their neighborhood's isolation and degradation; coming together to share their stories of near suicide and to redeem their own love; and building community in the face of terror.[1] They were telling their own stories and those of their foremothers and fathers. While anthropological or otherwise ethnographic work lags behind literary work in terms of chronicling and imagining friendship between women, Carol Stack's landmark ethnography *All Our Kin* (1997) illustrated the fact that survival networks of poor families were held in place by affect and interdependence; and Kath Weston's *Families We Choose: Lesbians, Gays, Kinship* (1991), another pathbreaking text, showed the ways in which chosen friends and lovers become kin, especially in contexts in which they had been turned away by their families of origin. Gloria Wekker's *The Politics of Passion: Women's Sexual Culture in the Afro-Surinamese Diaspora* (2006) is another example of work in this area, and she pushes it significantly forward. In this important work, we are made privy to intimate talk and thoughts shared between women, which we would not "hear" were it not for Wekker's keen ear and unflinching candor. As an insider and outsider—a member of the community of women who do Mati work (which I'll turn to shortly) but also different in terms of experience, national residence, and class—she reveals to the reader how she is complicit in producing particular knowledges. The book revolves around the social cultural milieux of an eighty-four-year-old working-class woman, Miss Juliette Cummings, for whom "even though there was no dearth of the offspring she produced, her sexual joy was overwhelmingly located in her connections with women . . . [which] were not passive and nongenital" (172). That is, Miss Juliette does Mati work. When the women in Wekker's study describe their sexual and love relationships with other women, they do not speak of such in opposition but complementarily. This complementarity is observable not only in terms of sexual and other relationships with men—which for women who do Mati work may be for pleasure, instrumental toward childbearing, or as a means of material survival—but more centrally in terms of the way they see their ethical, familial, and spiritual rights and obligations. To *do Mati work*, or to be engaged in these deeply meaningful, often troubled, and satisfying friendships is thus not *to be* "a Mati." Sexual behavior and intimate connection is precisely not held as a discrete ontological category but rather part of a complex, dynamic, at once spiritual and material experience. In a situation that is resonant with my respondents in Cuba and my experiences in the United States and other places, as well as reflected in black and Third World feminist readings of black erotic subjectivities, working-class "identity" among Surinamese black (and) Creole women who do Mati work is character-ized by additive, inclusive "both/and thinking" (Patricia Hill Collins quoted in Wekker 2006: 182). According to Wekker, the Mati work is "one idealtypical expression of black female sexuality in the diaspora. . . . show[ing] a sexual configuration where women unabashedly enjoy sex, are active sex partners, and can disengage sex from love. . . . [it is] genitally oriented and not the 'va-nilla,' cuddly brand that has so normatively been considered as the hallmark of feminine sexuality" (222).

The term "mati," like "oremi" (which I turn to in the next section), means friend.[2] The term is also very close to Audre Lorde's invocation of "Zami," used in Cariacou and Grenada (and in Trinidad and Tobago), which in her book of the same name she defines as *women who work, live, and love together.* Richard and Sally Price show that matis, originally shipmates who had sur-vived the murderous Middle Passage together, were close friends—usually men in "a lifelong relationship entered into only with caution and when there was strong mutual affection and admiration" (Richard and Sally Price quoted in Wekker 2006: 175).[3] Wekker reports that at present the term "mati" carries a "general, sexually neutral but affectively laden meaning of 'friend'" (178). Looking northward to the southern United States, E. Patrick Johnson's wise grandmother was among the first to teach him about the meaning of *quare* (2001). Certainly, she and most African Americans could likewise inform us what folks mean by "friend" in African American vernacular English. While a same-sex friend, without inflection or dramatic pause, may go unnoted among adults, inflected (or italicized) *friend*, without qualification (*girl*friend, friend *from work*, etc.), should be understood (but, like in Cuba, not declared) as sex partner.

DIONNE BRAND WRITES of women friends—in love and in revolution—in her *In Another Place, Not Here*:

> GRACE, IS GRACE, YES. And I take it, quiet, quiet, like thiefing sugar. From the word she speak to me and the sweat running down she in that sun, one afternoon as I look up saying to myself, how many more days these poor feet of mine can take this field, these blades of cane like razor, this sun like coal pot. Long as you have to eat, girl. I look up. That woman like a drink of cool water. (1997: 1)

In recalling Nicolás Guillén's "Caña," and the contrapunteo, we can think of "thiefing sugar" as taking the sweetness and sustenance that one has worked so long and hard for but that is constantly denied. These visions of raising consciousness, mending wounds, telling stories, moving between one place and another, and making new worlds, are the work of friendship. These visions of interdependence and passion are evident across time and genre and also across spaces of black diaspora, in the life.

To be *in the life* (non-heteronormative) in the black diaspora speaks not only to sets of common ethical principles and memory but also to material *facts of blackness* throughout the diaspora (to invoke Frantz Fanon), which condition similar circumstances and set the horizon for a limited number of combinations of action. For example, in Cuba *el ambiente* (the scene) is at once used to denote gay and lesbian space, and spaces of extralegality and potential danger. Further, in both Cuba and the United States, these nonmutually exclusive spaces often overlap. In the United States, Cuba, Suriname, and any other place or borderland where histories collide, this life in between is constrained by racialized, classed, and sexualized violence of the state, of global capital, and of the anxieties of desperate in-group elites. As one of Sharon Bridgforth's characters in *Love Conjure/Blues* (2004) explains apropos of one local example of these places, where one can *get one's life* (taken)—the jook joint—in this space "a whole lotta shit just libal to happen."[4] That a number of things are liable to happen is not for any reason intrinsic to the ethics of the people that attend the jook joint, hang out in el ambiente, or are in the life; but, for example, owing to criminalization (of cross-dressing and homo sex, for example) threats of attack, and crime emerging precisely to take advantage of vulnerability and invisibility. It is Thanatos (death) stalking the shadows of Eros. Nevertheless, *the life* is also a site of potential freedom, most centrally because it has to be. As Lorde states: "For the embattled/ there is no place/ that cannot be home/ nor is" ("School Note" in Lorde 1978). That is, home must be where one finds space to make it. And in the time one finds it. This instantiates queerness. As J. Halberstam writes:

> I am in a drag king club at 2:00 a.m. . . . and the people in the club recognize why they are here, in this place at this time, engaged in activities that probably seem pointless to people stranded in hetero temporalities. Queer time for me is the dark nightclub, the perverse turn away . . . a theory of

queerness as a way of being in the world and a critique of the careful social scripts that usher even the most queer among us through major markers of individual development and into normativity. (2007: 181)

As Halberstam demonstrates elsewhere, turning away from "the careful social scripts" has wildly disparate meanings and consequences for subjects for whom access to the scripts—and to status as subject, citizen, person, or any normativity whatsoever—is always already troubled. Indeed, the iconic sexualized black body is, as Hortense Spillers writes in "Interstices: A Small Drama of Words," "so boundlessly imagined" that the black person discursively "loses meaning" (2003: 164). So, in a land with no people (to speak of/ to speak for/to speak one's name) or cut off from among their people, black queers are multiply vulnerable. In the life. En el ambiente. En la calle.

A FRIEND IS ONE WHO SHARES in this process of knowing and becoming; one who shares in you *getting your life*. In transgressing societal rules about whom one is to love, make love to, or desire, same-gender-loving Cubans, like queers globally, seem to be well positioned to use their already existing friendships and networks to make new family and new society. They are positioned at the precipice (or more appropriately, the awaiting opening of new possibilities, veritably pulsating with anticipation and hope). We can also think of it as another facet of Gloria Anzaldúa's concept of a troubled but productive point of multiple contact and possibilities, "nepantla," composed of

> passageways, conduits, and connectors that connote transitioning, crossing borders, and changing perspectives. Bridges span liminal (threshold) spaces between worlds, spaces I call nepantla, a Nahuatl word meaning tierra entre medio. Transformations occur in this in-between space, an unstable, unpredictable, precarious, always-in-transition space lacking clear boundaries. *Nepantla es tierra desconocida*, and living in this liminal zone means being in a constant state of displacement. (1999: 237)

In what ways does friendship instantiate *una tierra desconocida* (a land unknown), a ground that is inevitably one of discovery? What might we learn from black diasporic erotic subjectivities that underscore friendship and communal connection within those interzones, in the life? In Foucault's now-famous interview "Friendship as a Way of Life," he attempts to push the focus of the gay individual to a collective project. He avers that "it would be better to ask oneself what relations, through homosexuality, can be established, invented, multiplied, and modulated . . . The problem is not to discover in oneself the truth of one's sex, but, rather, to use one's sexuality henceforth to arrive at a multiplicity of relationships" (1997: n.p.).

Friendship, Foucault avers, is potentially liberatory because it interrupts that which makes homosexuality "disturbing" to heteropatriarchal sensibilities. Friendship is a relationship of freedom: choice, intense emotion; obligations; sex and love; gendered, but not exclusionary. The multiplicity of relationships—of connections known and unknown—is predicated upon interdependence. You will recall from chapter 3 that Cole began to see the difference between the male comrades offered to him by the mass organizations, his socios on the block in his neighborhood, and Yaineris's friends. He had been clear that the brigadistas and communistas were loyal to the ideologies of the group, mired as they were in unchallenged assumptions about his blackness, but not to him personally.

Still, rather than encourage work that takes up and pushes cross-cultural, intergenerational, and cross-genre entreaties "to use one's sexuality henceforth to arrive at a multiplicity of relationships," some recent influential work in queer studies is characterized by its antirelationality and moves against futurity.[5] I have already asserted that black feminists offer that whatever our vision for progressive or revolutionary politics, the ground for transgression, transcendence, and finally transformation is the individual's recognition of her or his own intentions and desires. An effective mode for revolutionary becoming must therefore address deeper understandings of who we are and how we are connected to others.

Heiligeweg

Sex is one way to access or embody friendship. And should our toolkit for dismantling "the master's house" not include everything at our disposal, everything that we can ethically deploy to remind us of our humanity and connect with the humanity of a(n)other(s)? My respondents Delores and Yaineris both laughed hysterically as I explained to them how long it took me to understand the hand gesture that Cubans and other Latin Americans use to denote *lesbiana*. Fingers extended, they rub palms together as if flattening a tortilla to indicate the street lingo for same-gender women—*tortilleras* (tortilla makers). For weeks, when someone indicated tortillera, I thought it was a clumsy rendition of the common hand gesture for washing one's hands of a situation or person. It did not occur to me that this was an attempt to mime what people thought of as the sexual action between women. We joked about the fact that sex between women, when it is publicly presented at all, so often elides physicality—especially the genitals—preferring to imagine what Wekker calls "vanilla, cuddly . . . non-genital" affection. I told them that when someone finally explained the gesture to me, I was incredulous because the flat palms do not, as my heterosexual male interlocutor demanded, resemble any part of women's anatomy (other than a palm), and that the quick, barely touching pat-pat of the hands was probably not what goes on between the women I know. While sex between men is represented in everyday speech as animals devouring each other or other nonhuman activities; between-women sex is represented as mundane, domestic work, in this common shorthand for lesbian. Far from consuming or devouring for their own pleasure or survival, same-gender-loving women are imagined producing or cooking for others. As we talk, Yaineris, much to Delores's embarrassment and delight, begins doing the common hand gesture; she then lightly touches all of her fingers, moving vigorously, then slowly, forcefully then gently, through her finger webbings, after which she kiss-licked each finger. Finally, moving closer to Delores, she made a fist and seductively licked the opening of her left hand, paying particular attention to folds and ducts in her skin. Yaineris then carefully put much of her right hand in the opening in her left. Delores replied by laughing herself off of her chair and onto the floor. Challenged by Yaineris, who said "Pero . . . ¿es verdad, no? [but, it's true, ain't it?]" Delores replied, her head down but smiling, "Esta bastante correcto [that's so right]."

For Yaineris, sexual relationships with men had been "pleasant" if not frustrating, given that, as she reports, men do not take her attraction to women seriously. She explained to Cole that, for her, he just did not have the "requisites" for that kind of relationship with her. Contrary to assumptions of cooperative and egalitarian relationships between women, Yaineris tells me that her relationship with Cole is much easier than her sexual relationships with women. She and Cole understand each other, and he is affectionate, protective, and even a bit jealous—which she likes. But it is not the sort of jealousy and *candela* (drama) that she had endured with female lovers who she says acted as if they must totally possess her. Still, this is the way her blood beats, toward "beautiful women with curves" and not to men, no matter how attractive, intelligent, and devoted to her. Alas, she has tried. Sex, under the pretext of drunkenness on her part, was "very strong, nice" (she said while her face was contorted in that way as if to say, not really), but it still did not get her "where" she needed to go, she said. Reading Wekker years after this conversation, it occurred to me that her destination was the heady, exciting place of Heiligeweg.

"Yo no me parezco a nadie"

I had never before been to this section of Havana, which sits just beyond Miramar where avenues widen and homes seem no worse for the revolutionary wear. The collective taxi I was riding with Yaineris stopped a few blocks away from her friend Marilisa's home, and we carefully extricated ourselves from the crowded Chevy, full of Cubans on their way to visit family members or to do other business on this late Sunday afternoon. We, or I, had thought of splurging on a tourist taxi, since my first trip to the women's party was a special occasion. But Yaineris usually preferred to use peso-friendly Cuban transportation, even though it was often slow and always crowded. In any case, it was much cheaper to ride in the collective taxi, where we listened to the hushed conversations and occasional raucous entertaining banter, especially on longer trips or when the driver was feeling particularly gregarious. I kept my comments to a minimum, since after all I was passing as Cuban. Yaineris and her friends agreed that rolling up in a taxi was not very respectful of Marilisa, since the interest of her neighbors would certainly be piqued by a number of taxis arriving on a late Sunday afternoon. To be discreet, therefore, my crew thought it would be best to walk the last few blocks to her place. Still, I wondered what the neighbors would think of the fact that they had not been invited to the party, and that all but a few of the guests were women. This party, five years before the advent of the popular "Fiesta de Lila" and "Milagros," "Fiesta de Humo," or "Fiesta de la Burbuja," seems, now years later, to have been a kind of dry run for the women's parties that have become very popular. Indeed, they have even undercut the popularity of the men's parties (featured in the next chapter), since they are often closer to the city center and therefore more economical for Cubans to attend. Of course, like the twenty-peso parties, the venue changes each time—with those in the know using a telephone number circulated among friends in order to get the address.

We ascended the stairs to be greeted by a striking woman, whose long, fitted dress and short cropped hair made me think of Vannia from the timba band Bamboleo. As we entered the room, Isaac Delgado's "El pregón del chocolate" was blasting from one small floor speaker and the dance floor was alive: five or six couples were twirling, undulating, and laughing. Some sang along with the *coro* (chorus): "Tengo el chocolate pa' ti, el dulce que te gusta! [I got chocolate for you, sweet like you like it]." At the center of the floor, a circle of women had captured everyone's attention with their hip shakes and shudders. The gorgeous Vannia look-alike at the door was Marilisa's girl-friend of the moment, and it was she who had organized the event and now collected the entry fee and warmly greeted everyone at the door. Somewhere between what people were used to seeing as "feminine" and what they expect of "butch," she stood, confidently, apparently taking particular joy in multi-tasking. She sang the coro to the song, shifted her shoulders, shook and rolled her hips, folded the money, smiled and chatted up the guests.

In that two-story home on the outskirts of Havana, in this room with stripped floors and very little furniture, we witnessed a party alive and puls-ing with loud music, good food, and beautiful black women in various combi-nations of dress, complexions, hairstyles, and economic backgrounds.[6] Lycra rules in Cuba for women's party wear. Some wore it in bandeau tops with high-waisted shorts, jeans, or short skirts, and others in shifts that grazed or passionately embraced their bodies, but most, no matter what the style, wore it as if it were makeup—an application of color over the skin. It served as more than mere covering or "clothing." Flowered polyester or even cotton shifts and sleeveless shirts were worn by the more modest, with a leotard or tights un-derneath. At this party, distinctions between butch and femme seemed less apparent at first—at least to me—than those between class groups. Of course, I was far from the intended audience of the women present. Still, the women drinking beer out of bottles and cans, talking the most and loudest, and wear-ing pants, collared shirts, and sneakers, oxford shoes, or hiking boots, made their butch presence felt. A few could afford to accessorize liberally, and others, like the vast majority of Cubans, had to keep to a basic repertoire of one pair of shoes for going out and something to wear for everyday, and one good outfit for very special parties and other occasions, which is handled with great care. One partygoer told me that it would therefore be foolish for a woman, no matter how butch, to use her meager resources to buy things that she would wear only to these parties.

The fiesta seemed to intensify when the DJ played "Yo no me parezco a nadie" (I'm like no other). One of the many hits by Bamboleo, this song seemed to announce that there had never been a band like this, fronted by two black women who, like their bandmates, were graduates of Havana's school of music. Both stunning, with heads shorn bald, understated makeup, and long, trendy dresses, the title "Yo no me parezco a nadie" is more than apt. Here at the party, a woman with long curly hair and small stud earrings pulls another party guest onto the dance floor and the two of them *get their life*. The first woman's footwork—stomping each step in her rounded-toe hiking boots—and her manner of staring off seriously into the distance as she leads and spins her partner, betrays the flirty femme shirt she wears (tellingly worn oversized and buttoned over a tight leotardlike T-shirt) and loose jeans. For her part, the other woman moves wherever her partner will have her move, smiling and laughing as the *vueltas* (spins) get faster and change direction. First three to the left, then four to the right; to the side; then under the arm—a move that was pulled off elegantly even though the dance lead was a few inches shorter than her partner. As the typical timba break comes—all horns blaring and piano banging at the same time, until the timbales and clave change beat again—the long-haired woman lets go of her partner's hand to step up close to her. She shudder-shakes as the other woman rolls her waist with her hands on her hips, moving up and down with her legs astride, toes nearly *en pointe* in the flowered Chinese slippers that were so popular then. Rounded-toed boots are planted firmly, shoulder length apart. As Vannia sings the commands "Entonces, empujalo! [So, push it!]," arms go up and fists are shoulder height. The long-haired woman's shoulders are stiff, as her chest, stomach, and ass shake and shudder powerfully. The coro begins, high hats strike, and her partner holds on now, closer. Slowing her balletic grind in half time of the clave, she is syncopated with the piano. The party goes up. A roomful of women swoon. Finally, a smile comes from the long-haired mulata who has seemingly commanded this so well: she is obviously enthralled by the graceful femme. "She's got her now," Delores says. Pretty flowered slippers perfectly positioned for plié, the femme rolls up to her partner's betrayed delicate blouse, down those loose-fitting jeans, putting her hands tentatively on her partner's thighs, then, up again, lets them rest on her shoulders and whispers something in her studded ear. The music continues and they move steadily. Step/stomp one two three. Turn/roll four five six. The stomping woman tucks in her blouse-cum-jersey, and rolls the cap sleeves into her undershirt. Smile three four. Stomp/step one two turn. . . . The new intimate friend of the now-tucked woman takes her partner's long curly hair, smoothes it, and ties it in a makeshift bun at the nape of her neck. "Ay," Delores said, rapidly snapping her fingers in the air, "Imáginate! Es asi! [Oh, imagine it! It's like that!]" and everyone in our corner, standing close to the DJ changing a stack of burned or pirated CDs on makeshift table, giggles. Perhaps as a joke, the DJ switches unceremoniously to Los Van Van's "Esto te pone la cabeza mala" (This'll make you crazy!) and the re-dressed dancer laughs innocently. We finally see her teeth as she opens her mouth wide, then, a bit shy, whispers something to her partner and takes her off to a corner, where they stayed for much of the night, between repeat performances.

Dance is serious play. Cubans take learning how to dance and express oneself with another person on the dance floor as an important matter (though many of my respondents would disagree that it is "learned" at all). The courting dance at this party—a sort of butch-femme *pas de deux*—did not go unnoticed by the admiring crowd. The initial and apparent success of the dance-floor icebreaker challenged and emboldened other women in the room—some who looked butch and others who did not, some lead, some followed, and others did neither. Sitting there in a suburb of Havana—watching, and trying to be unassuming (mostly unsuccessfully, as one of only a few men and one of the people entranced by the ballet to which we were treated), I thought of Audre and Afrekete, in a brick frame house in Queens: "Dancing with her . . . I felt who I was and where my body was going, and that feeling was more important to me than any lead or follow" (Lorde 1982: 245). In making friends in spaces like this one *in the life*—sweat pouring, horns blaring, and bodies moving—one can begin to melt away the thick carapace of learned alienation from our desires and from each other. It is a catalyst for the creation of community.

Home

My friends' Ian and Anier's spacious high-rise apartment was a center of activity in Vedado. A number of the people that I met in Cuba I encountered on the thirteenth floor of that building, which so often threatened my undoing with forced hikes on dark, hot, narrow stairs during scheduled power outages. It seemed I was the only one unaware of the times there would be no electricity, and thus, no elevator. Ian, who is a white European, a longtime resident of Cuba, and a true believer in the Revolution, lived there with his black Cuban lover Anier. Also in residence were at least two or three other friends of theirs: a Cuban man who made street performance art, a white woman from the United States who worked with Cuban organizations to organize citizens' delegations to Cuba, and a British composer who made a living as a translator. There were always people around the apartment: men and women visiting Cuba or doing international solidarity work; expatriates, exiles, and escapees; Cuban writers, painters, stilt-walkers, laborers, and singers; and the odd foreign researcher. There were also always young Cuban men, seemingly no matter the occasion or the time of day. By no means wealthy, this household had what I have come to understand as the key ingredients for clearing a space for communion: critical acceptance, laughter, food, shelter, and no lack of two of the most important elements: a willingness to engage and a quantity of rum (or at least the will to send someone down the thirteen flights to get some).

When Ian invited me to accompany him and his friend Osjami on the quick trip from Havana to Los Cocos, the HIV sanatorium at Santiago de las Vegas, I went because of my friendship with Ian and empathy for Osjami, who had been staying at Ian and Anier's apartment over the weekend. But also I went out of curiosity about this place where in the United States I had heard that people living with AIDS were "imprisoned," while others claimed it as a place where Cuba had erected an HIV *spa* of sorts. Neither assertion was true.[7] I also could not help but think of a few dear friends of mine, back in the United States. That Cubans infected with HIV are being cared for at facilities such as Los Cocos does not mean that we should not ask the hard questions about protection of individual privacy and volition that critics of the system raise.[8] Neither should we ignore, as the large number of these critics do, the fact that the state's responses to this global epidemiological disaster reflects our common history of slavery, colonialism, continued racism, and heterosexism.

Osjami had been living at the sanatorium, what many Cubans call the "*SIDA*torio" (SIDA, síndrome de inmunodeficiencia adquirida, is the acronym for AIDS) for several months and as Ian told me, "his parents have not yet adjusted." His reticence to display immediately what the psychologists thought of as appropriate concern for abstinence had warranted an extension of his "orientation period."[9] As such, this was only his second or third time away from the sanatorium since his admittance. To tell the rest of the family where he was staying was out of the question, his parents thought. But they no doubt would learn through intricate networks of gossip that the twenty-three-year-old was not working for the television station in Havana, as his parents had been telling everyone, but rather has been a patient at Los Cocos. We delivered Osjami to his neat small house, which was better appointed than most others on "the outside," and we talked with a few individuals who had decided to stay at the sanatorium that weekend. Osjami reported that the facility offered him more plentiful food than he got at home as well as medicine, medical care and time to exercise and listen to his music, but he still planned to return to work very soon.

AIDS "BOUNDING" BLACKNESS?

While the Cuban government does not keep account of race and color in any of its statistics, many of the patients I saw during this trip to Los Cocos were black, and they were overwhelmingly male. I was reminded of wards I had visited at St. Vincent's Hospital in New York and Grady Hospital in Atlanta. Further, data from the United Nations on the numbers of people living with HIV on the island report that men who have sex with men account for over 80 percent of those infected. This is the case despite the fact that homosexual men were not the first Cubans discovered to be infected, but rather heterosexual-identified soldiers who had recently returned from central and southern Africa, where HIV was more closely associated with heterosexual sex than the "gay plague" it was touted to be in the United States at the time. While the HIV/AIDS pandemic has affected every corner of the globe, it appears that it has become a common threat in black diasporas, and tragically, in some communities of black folks HIV is nearly a rite of passage.[10]

Populations of African descent in sites around the globe present an incidence of HIV infection that is disproportionate to other groups within their borders. Globally salient racial formations find blacks suffering not only from disease cofactors such as poverty, lack of access to reliable information on sexual health, inadequate healthcare, a suspicion of state public health authorities (in some cases prudent),[11] and higher rates of drug use (including intradermal drugs), but also despair inflicted by persistent racism. The United Nations shares the view that poverty and lack of education are among the most important risk factors for HIV. There is compelling evidence that the fortunes of black Cubans are relatively positive with respect to infection rates of the rest of the region and around the world.[12] Yet, socialism is neither an HIV vaccine nor a cure for AIDS.

In the United States in the early 1980s, at the onset of the HIV/AIDS pandemic,[13] black lesbian and gay forms of making sex, literatures and other expressive practices emerged, thereby pushing notions of erotic experience beyond heterosexual sex and reproduction. After all, *Beloved*'s Baby Suggs's "life-giving private parts" that must be "love[d] . . . hard" in response to those yonder who would rather see you bound or dead, are not life-giving only because of their potential for heterosexual reproduction. Work by authors such as Audre Lorde, Joseph Beam, and Essex Hemphill showed that "loving . . . hard" means to honor the faculty of Eros to which we have access through our bodies. This site of the erotic—simultaneously embodying and invoking sex and death—is pregnant with transformational potential. That, for example, black lesbians announced that they (like to) fuck and black gay men, who were assumed to be fucking unconsciously and "unnaturally," added "now we think as we fuck" (Hemphill 2000: 155) at what at the time was the height of the AIDS epidemic, constitutes a profound contribution to radical praxis. At a crucial moment in which it was clear that, as Phil Wilson, director of the Black AIDS Institute, commented, "They are going to let us die," black lesbians and gay men created community out of crisis—in Nepantla, in the life, en el ambiente—complex, troubled, and riddled with *candela*.

The story and context of black community responses to HIV/AIDS in the United States is well chronicled in Cathy Cohen's tour de force *The Boundaries of Blackness: AIDS and the Breakdown of Black Politics* (1999a). Cohen highlights the slow and in cases indifferent response of local and federal officials, including that of President Ronald Reagan, whose inaction during the crucial moments at the onset of the epidemic cost innumerable lives around the world. One of the hallmarks of Reaganism was a disinvestment from state functions of providing health, education, and security (other than military funding), which was communicated to voters as an end to "big government."[14] Cohen argues that black gay men and lesbians had to confront stigmatizing institutional and cultural rhetorics and practices of both the state public health establishment, and black politicos and religious leaders, who held institutional power in black communities. Despite their vast resources, the United States state and black cultural and political institutions both responded slowly and weakly, largely as a result of a deeply ingrained homophobia and perhaps an indifference to what was initially described as a "gay plague." Cohen avers that her detailed critique of Ronald Reagan therefore is "not to excuse the lack of action regarding AIDS by black leaders, but to highlight the complex political environment confronting black activists as AIDS emerged in their consciousness" (1999a: 85). This political environment included the erosion of urban areas of the United States that large numbers of people of color call home.

I discussed in previous chapters the political situation in Cuba in the 1980s, in which the government had attempted a campaign to reconsider the increasingly contested policies and practices borrowed from European socialism. In response, the government decided to return more centrally to the philosophies of Che Guevara, who had insisted that revolutionary *conciencia* (consciousness) of "homeland or death" and moral incentives would be the only motivator that would work when faced with the decrease of material incentives. The vanguardist, patriarchal character of the Cuban state, which characterized the masses as unfit to make crucial individual decisions that impact the collective, is evident in their response to HIV and AIDS. Cuba's controversial former AIDS policy has been the subject of much polemical debate. The island's system of mandatory HIV testing and placement in sanatoria, set up in the late 1980s to combat AIDS by identifying and effectively quarantining HIV-positive Cubans, was seen as repressive and despotic by critics of their policies. There are others, however, who continue to defend the decision and cite the island's low HIV rate as proof that their measures were prudent. For my inquiry, however, the issue is not to determine whether these were "correct" measures; instead, I wish to examine the recent past for a deeper understanding of the state's decisions and of the responses of networks of friends in order to work toward more deeply humane and effective solutions in the future. In Cuba, as in many other parts of the world, HIV/AIDS has forced discussions that have been long silenced, at the same time that it impels unlikely alliances. It continues to demand huge resources of ingenuity and creativity to care for those infected and to prevent others from becoming infected. The opportunity presented by this unprecedented worldwide crisis includes increased revolutionary love.

"DENTRO DE LA REVOLUCIÓN, TODO; CONTRA DE LA REVOLUCIÓN, NADA"

While HIV/AIDS was not associated with gay men at the beginning of the crisis in Cuba, as in North America and Europe, gay and other men who have sex with men have become the group with by far the highest incidence of HIV infection on the island. In 2008, the Cuban National Program on STIS/ HIV/AIDS reported that over 84 percent of Cubans infected with HIV are men who have sex with men (Oxfam 2008). Members of this group have also become the leading educators and advocates in Cuba, just as gay men and lesbians have done in the United States and other places. The work of HIV/AIDS activists and volunteers in Cuba—largely carried out by gay men, lesbians, and otherwise same-gender-loving people—has gone virtually unremarked. These volunteers and activists, like those of Grupo de Prevención de SIDA (GPSIDA, or Group for the Prevention of AIDS), Lineayuda (Health Line), and Carito por la Vida (Little Van for Life) borrow some of the rhetorics and tactics of HIV prevention praxis from the North. This is, of course, both constrained and supported by the Cuban state. When I asked about this, a gay volunteer in one of the organizations quoted to me Fidel Castro's famous (and to many, infamous) line in his "Palabras a los intelectuales" (Words to the intellectuals), delivered on June 30, 1961: "Dentro de la Revolución, todo; contra de la Revolución nada," or "Everything within the revolution, against it, nothing."[15] Read generously, one might understand Castro promising an expansive, intellectually open revolution. The test has been whether the Revolution can accept what revolutionaries who had been on the outside bring to the table. The work of HIV prevention "within the revolution" not only highlights the emergence of civil society in Cuba but also the willingness of the state to change public policy based on their own perceived errors, and the efforts of citizens and solidarity workers in the field, if not also the critical—literally life and death—importance of the matter.

GPSIDA was created at Los Cocos in 1991. One of its founders, Dr. Armando Alvarez, explained in an interview that the group was composed of mostly HIV-positive sanatorium patients in order to offer support for those living with HIV/AIDS and to meet the population head on with an education campaign.[16] Most of the members of GPSIDA, which did most of the early HIV prevention outreach, were same-gender-loving men. They advocated for an end to the quarantine system and for more-aggressive HIV prevention education, both widespread and targeted. They convincingly argued that Cubans would not understand or be able to protect themselves against HIV if they were isolated from people infected with the virus and therefore thought the threat of HIV was being "contained" within the gates of the sanatoria. This argument proved to be prescient.

The government now sees HIV/AIDS education and prevention as a priority of the revolutionary project. The National STI/HIV/AIDS Prevention Center was opened in 1998. It currently provides HIV/AIDS education through the island's main media outlets, including television, radio, public billboards; school presentations; and the national AIDS hotline. The new stage in the health authorities' campaign, begun in 2001, involves community, grassroots *cara-a-cara* ("face-to-face" or one-on-one) work, as well as peer education. Increased grassroots community work has expanded since my initial research. Cara-a-cara counseling centers are attached to local neighborhood polyclinics. They are staffed with trained counselors from the Ministry of Public Health, and they exist in all fifteen municipalities of Havana and throughout the provinces. Like the peer-educator models now popular in urban areas of the north and all over the globe, gay counselors work with gay and same-gender-loving communities; specially trained inmates are working in the nation's prisons; residents are being taught to counsel their neighbors in the solares of Old Havana and Central Havana; the FMC (Federación de Mujeres Cubans) has begun education programs aimed at women; transsexuals are currently organizing similar efforts through CENESEX (Cuba's Center for Sexual Education); and the country's CDRS (Committeees in Defense of the Revolution) discuss HIV/AIDS on a block-by-block local and national level. Moreover, the staggering incidence of men who have sex with men (MSM) infection "has driven Cuban health officials, educators, and advocates to develop programs, undertake research, and seek innovative ways to reach Cuba's most vulnerable group . . . [including] the national MSM Project [Proyecto HsH], that designs educational materials, convenes video debates and organizes MSM-dedicated film festivals. . . . [Additionally] GPSIDA directs several MsM projects on a local level.[17]

The National Center for the Prevention of STIs and HIV/AIDS also runs a successful project called Carito por la Vida, which is composed of a small recreational trailer towed by a twelve-seat minibus that travels to the beaches close to Havana and to densely populated communities, as well as to areas frequented by sex laborers. The Center also houses and supports a non-governmental organization called Population Services International. Funded by sources in the United Kingdom, it has begun a social marketing program that has introduced a new, low-cost, quality condom to the Cuban peso market. Current measures—while steps in the right direction—do not, however, address some of the more profound structural issues of racism and heterosexism that lead to increased HIV risk. In order to prevent HIV infection and care for those already living with HIV/AIDS, an aggressive assault against the root causes of disaffection and exclusion in Cuban society is needed.

Oremi, Again

By the time I returned to Cuba for a short visit in 2005, the Cuban economy had shifted once again. Along with the change in the economy, there also were social shifts. The Special Period was said to be over, and closer business relations with China and Venezuela, for example, seemed to be fueling more development on the island. Still, despite significant increases in GDP reported by the government, people told me that there is less money circulating among ordinary Cubans than there was a few years ago, a situation evidently linked to Cuba's delegalization of the United States dollar. In 2004, the George W. Bush administration, openly citing its objective to "squeeze" and destabilize the current Cuban regime, had restricted travel to the country by students, artists, and other professionals from the United States, and severely limited the number of visas granted to Cuban performers and intellectuals to visit the United States. This sort of thing had long since become a de rigueur election time maneuver for the votes of Cuban Americans in the "battleground" state of Florida, but the George W. Bush administration had increased the stakes.[18] In a surprisingly bold move that made for uncharacteristically anti-Republican chatter on Cuban American radio in Miami, the Bush administration also placed new restrictions on the number of trips that Cuban American family members could make to visit the island, and limited the amount of remittances that could be sent to family members on the island. As we eat pizza with a group of friends, around the corner from our favorite nightclub, Delores echoes what other friends and respondents have said since my return to Cuba: fewer family members visit, and it seemed that there were fewer North American tourists than the year before. There was also an air of uneasiness after a few crackdowns and seeming closures of cultural openings in the nearly two years since I had completed my major research in Cuba.

I asked Delores about the hopeful, exciting bits of news I had heard about an emerging organization, or gathering, of lesbian and bisexual women, called Oremi.

At the prompting of a group of cultural workers, intellectuals, and (lesbian) researchers, CENESEX director Mariela Castro Espín invited a few lesbian and bisexual women to the center's offices to reflect on their lives, issues, and visions in a type of focus group. The sociologist Tanya Saunders notes that "the group [which was later called Oremi] received institutional support largely because several independent, unpublished, state-recognized Cuban studies about homosexuality . . . showed that gay men [had] benefited from state efforts at eliminating homophobia, while the situation of lesbians has stagnated and, in some measures, slightly deteriorated" (2009a: 168). Scores of women showed up at that first CENESEX forum—mostly women of color. Like Saunders's respondent who whispered, "I want to start an organization just for black women" (169), many had longed for such a space. They knew that surreptitious gatherings had occurred and short-lived groups had formed and dissolved in various places on the island. This had been impossible for most, since collective action outside of official state organization is not only difficult but also strictly forbidden.

Oremi literally means "close friend" in Yoruba. According to my respondent, Yaineris, Oremi is also the name by which a group of non-heteronormative nineteenth-century Cuban women adherents to Lucumí (as Yoruba religion is called in Cuba) were known. Yaineris learned through a local santera in Regla that these women loved one another sexually and formed a mutual-aid society. Their reported sale of tortillas has become a bawdy sexual double entendre, leading some to claim that the colloquial term for lesbians, "tortilleras," references these women. Though unverified, this claim seems an apt homage. The evocative scene of the historic Oremi of Regla, making and selling tortillas on the streets during festivals, connects contemporary Oremi to their foremothers who provided for the community, but on their own terms. The twenty-first-century resurgence of Oremi was born in this space between state hailing (this time, it seems, for a beneficial if not neutral purpose) and erotic connection. Delores and Yaineris attended the first meeting. Delores was very heartened to see "women you had thought might be, but were not sure." She said there were some "dykey . . . very strong-looking women, delicate women, and . . . a few natural women like me . . . bisexual, lesbiana . . . y [laughing] bueno, y [pause], no se . . . les gustan haciendo sexo con mujeres [well, that just like having sex with women]." We all understood it took more than just liking having sex with women to show up to face the unknown at such a historic event. Delores's description of herself as "natural" was made with respect to her unprocessed hair and lack of makeup, but it was also a reference to how she saw herself as perhaps more cosmopolitan, or intermediate between those she saw as "dykey" and other very "femme" women. Her own gender performance indexed her class status, education, and familiarity with styles worn by black women in the United States, that she learned from visitors, and the videos and magazines they left behind at YaYa's.

The conversation at the first Oremi gathering was "interesting" but had stops and starts, she said. By the next one, the numbers had swelled and CENESEX was unprepared for "what seemed like a sort of movement," in the words of another woman who attended the second meeting. This woman was anxious to attend the gathering, along with a few other individuals who did not necessarily fit or identify with Delores's categories of description, but who were nonetheless committed to women's liberation and to supporting their same-gender-loving sister-comrades. CENESEX was not prepared (at least not at this time) to oversee or champion an interest group of lesbians and other same-gender-loving women. Some of the women themselves felt less than comfortable being "out" in a gathering that was not only held under state auspices for scientific purposes but also was growing larger in size. I was told several stories by women on either side of Delores's schematic, as well as by the sociologist Tanya Saunders who has carried out extensive fieldwork with members of Oremi. Some of the women were uncomfortable not with the size of the group or the fact that "Raúl [Castro] could be listening," but rather with being seen walking into the sex education office at the same time as women who appeared to be lesbians. Some women used this rare and exciting opportunity to meet and have sex with women. And I heard anecdotally from a few attendees that some, much to the chagrin of neighbors of the CENESEX office who were treated to scenes of women holding hands and kissing in doorways and halls of CENESEX's neighbors, took this rare opportunity to make connections. A few of the women had begun to openly discuss the fact that the group was overwhelmingly black and mulata. There were early rumblings about the long-term-resident foreign women present, and they were summarily excluded as subsequent meetings were held by invitation only. Finally, there were others who wanted to continue the momentum of the meetings, and thus gather together informally at their homes, bars, and other locations.

In 2005, when I asked Delores what was up with Oremi, she sighed. It had been "so beautiful," she said, but it could not exist without the support and covering of CENESEX, which seemed to be overwhelmed with its work and a bit taken aback by the immediate calls to organize. After a short while, the CENESEX space was no longer made available. With the fate of the feminist network Magín sealed so recently (Fernandes 2005), it seemed clear that the group could not survive. As Delores explains:

> It is like us sitting here talking, Jafari. We can talk, all of us at this big table. We can meet here for pizza and talk twice, three times. Then the fourth, people notice. Then the fifth time. The same people at the table? *tsk tsk tsk* questions—Who are you? [she touches my shirt, indicating my foreignness] What is this about? [there was a long, sad pause. Then, she picks up a water glass]. Someone says, "We all like water glasses here, we are the society of water glasses" . . . no, no, no, *tsk tsk tsk* not here. It is not possible. Understand?

Of course, I did understand. I reminded her of our gatherings at YaYa's and how after a while she was called on to answer questions about them, and how finally they ended. With this, Delores sighed again. And her face showed that look that I had seen so many times before on the faces of Cuban friends, collaborators, and respondents. Although previously I had seen hope too, on this day it was harder to see. I prayed it was because I had been away so long—that my eyes were ill accustomed to Cuban realities; *aqui nada es fácil*, I remember being told my first day there: "here nothing is easy." Had my sight become

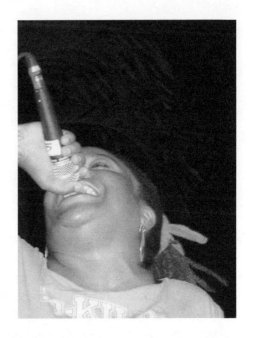

FIGURE 2. "Now there's the real question: Can we all get along long enough to make a revolution? Perhaps, but history tells us that it will mean taking leadership from some very radical women of color ... What the old guard militants really need to do is give up the mic for a moment, listen to the victims of democracy sing their dreams of a new world, and take notes on how to fight for the freedom of all" (Robin Kelley 2002: 156). Photo by the author.

jaundiced by academe, by the workaday world, by the political possibilities that seemed to be fading fast at home in the United States? Another sigh, collective now. YaYa sees Delores and I sitting wordlessly, and she saunters between us, in that regal way she has about her—smiling and holding us tight as if Delores and I were two sides of a piece she must connect. She brings us tighter and showers us with her kisses, perfumed by the cigarettes we have encouraged her to quit. Her presence stokes our resolve and focus. She reminded us of our date tomorrow, at the long-awaited Women in Hip-Hop concert starring Las Krudas (The raw ones), Majia, and others: "Y mañana," she begins, entertaining us by stretching out the words in her rendition of a Santiaguera accent, "la concierta de las mujeres de hip-hop!"

The Raw Ones

The next day we traveled to the Almendares forest at the edge of Vedado, where the concert would take place. At the end of a long bridge, intense, heavy greens greet you as you descend into the forest, as if entering another world. Almendares is a tropical forest sitting on a small river in Havana, where the neighborhoods of Vedado, Marianao, and Playa meet. The forest is a space of magical realness—serene and covered in trees, grasses, and vines—palpable sensuality in the heavy air. I remembered the stories that some of my gay male friends had told me about "hunting" for sex there among the ancient ficus and the sacred ceiba trees—their roots forming private cocoons. They talked about how the park gets so dark and still that one forgets that it lies within the city of Havana. Undoubtedly, there is cruising going on here tonight. I can sense it in the sweet wet air. But the feeling in the air is also anticipation for the women of hip-hop concert.

As we approach the Almendares amphitheater, the number of people wearing baggy jeans, long T-shirts, braids and twists increases. There are a few familiar faces from the days of La Pampa, and concerts at Alamar. Although I have attended a number of hip-hop concerts and performances, including the famous Black August hip-hop festival organized to raise awareness of political prisoners in the United States, this was the first I had seen exclusively featuring women: Las Krudas; Leidis; Magyori aka La Llave from EPG, whom I had never met but had seen at various places; and Majia (from the duo, Obsesión, with her husband Alexi), whose conscious and uplifting lyrics, strength, and warm personality I had admired since living across the street from her mother's home in Central Havana. Obsesión and other rappers have made tremendous contributions to cultural and political shifts on the island.[19] Still Las Krudas has made a singular contribution with their music and through their presence as progressive feminist lesbians. Although I had met Pasa Kruda (Odaymara Cuesta), Pelusa Kruda (Olivia Prendes), and Wanda Kruda (Odalys Cuesta) a few years before through my friend Llane, who had performed with them stilt-walking in Plaza de las Armas, this became most evident for me on the evening of the Women in Hip-Hop concert. Ronni Armstead in her essay "'Growing the Size of the Black Woman': Feminist Activism in Havana Hip Hop" quotes Pelusa as follows: "[We are] in theater, but we have to do our own theater because we don't want to join the [established] Cuban theater . . . We do our own where the black woman is protagonist, because the rest of the time in Cuban theater it's not that way. . . . where the black woman is protagonist and her life is a victory. *Entiendes* (Understand)? So then, we, through our theater projects, try to grow the size of the black woman" (2007). Here, and in the work of Tanya Saunders, who has profoundly engaged with the group over a number of years (2009b), we can see the emerging correspondence to the "Black Feminist Statement" by the Combahee River Collective (Smith 1983). Both champion the need for complementary analysis and action and enlargement or amplification of black women's voices.

The concert was far removed from the hip-hop shows that I had witnessed in Cuba and the United States where male MCs, accompanied by a posse of men crowding the stage, come out and spit lyrics, pace up and down the stage bumping and grinding, or employ a coterie of scantily clad women who do the bumping and grinding by proxy. The women's concert included all of the lyricism and swagger of the others I had seen, but also offered dance, short skits, and background work by many of the artists in support of their colleagues. From religious hypocrisy to various forms of patriarchy—in the home, on the street, and in the hip-hop community in Cuba and beyond—each woman performed their best material. The crowd was composed of the usual number of foreigners with video and still cameras, and those with requisite rum in recycled bottles. At the same time, however, it was different from other shows. First, more women than usual were in attendance. Groups of young men sat or stood in the back, as rapt as the rest of the audience but not throwing their hands up and becoming a part of the scene as might be expected. Instead, it was women who participated. It seemed that the raperas were speaking to them personally: hip-hop pitched to young women. The song "Soy gorda," a manifesto of bodily pride, featured Wanda flaunting her ample body while the other women posed, at first as hip-hop video dancers and then, after bursting out of these, they struck strong, defiant poses meant to show their own worth and creativity. Olivia appeared on stilts; costumes included priests, nuns, and santeros. In their track "Pa'ketenteres," Las Krudas had already exhorted women to own their own bodies, regardless of the sex/gender system that finds them "against the wall," but also sexually—wearing masks of heterosexuality while desiring other women. As the song tells it:

> hasta donde? contra la pared
> somos personas . . . siempre el mismo drama
> el macho pa la calle, la hembra pa' al cama
> [where does it lead? back against the wall
> we are people . . . always the same drama
> the man for the street, a woman for the bed]

The song continues:

Mujer, eres duena de ti mismo
de tu destino
eres tu quien determina como sigue tu camino eliges a quien amar
eliges como pensar
elegies como quien sonar
[Woman, you rule your own destiny
you determine what path to follow choose who you love
how to think
choose who you dream with]

Still, the crowd was surprised by the declaration that many had already understood but had not heard declared. As we continued to bounce and bop to the beat of Wanda's flow, Olivia moved from downstage to Wanda's position, looked into her eyes, smiling, and raised her hand. Then Wanda said, "My woman. . . . many years. . . . together. Krudas. . . . ¡Vamos a vencer!" "Vamos a vencer" (we are going to win), is a more popular way of expressing the notion "venceremos," perhaps because it lacks all of the heavy ideological baggage that one may find attached to it. In this instance, it referred not only to the people, or all women, or all black people, or lesbians, but also personally to Wanda and Olivia. We will win, together as a couple committed to loving each other. Oremi surrounding me, I felt the chill of affirmation. A flash. Perhaps too enraptured by the moment to read the crowd or start asking questions, I could feel surprise at the utterance; a flash, and then the party continued. For Delores, however, this was a watershed moment that could not be forgotten in the next beat. "Whhhhhewwww!" she said, beaming as she stood beside me. "Bastante fuerte." Very powerful indeed.

That evening, Las Krudas ended with "Eres bella" (You are beautiful). And this is the signature song/rap that they opened with two and a half years later when I saw them at Austin's Ruta Maya in their first public concert since arriving in the United States. Just a few months earlier, I had received a cryptic e-mail message from a friend in common, asking whether Austin was close to where I lived and worked. As it turned out, they eventually settled less than ten minutes from my home. That night, at Ruta Maya, with Pasa drumming to recorded Orisha chants, they arrived onstage and began their invocation, their statement of their mission as "Uniendo familia amor, arte y activismo, y la lucha por revindicar los derechos de la nueva mujer del mundo" (Family united in love, activism and the fight to vindicate the rights of the new global woman). And then there was the song:

> Dedicated to all the women in the World
> To all the women who, like us, are struggling.
> To all the warrior rural women, urban women
> To all of the women
> Especially the blackest, the poorest, the fattest
>
> . . .
>
> You are beautiful being you, ebony flower, black light
> Your body isn't your only virtue

It was a great performance. Austin welcomed them by dancing, applauding loudly, listening intently, and dancing long into the night. But still, I was a little sad. I wondered what it meant that they had moved to the United States. I could no longer ignore how the various circles of respondents and friends I had grown close to in Havana had diminished in size. I had grown tired of asking after people during each trip, because so many had gone. Some left the island "the right way" of seemingly endless and costly permissions and visas for betrothal, marriage, or family unification, or to present work in a concert, exhibition, a conference, and the like. Others, as one of my respondents joked about his sister, simply "forgot"; that is, she missed her flight back to Havana when she was out of the country for a sports match in Mexico City. Another missed a flight in New York; another (long awaited and planned) in Madrid. It then occurred to me that this too is part of the continuing Cuban Revolution. It is not exporting socialism the way Fidel would have liked—through doctors, ballet, hurricane assistance, and the like, but their hard-won mobility, as a family, indeed grows the size of the black Cuban womanhood. In the next chapter, we will examine more controversial forms of mobility and "friendship."

¡Hagamos un Chen! (We Make Change!)

6

AS SCHOLARS SUCH AS Kamala Kempadoo (1999, 2004; Kempadoo and Doezema 1998), Denise Brennan (2004), Mark Padilla (2007), and others have shown, sex work is taking place throughout the Caribbean. Nowhere is this more remarkable than the *ambiente* (environments or scene) of sex labor in Cuba. Owing to the obvious irony involved in the "reappearance"[1] of streetwalking, long after the revolutionary government had stamped out female "prostitution" in the wake of their triumph in 1959, Cuban sex work has gained international attention in scholarly work and in the popular imagination (Cabezas 1998, Fernandez 1999; Fusco 2001; Hodge 2001). In this chapter, I will explore some of the historical, affectual, and political-economic factors that both underlie Cuban sex labor as a practice and give it salience as a metaphor. The Special Period's reglobalization of Cuba recruited black Cuban subjects to late capitalism's global market of commodities and ideas as consumers, yet global capital also requires the consumption of black bodies, as it always has. Tourism-related sex labor is one of a growing number of spaces in which commonsense understandings of racial and sexual identity are represented and exploited toward related aims of material "survival," commodity acquisition, mobility, and becoming a cosmopolitan subject.[2]

Through an interpolation of registers and sites, this chapter will consider myriad practices and likely subjective intentions of men who rent their time, talents, and bodies. The chapter follows a new sort of triangle (sex) trade—from the provinces of Cuba, to Havana, and beyond. We begin with a brief "tour" to Miami.

From El Malecón to La Avenida

One evening in 2002 at Sugars, a black gay dance club in North Miami Beach, Florida, I could scarcely believe my eyes when I noticed a handsome, muscular black man who was returning my stare of disbelief. I should not have been shocked, after so many years of engagement with Cuba. Ramon, one of my respondents in Cuba, had made his way to Miami. I understood that he, like many *pingueros* (male sex workers) and other young people I met had been working simultaneously on a few plans that would get him off the island. But one does not expect "the field" to collapse in on one so dramatically. From our first meeting, Ramon had been among the cagiest of my respondents. He was also the first to ask that he be remunerated for the time we spent talking. I thought this move indicative of a particularly ruthless goal-oriented professional—and also, of course, fair. After all, I was imposing on an entrepreneur during working hours. Still, other pingueros I met seemed to genuinely enjoy talking and were pleased with the fact that I purchased dinner, or beers, and that I politely moved on when duty called them away. However, Ramon also seemed more suspicious of me than others. He told me that I would have to give him one hundred U.S. dollars for his services.[3] When I told him that I did not want to have sex, but instead wanted to chat with him, perhaps interview him, he was incredulous. During our Miami meeting, he was perhaps a bit more forthcoming because of the surprise and the fact that I was familiar. He said that I reminded him of home. Still, by our lunch interview two days later, he was again cool and professional, perhaps concerned to not give too much information that might effect his plans for immigration, or the position of his various Miami benefactors and clients (incidentally, none of whom would be seen in a "low bar" like Sugars).

While he gave only sketchy details, it seems a customer-friend had arranged an invitation for Ramon to leave Cuba to work in Brazil. In the end, he was able to leave Cuba, go to Brazil for a short while, and then make his way to the United States. Of his benefactor whom he says he left in Brazil, Ramon says, "We are friends." Upon his arrival to the United States, Ramon had quickly made contact with his cousin, Ariel, who had arrived on the Mariel launch two decades earlier. Ariel arranged a room for him to rent in the home of a friend of his, to share with recent arrivals from Central America, and a job as a busman in a South Beach restaurant. In his work bussing tables, Ramon was sure he would be "discovered" by a model's agent or a wealthy older man, whichever came first. In the interim (faithfully reproducing narratives of immigrant industriousness) he quickly found another job. His new job was at Avenida, a gay strip club well known for a variety of Pan-American male erotic dancers. It was a chance for untaxed tips, in cash; bright spotlights and constant attention; and opportunities for freelance sex work outside the club. The American dream. Martin Manalansan argues that queer theory's understanding of sexuality contributes to a broader and deeper understanding of (im)migration experiences (2006: 224). Manalansan, who in his signal contribution, *Global Divas* (2003), theorized identity and movement among non–gender normative (and) gay Filipino men, argues that migration researchers should rethink prevailing notions of gender and sexuality, not only by including queer persons but also by taking up some of the theoretical or conceptual tools of this enterprise of queer theory. This centrally includes looking past commonsense or received knowledge to ask what and or who is missing. These are certainly sites for exploration in terms of not only how these various iterations of sexual play and sexual behavior and structuration of desire condition particular experiences *at home* but also the ways in which they change across sites of difference such as gender, class, race, color, and sexual expression; how they might be differentially regulated by the home state (and potentially by the act of emigration); how they inspire or necessitate *sexile*, or condition decisions of when to immigrate and with whom; and finally, how they make their sexual lives in the new home country and how this changes as they travel back to the original location.

It is well known among blacks in Miami that many in the Cuban American exile community identify as white and reinscribe racist practices of prerevolutionary Cuba that make Cuban Miami very inhospitable for blacks. Nevertheless, when I lived there for a short time I naively went looking for black Cubans in the Cuban American sections of the city and at Cuban events, restaurants, and churches. I found only a few—none of whom lived in the center of Cuban Miami. And like Ramon, Ariel, and many other blacks in South Florida, I too have heard racist comments on Cuban American radio and while indulging in the sweet nostalgia served in cups and on plates at Versailles, La Carretera, and other Hialeah haunts. Having read the work of Lourdes Arguelles and B. Ruby Rich (1984), I was prepared to hear folks say, for example, that "the only good thing about Castro is that he got rid of the homosexuals," but I did not think I would hear it as often as I did or in as many ways. Black Cubans, with the exception of those who made their living in the entertainment and Cuban nostalgia industry, seemed integrated only into (already disempowered) black Miami—well west and north of the beaches that adorn travel brochures where the world's elite play tropics in North America, and southeast from where Cuban Americans have erected their version of a Castro-free Havana, known as Little Havana. I met more black Cubans in Little Haiti, Overtown, and other areas of northwest Miami than I did in the traditionally Cuban areas. Other black Cubans had left South Florida for more welcoming Cuban enclaves in Union City, New Jersey, and the New York City area; or San Francisco where in the 1980s, gay North American men had advocated for the acceptance of Cuban gay men reportedly fleeing homophobic persecution in Cuba (and were reportedly introduced to United States–style racialized sexual objectification, according to Arguelles and Rich).

For his part, Ramon had been counting on racialized objectification, his stock in trade. At Avenida, he danced alongside Jamaicans, Puerto Ricans, Dominicans, and Brazilians—each of whom alternately performed cultivated versions of national and ethnic distinctiveness, and generic black and brown "macho" for the crowd. He was therefore not ready to leave Miami, which offered so many opportunities of men willing to pay to see him dance onstage at a place like La Avenida, in midtown, or to have him over for an "out call" to a tony hotel in South Beach or Coral Gables. He seemed, like many of the Cuban *pingueros* and *jineteras* that I had observed over the years, savvy about his role in the reproduction of exotic fantasies, both in Cuba and in his new home. For black Cuban subjects, the transnational "triangle trade" of desire, constituted by not only the northern gaze but also by the performance of "tropical" or "exotic" black sexualities by individuals with severely limited repertoires of agency, illustrates the interplay of sexual interpellation and self-making and the political economy of globalized black sexualities, both *here* and *there*.

¡Hagamos un Chen! (We Make Change!)[4]

Sitting in an open square in a town in the Oriente Province of Cuba in 1999, I was waiting for an appointment and writing in my notebook when Esteban appeared. At a lanky five feet ten, and with light-brown skin, coarse curls, and dark-brown eyes framed by long thick eyelashes, he looked to me every bit the naive eighteen-year-old. We chatted about the heat—which is an amazingly common topic on this island that is hot so often—and Esteban suggested that he would like to go for something cold to drink. I explained that I could not go for long because of an appointment, which he then implored me to break. I explained that I could not, but I promised to meet him the next day at the same time and place. The next day he showed up as agreed. We talked about his impressions of the attractive women who passed us in the park and at the ice cream stand: "I like black women because they are much more caring and sensuous." he said. "Her skin is the color of yours . . . she is very pretty even though she has fake hair [braid extensions]." Esteban seemed a bit nervous and very chatty, as if there was something else he wanted to say. He then continued, "She looks very *civilizada* [in the know or sophisticated] and *educada* [educated] . . . I am a laborer, and I am not *muy negro* [very black], but my mother is like her. I am always attracted to *negros* [generically dark-skinned "black people" but specifically, by use of the masculine form, dark-skinned black *men*] even though people say that they are ugly." He relaxed when I told him I was a researcher studying sexuality among Cuban men, and he was among the first of many to say "with me, you will experience everything you need to know." We both laughed, then I shifted the conversation to his life at home. He was considering dropping out of a vocational training program because he saw few prospects for well-paying jobs in Oriente. Finally, Esteban told me that he had a girlfriend, but would go to Havana soon "to do business . . . make some money." Then, softly, his eyes met mine. He demurely cast them downward, confiding, "I have male friends who I see also. They help me." He rankled a bit when I chuckled at his melodramatic performance. I told him that I meant no disrespect. Esteban and I met to chat a few times during my stay in Oriente. As it turned out, the friends who "help him" were older Cuban men who assist him with clothing, access to the places they work, and, occasionally, money.

Esteban did make it to Havana. I unexpectedly ran into him in the winter one year later on La Rampa, the area near Hotel Habana Libre that is well known for cruising among men who have sex with men. To Esteban, and many young men and women like him, Havana is the main place to encounter not only foreign people and ideas but also their currency and commodities. Although there is certainly sex labor in various places on the island, it is most prominent in Havana where there is not only a larger number of foreigners but a larger population overall, thereby supporting a degree of anonymity (or plausible deniability) impossible in places with closer family scrutiny. Esteban explained then that although his family had a room for him at home, he preferred to come to Havana to ply his new trade as a pinguero (male sex worker). Still, I was surprised and a little concerned for the emotional safety of this boyish young man who had arrived only hours ago from the provinces, with no bag and no money. Esteban had completed half of his training program, but he preferred *"luchando* . . . anything but getting fucked." Later that evening, before he had a chance to meet a willing *yuma* (foreigner) who would test the boundaries he had set for himself; he was taken to jail where he says he spent the evening in a cell with fifteen other young men from the provinces. Like him, these men—according to Esteban, "strong-looking black men"—had left home to (be) trade and were picked up by the national police for loitering in tourist areas and having no legitimate business in Havana.

When I offered to purchase a train ticket for Esteban to return home, he asked instead for the money I would have spent for the train ticket, along with some clothing and a shower. Later, standing in the doorway of my apartment wearing my clothing after a light meal and a shower, he seemed confused as I said goodbye to him. I had not given him any cash and we had no sexual contact, which he seemed sure would have turned me into his benefactor, rather than the position of friendship that our nonsexual interaction had proffered. He said, in what sounded like a recently rehearsed seductive tone, "You could be the only one who helps me, and I would not have to do this." Once more, I suggested giving his training course in Oriente another try, or finding a course that was more interesting—perhaps even selling bootleg jewelry or cigars, until he seemed savvy enough not to land in jail. He scoffed, "For me this is all too much trouble." Then he made another appeal for my designer sandals.

Amalia Cabezas, in her review of the literature on race and female "prostitution" in Cuba, argues that much of this work betrays notions of female propriety and sexuality that fail to historically and politically contextualize the issue. "What informs these studies," she writes, "is the continuing construction of prostitutes as pathological, deviant subjects" (1998: 48). Putting a finer edge on this issue in her provocatively titled *Vindication of the Rights of Whores: The International Movement for Prostitutes' Rights*, the scholar and sex-work activist Gail Pheterson asserts that for women, "prostitution" is a heavily stigmatized social status, which in most societies remains fixed regardless of change in behavior (1989). This lies in stark contrast to the view of male clients. Moreover, heterosexual-identified male sex laborers are thought to play roles as "gigolos" or "studs," often regarded as a temporary activity. Paulla Ebron, who writes about Bumsters (male sex laborers in Gambia) in her book *Performing Africa*, nicely summarizes ways in which the study of male sex labor—"different enough to be illuminating"—holds great promise as a site from which to observe and theorize sexual sovereignty, labor, agency, and self-fashioning. As she states:

> "Traffic-in-men" narratives disrupt our taken for granted axioms about the gendered locations of sexual agency. . . . Despite the attempts of feminist scholars to participate in this rethinking, our scholarly tools have not been very helpful. . . . This subjective sense is constructed out of "Agency" as erasing "oppression"; where there is a clear power imbalance, we reasonably want to show cohesion and vulnerability, not self-fashioning. The Gambian "traffic" I describe is perhaps different enough to be illuminating. It is difficult to imagine any of the participants as victims, for none will let themselves be described that way." (2002: 169, 188)

In the cases of both men and women in the Cuban tourist sex trade, framing the "problem" as moral turpitude, counterrevolutionary, or false consciousness, or simplistically posing these subjects as victims of global capital—to name a few impulses in the popular imagination and in some cases in scholarship—elides the dynamic relationship between sex laborers, their foreign clients (or "friends"), and a four-century-long racial-sexual ideology in which black bodies and feminized bodies are interpellated as always accessible sites of pleasure and danger to be exploited. This follows Caribbean and black feminist critique (Reddock 1990; Gilliam 1991; Alexander 1997; Mohammad 1998), which insists that the history and political economy of the Caribbean and the raced, gendered, sexed, and classed subjectivities of each of the actors be interrogated. While we can agree that an individual sex laborer's ability to act and choose freely, or the degree to which he is in fact "forced to choose" (Doezema 1998), is in part located in his subjective sense of authorization, control, and effectiveness; feminist theorization on sex work must push beyond the sort of either/or proposition that Ebron points out. Agency does not in fact erase oppression any more than "choice" means that all alternatives are attractive, planned, or desired. Neither should this be confused with the fantasy of a "free" choice or action, unlimited by cultural, historical, and material structures. As I have tried to demonstrate through the experience of other Cubans making their way under difficult conditions, "subjective sense" is not neutrally produced. Personal agency does not follow any particular telos.

Moreover, we must move beyond moralizing rhetorics that pose sex work as a singularly or especially debased activity. This is key to any serious interrogation of the current meanings of sex labor and the experiences of the individuals who engage in it. This is complex and difficult to navigate. One of my long-term Cuban respondents and friends constantly challenged me on what she saw as my relativistic position on sex work. Annoyed, she told me: "My refrigerator is not full . . . it is actually broken . . . Still, you don't see me going around with foreigners[5] or wearing those tight dresses and too much makeup . . . It is a matter of respect and education. These girls lack these things and should know better—that they have other opportunities."

To my friend and to many others, the return or shift to tourism and sex tourism in Cuba is a painful reminder of the limits of the success of the Revolution. Post-revolution sex labor had been limited to small sex-for-commodity exchanges with Soviet and Eastern European functionaries visiting the island. But the financial desperation of the Special Period is clearly not the sole reason for sex labor. If it were, we should have observed a decrease in the practice in an inverse relationship when there were improvements in the Cuban GDP and food distribution. This has not been the case. Moreover, one cannot eat a Nike shoe, a gold chain, or a designer-label T-shirt. In the late 1990s, yumas paid in clothing, jewelry, and other commodities much more often than in cash. Notwithstanding Cuban, and more broadly Caribbean, political economy and history, the subjective desires and intentions of agents on the ground are equally important as economic crisis.

The desire to consume in the ways that foreigners do and to exercise the types of personal and sexual freedoms that northern foreigners seem to practice, is a powerful enticement to sex labor, especially in a changing global landscape in which, more than ever, to consume in particular ways signals full personhood. For many, especially young people, the lack of what seem to be sine qua non markers of global personhood and citizenry, can engender feelings of isolation from what is increasingly represented and broadcast in worldwide media as a "global community" seemingly defined by state-free and politically neutral individuals who consume commodities and enjoy a carefree lifestyle. So, while luchando pa' la calle like sex labor does not necessarily suggest a moral failing, false consciousness, or lack of revolutionary resolve, it certainly does point out important social shifts and cleavages. The ambiente of sex work in Cuba is thus constitutive of a particular sexual culture that has developed since the founding of Cuba's slave economy in 1512; the stark economic power imbalance between Cuba and the overdeveloped North; the imbalances between whites and blacks, women and men, and machos and maricones on the island; as well as the subjective desires and intentions of individuals to become cosmopolitan, global subjects.

Fidel Castro lamented that he wished Cuba could export its beaches. He held that to embark on tourism as a development strategy was, in fact, like making a pact with the devil. He made the pact, nevertheless. And while "the devil" for former President Castro may be the specter of capitalist excesses "returning" to the island, for black and other dark-skinned Cubans the re-emergence of tourism and related sex work—to go "back to the future" as Nadine Fernandez (1999) puts it—hearkens back to pre-revolutionary structures of feeling. This includes contending with a tourist gaze that casts people of the South—especially blacks—as objects of their pleasure. In the words of one of Coco Fusco's respondents, "No one comes to Cuba for ecotourism. What sells this place is right on the dance floor—rum, cigars and la mulata" (1998: 152).

Until 1881, the slave trade constituted black and brown bodies as chattel, bought and sold in actual markets. Mythologized as at once savage and desirable, Africans were the express property of European Creole (structurally white) males. After blacks were grudgingly granted the emancipation they won in the War of Independence, during the Republican period it was common for moneyed men to access the bodies of poorer and darker people, whether through "consent," coercion, commerce, or outright violence supported by the juridical system. Notions of negro savagery and the morally dissolute mulata were codified in popular and scholarly discourse. The effects of this sexual/racial ideological effect still obtain today. It can be seen in the reasoning given for romantic object choice, which Nadine Fernandez explores among young heterosexual couples in her *Revolutionizing Romance: Interracial Couples in Contemporary Cuba* (2010). Likewise, Ian Lumsden contends that "Cubans expect blacks to be 'symbols of virility,'" and further, quoting an "old homosexual" respondent, "The lower classes had much more *sabor* (flavor). Decent people had no *sabor*, no spice . . . Did we often pay for sex? Of course we did" (1996: 96).

As I have noted, Havana in the 1950s was the original "sin city" for United States and Latin American elites. The revolutionary program sought to invert the country/city disparity of resource allocation, which found the countryside without basic infrastructural support, and tried to "free" laborers from work in hotels, casinos, brothels, and on street corners, which the revolutionary government deemed alienating. But the city also stood as a symbol of freedom and pleasure for Cuban and foreign sexual minorities and sex enthusiasts, and it was an important site of work for poor black Cubans, as opposed to the countryside where there was little or no work, and certainly no excitement compared to the bustling international city of Havana. Havana then—as now—held various meanings for different individuals, including the chance at *sexile*. Now, visitors who see Cuba as a relatively inexpensive alternative Caribbean "playground" or as a unique destination "frozen in time" and therefore providing a simulacra of socialism and machismo, for example, contribute much-needed hard currency to the local economy. As agents of not only their own pleasure, but the global hegemony of the North from which most come, the demands and perceived preferences of these visitors drive supplies of old Cuban music, old Cuban costumes, old Cuban racial hierarchies, and the reinscription of old machista structures of feeling and gender/sex roles.

To pose these young men as innocents whose "natural" course of gender or sexual formation has been impinged upon, does not reflect complex contemporary realities. It would be erroneous and particularly heterosexist to presume that because some young men trade companionship and sex, they have been interrupted on a particular ("natural") trajectory of (hetero)sexuality, or turned off of nonpay sex. Capitalist re-incursion has not *turned out* every young man in Cuba. Rather, discursively denying them the agency that they in fact exercise daily is counterproductive intellectually and enervating to the revolutionary project, which needs and deserves healthy debate, criticisms of its choices, and an honest assessment of the forces that indeed seek to render the entire island of Cuba an outpost of global capital.

The Twenty-Peso Party

After my first unaccompanied visit to a twenty-peso party,[6] I visited the home of friends in Cerro. When asked about my impressions of the party, my full report followed. Unlike other gatherings that I had attended in Santiago or Havana, either with these friends or with other acquaintances, and in stark contrast to the parties in neighborhoods like Cerro, Cayo Hueso, and Old Havana, no one approached me to talk, dance, or even held a glance very long when I attempted to initiate a dance invitation or a conversation. Uncharacteristically, I had been a wallflower content to observe more than I had participated that evening. Laughing, my friend's lover asked me two questions: first, *What did you wear?* then, *Did you speak English?* I proudly explained that I spoke only (my best Habanero) Spanish, and that I had worn the guayabera and plain sandals I had traded for my running shoes and Morehouse College T-shirt a week before. Laughter ensued, at my expense. When he recovered, my friend's lover gave his advice—very slowly, since it must have seemed to him that I was completely socially inept, having made such a terrible bargain and fashion choice: "Next time, speak English—very loudly . . . Go first to the bar to buy a bottle of rum. You will have many friends before you even open the bottle." They explained that the partygoers thought that I was Cuban, and a *guajiro* (country boy) at that—wearing a guayabera like an old man who just came in from the provinces! As a foreigner, I had been misplaced in the economy of the twenty-peso party.

For young men in Havana and elsewhere on the island, twenty-peso fiestas—the weekend pay parties attended by foreign and Cuban men who have sex with men—are important weekend diversions and a center of the constitution of the emerging *gay* public. They range in style from small gatherings in nontourist areas—attended mostly by Cubans and a few foreigners—to more grand affairs in lush gardens, dominated by foreigners and more well-heeled (and whiter) Cubans. I will limit my exploration to the latter style of fiestas because they constitute a key element of male-male sex labor and thus are more germane to the topic. This is one example of the interplay of the desires of Cuban pingueros and foreigners who attend these parties and other spaces in which they gaze upon "objects" of their desire. The twenty-peso parties are often spectacular affairs, sometimes including *espectáculos de transformistas* (drag shows), but they always have a cash bar well stocked with bottles of (mostly popular nontourist brands or homemade) rum, mixers, and beer; and the festive structure of feeling does not seem dampened by the fact that it is "hidden" (in plain sight, just farther away). One popular venue is near the airport, at the end of a long, dark road. In another, one enters into a large courtyard ringed by mango trees and royal palms, with lighting rigs on large poles and a large dance floor populated by perfumed, coiffed, and jubilant young men and some women, dancing to global Top 40 hits; timba, charenga, and other homegrown Cuban favorites as well as Latin American dance music; and occasionally, European techno music. Rap music and la monia are not customarily played, but as the reggaetón craze has expanded it has found its way to these parties.

Since these parties are officially extralegal, like any paid gathering not licensed by the state (though I have attended many parties where the national police have pointed out the site of the party along a dark road) and not advertised openly, the best way to find out about the twenty-peso party used to be to hang out on La Rampa (the main drag in Vedado close to Habana Libre Hotel) in front of Yara cinema on a weekend evening. From the moment a yuma arrives at any of the places where men who have sex with men are known to gather, like La Rampa or the eastern beaches of Havana, he is scrutinized closely, then approached—often boyishly aggressive—by one or more of the young men present. This aggressiveness is not to be perceived as threatening, but rather as masculine. It seems also, from conversations with yumas (who for the purpose of this discussion do not have to be from the United States, but are foreign), that this aggressive, so-called macho attitude is titillating to them. The Cuban will decide, given who is available, which yumas they will approach and ultimately engage. In echoing the majority of those I talked to, one young man told me: "for me to go with him, he must be attractive and clean, and look like a good person." In any event, regardless of what he looks like, a yuma will eventually be approached by a Cuban who will break the ice with some form of "My friend . . . where are you from? . . ." On weekends, if the young Cubano wants to attend the twenty-peso party, he will mention it if the yuma does not. After he agrees to go, often the young man—now the yuma's host for the evening—will invite his friends to join their party. They may share a colectivo if the yuma is passable as Cuban and the young man is budget conscious. More often, however, they will use a tourist taxi or privately hired car and the foreigner will pay. Once at the fiesta, the foreigner will pay twenty pesos (one U.S. dollar) each for the entry of the Cubans. For himself he will pay two or three dollars—always more than the dollar for Cuban entry. This "double-standard" is a common practice all over Cuba, where foreigners must pay more than do Cubans for entrance fees and cover charges at state-run events in order to gesture toward equalizing the tremendous gulf in financial ability and providing Cubans access to Cuban cultural events. Once they have arrived, the Cuban host, following local rules of masculine etiquette, will make sure that everything is okay, that the rum is flowing (from the pocket of the yuma), and that the yuma enjoys himself dancing, drinking, and being attended to by his host(s). Despite the fact that he has not paid the entrance fee and is not providing the cash that facilitates the drinking, the Cuban young man remains the host and will in most cases take very seriously his role of making conversation and joking, paying close attention to the yuma, and maintaining visibility as a center of attention. By the end of the evening, the young Cuban will, as a pinguero friend told me, "know whether he is generous or stingy" and therefore whether he should continue attached to him or risk finding another yuma if a Cuban friend with access to transportation is not available. The more or less typical scene of the twenty-peso party described here can have various endings, and not all yumas are interested in the fiestas. Similar in spirit are trips to parts of Havana's eastern beaches. There are also other scenes (which Ramon claimed to participate in) in private homes and among well-heeled travelers in which more sought-after young men—usually athletes and entertainers—may not have to work as hard to entertain and are remunerated better for their time. In other cases, of course, "some [tourists] prefer to just stay in their rooms and get fucked," as one pinguero told me.

If, like Alejandro, one happens upon a foreigner who has a large amount of leisure time and money, a young Cuban man might have the opportunity to travel to various places around the island. Alejandro returned to Havana talking as if he had just returned from holiday himself, rather than a ten-day "business trip" with an Italian tourist. Alejandro reported traveling to "Varadero, Matanzas, Trinidad . . . I have family there [in Trinidad] but had never been before . . . I just had to massage him and hold him . . . be nice, get sucked, fuck a couple of times . . . he gave me a lot of money." He bragged that his friend would continue to send him money, and had given him an Italian horn pendant on a gold chain and a Tissot-brand Swiss watch, which he proudly showed me. As we silently admired these trinkets over cold beer and small Cuban "pizzas," he said: "Maybe I can get a work visa invitation to go to the Alps to see how life is there."

Consuming Ga(y)ze / Working Guys

Vacationers get to invert their everyday experiences while they consume experiences and bodies, the likes of which they would normally have no access. As John Urry contends: "The gaze . . . is constructed in relationship to its opposite, to non-tourist forms of social experience and consciousness. . . . Places are chosen to be gazed upon because there is anticipation . . . of intense pleasures, either on a different scale or involving different senses from those customarily encountered . . . in some sense out of the ordinary" (Urry 1990: 83). The twenty-peso parties provide some cultural legibility for these North American and European travelers who experience the often-disorienting singularity of Cuba in other realms during their visits. This feeling allows northern gay yumas to be comfortable in the familiar scene of young and attractive men dancing and drinking and flirting. The traveler from Canada or Western Europe may not know how to read cultural signals from young Cuban men at the beach or at the theater. They may not understand socialist politics or policies and may be completely mystified by the implicit rules of deportment in the country. Still, the signs and significations within the "gay club" are similar the world over—one indication of globalization's attempt at homogenization, even at the margins.

What is pleasantly different here for the foreigner is that his status as a foreigner at the fiesta and in the wider milieu of male sex labor, is privileged in ways that most men could not experience in their home countries. This is especially true for those who are perhaps over "a certain age," or are otherwise less desirable in the economy of gay desire in the North, which famously favors youth and stereotyped standards of beauty and carriage. Those who would be seen as surplus to the gay economy of desire at home may in fact become central to the scene in Cuba. Moreover, for gay men, Cuban tourism provides an uncanny and unexpected inversion of the surveillance and suspicion that they may face at home, as well as a relaxation of competition for attractive partners and barriers to affection, sex, and romance. One yuma from Canada explained to me that "it's not 'just sex,'" while another from the United States pointed out how "comfortable" and "safe" he feels with his Cuban friend at the parties and on the streets of Havana in comparison to being alone in Dallas. As Jerard, from New York (the only black American tourist I met at the time), confided to me, "They are as fine as the Dominican and Puerto Rican trade [an impeccably masculine "top" partner or sex laborer] back home, but you don't have to worry about getting bashed in the head . . . they are so sweet!" In this case "trade" not only satisfies sexual desire but seems to care and is economical to boot! This is not just my attempt at humor at Jerard's expense. The perception, at least at first, of many yumas is that these young men are innocents, not the reputedly callous and uncaring but therefore also hypermasculine and attractive young black (and) Latino men of the North. This is a sort of tropicalist thug fantasy—interpreted by young Cuban men via local understandings of guaperia.

The combination of the perception or experience of care, sexual proficiency, and security is central to why the experience of a tourist in Cuba is different from that of a gay man from Illinois visiting Miami, for example. As such, this combination is a key constitutive factor in the tourist's consuming gaze. Yumas feel safe in Cuba, not only because the national police were patrolling the street and harassing young men by asking for their carnets, thereby moving them out, or more accurately, cycling them through different tourist areas, but more profoundly because the men were (or appeared to them to be) arrayed there for their pleasure and consumption. Further, in the words of a Canadian tourist, repeated by many others, they felt safe because "these are real men." The market for male sex laborers is driven by strongly held notions of hyperactive Cuban masculinity (machismo), romance, and sexual organs of legendary proportions. Further, Cuban achievements in music and art have been exported to a global market primed for images of dancing, singing, and hospitable "natives." This is not to say that these images and ideas are always or necessarily "false," but certainly unreconstructed. Sex laborers exploit this, mostly in a very self-conscious way.

As I explained one afternoon to my respondents Pedro and Ilanisvany, in the United States notions of black male physical prowess are similar to those that circulate in Cuba. While in my experience black men in the United States refuse representations of themselves as lazy, criminal, or unintelligent, parallel ideologies of superiority in sports and sex are constantly reified by black men and women themselves. Ilanisvany, whose reaction was more or less typical of the commonsense of Cuban race/sex ideology, looked at me incredulously as I talked, then announced with no hint of irony, that this *fact* of sexual and physical prowess is a result of the inheritance of Africa, and conditioning in slavery—black bodies, he offered, are more well suited to making love and working. Pedro and Ilanisvany laughed and rolled their eyes when I suggested that this was a myth—and a racist one at that. Later, I mentioned to them that I was told that a gay magazine in the United States had warned gay travelers that *the only bulge in your pants that Cuban men are interested in is your wallet*. The laughter gave way to confessions that if not for the "help" that foreigners give, these men would be less apt to routinely have sex with foreigners. Still, they sharply critiqued the sardonic assumption of middle- and upper-class foreigners, evidenced by this comment, that all poor Cuban men can be seduced for the right price, and further, that money was the only motivator. In Cuba this is recognized as an "imperialist" gaze that seeks to expand its ownership of not only the means of material production but the bodies of the "natives." This is a familiar relationship in Cuba, where historically, younger, darker, and poorer *bugarrones*, or insertive partners, were sought by local elites for pay or favors, which seems to be the interaction Esteban was engaged in before his migration to Havana.

Jasbir Puar points out in "Circuits of Queer Mobility: Tourism, Travel and Globalization" that while on one hand the phenomenon of "queer[s] [on] holiday" is seen to disrupt what is posed as the heterosexual space of the tropics, the exotic is also signaled by discourses of homophobia. She shows that in the case of international gay travel organizations condemning Jamaica and other "homophobic sites," "the gay and lesbian tourism industry is indebted to the culturally constructed homophobia of another place," which she argues is intrinsic to the framework of modernity and enables, rather than deflects, tourist interests as well as fantasies of sexual transgression (2002: 104). She adds: "The assumed inherent quality of space is that it is always heterosexual, waiting to be disrupted through queering, positing a single axis of identity which then reifies a heterosexual/homosexual split that effaces other kinds of identities . . . Rarely is that disruption interrogated also as a disruption of racialized, gendered, and classed spaces. Nor are such disruptions understood in tandem with a claiming of class, gender and race privilege as well" (111).

There seems to be a concomitant misuse of the tropics and tropical subjects in some streams of scholarship on transnational sexualities in which, too often, as Puar and others have begun to assert, the only mobile subjects are white, middle class, and male, while those of color are cast as immobile and unchanging. This is particularly the case in transnational queer studies.[7] An examination of the queer studies literature may leave one with the impression, from the absence of black subjects, that while other groups are traveling, changing their minds and sex partners, and exchanging goods and ideas on the global market, black subjects remain the primordial, fixed, object. As such, the Third World subject is denied voice in narratives of queer sexual encounter. Ramon's globetrotting trade certainly refutes this assertion, as does Jerard's transnational sex tourism. A formidable body of creative literature documents and imagines the vigorous travel and migration patterns, filial and affective ties, and consumption of cultural production from a variety of sites around the globe of black subjects.

I MET TWENTY-YEAR-OLD George, a handsome athletically built baseball player, at La Pampa in 1999. This putatively heterosexual hip-hop club was located just steps around the corner from El Fiat cafeteria, which at the time was a late-night haunt of men who have sex with men. George, who identified himself as bisexual (something he does not disclose to his female partners who would be horrified by this, he says) could have just as easily been available for homosexual or heterosexual relationships—a young female student sampling Cuban hip-hop and la monia at La Pampa, or a man enjoying the homoerotic ambiente at El Fiat. Both were located across from the Malecón. Some weekends, I witnessed a few hundred men of various color descriptions gathered there, enjoying the cool and scenic Malecón while cruising, talking, and laughing with old friends and new ones. George seemed at ease with the mix of men who have sex with men and a few women—transgender and those assigned female at birth. At La Pampa, directly diagonal to where we stood together, the crowd had more teenage and twenty-something male and female partygoers and was almost exclusively black, with the exception of a few foreign students and tourists. George seemed unconcerned about moving between La Pampa, El Fiat, and the crowds of men on the sea wall, although young men like him who are (or are rumored to be) members of various national sports teams are rarely seen hanging out at places like El Fiat, which at the time was known—at least to those in the know—as a "gay" space. He told me, perhaps naively, or merely counting on the power of denial, that "people do not know what these guys are doing here." The next week, I met George at a rap concert. When I asked him about his foreign friend from the previous week, with whom he had spent the rest of the evening after our short conversation on the Malecón, he explained that Michel was an executive at a French corporation that could invite him to France to work. George explained to me that although he was not sexually attracted to Michel, he "did not mind being sucked by him," though he reported that he drew the line after being massaged, fellated, and masturbated. When I asked whether he thought there is a difference in sexual orientation between those who suck and those who get sucked, he replied that "it is simply a matter of what you like, and with who . . . With Michel, I might only do that . . . I might do more, maybe suck you. The machista attitude is an old idea." Later, on the same score, he offered, "This . . . is not a matter of shame, but a matter of what I like. . . . I might get fucked one day too."

While not denying that they have sex for some form of remuneration, male sex laborers in Cuba hold that the way that they do it as a form of friendship—for example, not just having sex but by showing off the island and other such activities—that sets them apart from "prostitutes," who they think of as full-time (female) professionals who trade only sex for a set amount of money. They insist that their practice constitutes a particular genre of work, a service to the foreign visitor and a peculiar form of interpersonal exchange that includes the pursuit of leisure and play. I use the term "labor" rather than "work" (i.e., "drudgery") in order to remain true to the lived experience reported by my respondents and observed in my research. With much of the irony that I have come to expect, many Cubans also say that "there are no prostitutes in Cuba, only *jineteras* [literally, jockeys] who ride men for their money." Fidel Castro offered a similar definition. Like the distinction between jineteros and pingueros, this is differentiated from the way pingueros pose their own practices as mutual and nonexploitative—thereby preserving for themselves one of the important axes of masculine respectability. Pingueros insist that theirs is an interpersonal exchange that includes the mutual pursuit of leisure en la calle.

In Cuba, male sex laborers of various descriptions engage in a variety of levels of practice and have various intentions apropos of what they hope to gain or experience. Sex laborers may be students, like George, or as in the cases of various folks we have already seen "hustling" within Cuban informal markets, they may be professionals, workers, or un(der)employed, like Domingo. For the purposes of this discussion, romantic excursions and the cultivation of relationships with (the implicit or explicit promise of) sexual contact in exchange for a foreigner's (implicit or explicit) promise to give monetary or other material support or (a promise of) emigration can be termed "sex tourism labor." By opening a broader array of intentions in this manner, I hope to expose exoticizing and pathologizing tendencies that pose all sex work or "prostitution" as quick a la carte sex acts, and detached exchanges for money, that are always already dehumanized—often termed "selling" one's body. I want to encourage us to think through entrenched gender biases and moral judgments against "prostitutes" that assume and perpetuate unmarked status as consumer for heterosexual men. Male sex laborers (pingueros) are sometimes erroneously called jineteros or "hustlers." While there is overlap in these admittedly imprecise and not mutually exclusive categories, in my experience pingueros often insist on the difference, though the common sense of most Cubans may not always make this distinction. One sex laborer, a twenty-two-year-old man who identifies as a pinguero, explains the important difference this way: "Jineteros rip tourists off . . . [but] pingueros work hard offering sex in return for clothes, a good night out, . . . or dollars." Jineteros are unofficial market procurers who most often do not offer direct services. In the economy of *maquinando* (machinating or "running game") they are the "middlemen." Jineteros may sell counterfeit or stolen cigars or suggest *paladares* (restaurants) and accommodations—to which they often accompany the foreign client. Sexual contact may occur, but this is incidental to other sorts of services. Pinguero comes from the word *pinga* (cock) with the suffix *ero*, which denotes that this is what the individual offers, services, or specializes in—quite like a *zapatero* specializes in shoes, for example, or a *rumbero* is expert at playing or dancing the rumba. Quite apart from the accent on the hustle, emphasis is placed on masculine sexual prowess and pleasure. This points to an inescapable gender arithmetic—most of these men, at least initially, present themselves, or *perform*, in the most "masculine" fashion they can muster—as "normal" men and therefore the penetrator. Still, according to Alejandro, a twenty-seven-year-old pinguero whom I have known for four years, a sex laborer can be "heterosexual, bisexual, or homosexual . . . macho or [effeminate]." He may perform either heterosex or homosex—as a penetrator or penetrated—depending upon his own boundaries and desires and those of his partners, very much like other young men. According to local culture, young men are expected to "sow wild oats," as it were, and to experiment. The experiences of my research respondents certainly corroborate the fact that masculine sexual imaginations and practices in Latin America include sex with multiple partners, and not infrequently of both genders— which Roger Lancaster (1992), Richard Parker (1991, 1999), Ian Lumsden (1996), Hector Carrillo (2003), and others have already demonstrated in their work in Nicaragua, Brazil, Cuba, and Mexico, respectively. Predictably, these preferences run along particular hierarchies in which masculine performance (oral "passive" and anal "active") is valued more than its inverse, which is read as effeminate. Among Cuban men, foreigners are already read as less masculine than Cuban men. Europeans and white men from the United States "are known to be *pasivos*" ("passive" anal partners, or "bottoms") according to twenty-six-year-old José, who reported that he enjoyed having sex with foreign men because he can realize his "sexual fantasies" with them. He claimed that he found it difficult to find "real bottoms" among Cuban men his age, and added that his foreign "friends" are always the passive partner.

At the same time, this is the generation whose dreams of consumption and perhaps cosmopolitanism are more easily indulged by what yumas have to offer—money, access to material goods, experiences in Cuban nightlife and travel around the island, attention, and in many cases sincere affection. As Ulysís begins to tell me, "Young people think everything is supposed to be easy . . . Fidel told them not to worry, that everything would be given to them if they study and work hard. . . ." Then Carlos interrupts: "Those who are attracted to such relationships . . . are mostly those who do not study hard, and do not have much hope. . . . It is possible that a successful foreigner can give them something to aspire to."

Heterosexual Sex Labor

It is more difficult to pin down the intentions and elementary forms of hetero-sex-practicing laborers because their practices are shrouded in heterosexual privilege of "romance." This is an effect of the different demands among heterosexual women and homosexual or gay men, and not necessarily a differ-ence in sexual orientation, since some pingueros, like Domingo and George, might be available for both. There is a range of intentions—from those who work hard to be sure that they have a comfortable place to live each night to those who only occasionally date foreign women whom they really like. By forcing this juxtaposition of what is termed the "romance" of heterosexual women by presumed heterosexual men with the "hustling" of gay men by men, and female "prostitution," I intend not only to critique the heterosex-ist and misogynist foundations of discourses on sex work but also the pre-sumptive impulse that seeks to sanitize the messiness of personal agency and desire.

Thirty-three-year-old Camilo seemed perplexed when I asked him what he was "exchanging" with Erica, his Canadian girlfriend of six months. After a long pause, then an explanation of his situation of great material need and inability therefore to provide for a Cuban family in the way he would like or would be expected of him, he said that Erica had much *cariño* (caring and affection) for him, and that "there might be a future [for them] . . . which is impossible with a Cuban woman at this moment [because of the financial situation]." Unlike Jamaica and Barbados, Cuba does not receive large num-bers of women who come for the express purpose of sex tourism. And as one heterosexual-identified long-term respondent remarked, "women do not *pay* for sex," although many readily help lovers and romantic friends with everyday finances and other resources. Cuban men who exclusively seek out foreign women seem to be older and more educated than those who hang out on the eastern beaches and the streets of La Rampa, or those who attend pri-vate fiestas with foreign men. They may meet their foreign friends at cultural events, parties, or through friends, as well as tourist sites, as opposed to the street venues frequented by younger men, who along with other young black Cubans face tremendous scrutiny and profiling as jineteros and pingueros. Foreign women (mostly young, as opposed to male "clients" who are usually between the ages of thirty-five and sixty) who come to Cuba as tourists, to study, or perhaps with a socialist or humanitarian solidarity brigade, meet Cuban men who share their interest in Cuban music, culture, or politics, for example. In rare cases this may lead to emigration or long-term sexual relationships. In other cases, it can be a transitory sex for money or commodity exchange, depending on the circumstances and intentions of both individuals. Sex labor with women thus takes on very particular dimensions of "romance." This is enabled by heterosexist policies and structures of feeling in which these relationships, unlike those described earlier, can be sanctioned officially in marriage. This is increasingly changing, as nations like Canada and Spain allow same-sex marriage and emigration of spouses. Still, the effect of the romance discourse is largely to reserve the narrative of meeting a tall, dark, handsome exotic (i.e., getting "one's groove on" during holiday)[8] for heterosexual relationships, regardless of the geopolitical and ethical implications of consuming the Third World other.

Camilo and his Canadian girlfriend, who was originally in Cuba for a three-month language program (and therefore was not subject to the rule that foreigners staying for longer than this length of time be tested for HIV), had never used condoms. However, he reported consistent condom use with another girlfriend, a mestiza student from Central America whom he had known longer and whom I surmise had in fact been tested, since she had been on the island for more than a year. He decided, or negotiated, whether to use a condom based on nationality, class, color, and his assessment of the woman's relative "virtue," which is imbricated with each of the forgoing. He occasionally used them with his Cuban girlfriend—not because of HIV, he says, but because she had stopped using her birth control method for a short while and insisted that he use one. This made him suspicious. It seems from anecdotal evidence that, for heterosexual sex, condoms are used only occasionally for insertive vaginal/penile sex among Cubans who know each other well. Anecdotally, it seems that men who have sex with men use condoms with male partners more reliably. This inconsistent or discretionary use of condoms, based not on a promise of monogamy but a personal assessment of risk with a particular individual, points not only to the overlapping "vectors" of infection but also to an important and potentially dangerous gap in Cuba's new system of sexual health education. A larger study undertaken a couple years before my work found that nearly 90 percent of sexually active women using no barriers felt that they had zero chance of becoming infected and only

14.4 percent had insisted on condom use. This certainly is an inheritance of machista practices wherein women may not feel authorized to make these demands on men, especially husbands, but it is also a result of the belief, contrary to everyday evidence, that sexual risk is rigid and identifiable.

HAVING A DRINK IN the posh Jazz Café, a jazz club and bar overlooking the Malecón, Roberto, a tall, dark, and handsome black Cuban man in his late thirties, regaled me with stories of his "adventures" with foreign women.[9] Charming and intelligent, he spoke slowly and listened to my questions intently. At about the same time that we both finished our second drinks, he announced that we had made the white women who had been staring at us from across the room wait long enough, and he invited me to join him as he went to play. The women appeared to be hard-working midlevel career women taking advantage of their short two-week vacation to get some attention, sex, and perhaps to find love. My new debonair friend held the French Canadian women in his thrall, alternating between (good) French and (serviceable) English for the non-Spanish speakers who told us about their love of Afro-Cuban music and culture, the heat in Cuba, and "the beauty of the people." When they realized I was from the United States and had Anglophone Caribbean ancestry, they complimented me on my Spanish and began telling me how much they had enjoyed the handsome men of Barbados on their last Caribbean excursion, and how they really loved hip-hop music's "cool urban masculinity." I excused myself from the table. In my notes that evening, I wrote: ". . . polish and professionalism. He probably would not even have to have sex with them—just his attention and his suavete is enough." Paulla Ebron's Bumsters in Gambia read remarkably like their counterparts in Cuba, men like Roberto. For the Bumsters, style and charisma, along with European fantasies of extraordinary sexual prowess, become a calling card to female visitors. Bumsters, as she defines them, are "professional friends" who move alongside tourism. Not paid a wage, their services are multiple and may be compensated in a number of ways. Stories of their exploits circulate among men and become part of local cultural lore. As Ebron writes,

> The northern women in these stories were uncontrolled sex zealots. In contrast, the southern men were adroit businessmen ready to design their success by capturing raw European passions. . . . Stories of Gambian men

crafting a masculine national trajectory in which political and cultural agency depended upon African male abilities to fashion themselves as entrepreneurs who could shape themselves to suit European desires . . . catchers of opportunity. (2002: 169)

Roberto certainly saw himself as a "catcher of opportunity." In fact, his calling card actually read Roberto Sarduy Guerrero: "Translator. Guide. And More." Weeks later, he scoffed when I told him that I had guessed he would not have to have sex with these women (that he said were below his usual standard). He had sex with one several times during their weekend in Havana, and he referred a friend to be a "guide" for the other woman, who had taken a side trip to Varadero beach. In exchange, he received "cash . . . and made a friend in Quebec" who promised to send for him as soon as she could get the documents and fees for a fiancé visa.

Back to the Street

As we have seen, la calle is where men are expected to provide for the family through labor, as well as to bond with other men. Implicitly also, men are expected to have sexual liaisons in this sphere, populated by men and "fast women." Sex labor is one option that is successfully undertaken by men in an atmosphere and spirit of friendship, leisure, and pleasure, at the same time that those relationships are variously remunerative. Robin D. G. Kelley's notion of play-labor may provide some insight to understand the sense that my respondents conveyed that their activities were income-generating but not onerous "work." As Kelley writes, "Play undeniably requires labor, but it is usually thought to be creative and fulfilling to those involved; it is autonomous from the world of work . . . [suggesting that] the pursuit of leisure, pleasure, and creative expression is *labor*" (1997: 90). The notion of play is also advanced by Coco Fusco. Her notion of the streets of Havana as a sort of theater for performance complements another connotation of theater—a space for war or conflict, which is captured in the phrase "luchando en la calle." Fusco notes that although sex labor in Cuba is not an artistic phenomenon as such, it is still a performance: "Tourism in Latin America is a theatre for the playing out of colonialism's unfinished business," she writes (2001: 137). Cubans are aware that they play in a market full of images of Cuba as the land of 'women, rum, and Cuban cigars.' This market seems to be regarded and consumed as simulacra—as if in a "time warp" of socialist politics, old cars, and dark virile "macho" men. Sex laborers, the government's Ministry of Tourism, and various other Cubans who have contact with foreigners have all become quite adept at reproducing attractive representations-as-commodity for those whose hard currency helps them stay financially afloat, which in turn invites them to enter the mode of subject formation now entrenched in late capitalist countries: I consume, therefore I am. Ylysis, whom I have known since our first meeting in 1998 at the Fiat cafeteria, states the following: "They [the police] treat us as if we do not deserve respect . . . but we are out here struggling like everyone . . . Why are all of these foreigners here [on the Malecón perusing the crowd] and buying things in Cuba? . . . We work hard and he [pulling on his chin in a pantomimed rendition of Fidel Castro's beard] knows he needs us to take care of the maricones just as the jineteras ride the yumas. [he laughs] . . . How else can I go to the [U.S.] dollar store? I am trained to be an agricultural statistician—how else [can I] meet foreigners with dollars?"

The Cubans who engage in sex tourism assume roles in their interactions with foreigners, roles that are meaningful and valuable insofar as they resonate with tropicalist stereotypes. If convincing in their role, their chances of acquiring money and commodities, or of emigrating increase. Fusco writes, "I sense a bit of snobbery in the moralizing that too many privileged Cubans indulge in over this issue . . . What really bothers some people now is that *el pueblo* (the regular people) is having a ball, and that these white foreigners prefer mulatas and negras . . . Few among them seem willing to admit that most artists, musicians, and professionals with exportable skills are also looking for opportunities to socialize—and occasionally have sex—with foreigners to secure invitations abroad and even foreign jobs, not to mention to enjoy the best of Havana's nightlife" (137). Echoing my concern with male sex work and the ways in which heterosexual coupling with foreign women is unproblematically accepted as romantic rather than commercial, Fusco points out that "when Cuban men do it, everyone looks the other way. It's women who always take the heat" (137). Still, if according to Fusco black and brown Cubans are "having a ball," there remain incommensurable differences in male and female sex (and play) labor. Owing to principles of labor and leisure in the socialist context, underemployment, and culturally structured asymmetrical gender responsibilities in which all housework is "women's work," the lives of men and boys en la calle in Cuba are characterized by play-labor at least as much as work. In Kelley's essay on the commoditization by black urban youth in the United States of their own expressive culture (in which he theorizes play-labor) he distinguishes female "prostitution" in that context from the play-labor of the almost exclusively male domain of graffiti artists, rappers, break dancers, and athletes. He points out that the choices of young women to earn money in the realm of pleasure are dramatically fewer than those of young men. Likewise, in Cuba women and girls are, to a large extent, shut out of other hustles, thereby leaving few choices for play-labor. They have less access to life en la calle, which is where money is made in the unofficial tourist economy, whereas men may choose various hustles other than the sex trade. Moreover, as one jinetera who also sells contraband cigars, bootleg Cuban music CDs, and other alternative tourist-related goods told me, as a woman "no matter what you are offering . . . socially [and culturally], [both Cuban and foreign] men always think that sex is what is being sold . . . Why not [turn a profit]?" This certainly impacts the differentiation in the stigma against and economy of women's sex labor relative to that of the men described here.

Luchando in the Special Period: Racialized Genealogies

Sex work is an industry, albeit largely informal, and it is one that depends on particular technologies and new subject positions. These include, on the demand side, travel and disposable income in hard currency, along with access to information on the Internet and other media advertising Cuban vacations and sexual adventures for the foreign consumer. On the supply side, pingueros and other sex traders tend to be very aware, through international media, of a spectacular array of increasingly homogenized commodities and styles that without the aid of foreigners with U.S. dollars would be impossible to consume. Their trade is inextricably tied to global notions of what it means to be a full agent—that is, the ability to consume and to style oneself using certain signs of this consumption. Sex laborers find themselves pulled in by the web of consumerism, and thus bound they help to create an even tighter spool of desires and intentions wrapped up in consumption. This may be less the case with those, like Domingo, who have adult family obligations, but it is certainly true of young men who do not have families and children to support, and it is striking among young pingueros who cite the adventure and excitement of "the hunt."

It is the researcher, consumer, or observer, therefore, and not the actor himself who essentializes and "concretizes" young Cuban men as "sex machines" or "functionaries" by describing them by an activity, job description, or behavior that they may or may not retain or perform for the long term. Pingueros themselves understand their own practice as complex and nuanced. In my experience, the "beach boys" (as I described them in the shorthand of my field notes)—that is, the young men who hung out at the beaches of East Havana and other places—might also be art students. Those whom I met at El Fiat cafeteria early on could be members of a national sports team. The "Copelia queens," that is the fastidious, fashionable—*micky*—men eating ice cream at the famous shop, turned out to be friendly people with interests in opera and modernist architecture. "Hombres de alta cultura," on the lookout for stimulating conversation, sex, companionship, and perhaps an invitation to lecture, teach, play, or dance abroad, I found, were intellectuals, artists, rap enthusiasts, engineers, and laborers. Each of these hastily sketched categories that found their way into my field notes reflected where I found these individuals. This had to be complicated, however, by talking to them about their feelings and thoughts beyond that place, by engaging and participating in their nonsexual activities that reveal, after a while, deeper levels than the sexual activities that they engaged in for excitement, for money to pay for medicine or rent or travel, or for the ability to constitute themselves as cosmopolitan subjects therefore worthy of admiration. As we have witnessed in the changing fortunes of Domingo's family in chapter 5, before the Special Period one's performance as a proper socialist subject or association with card-carrying members of the Communist Party were the only ways to gain extra material things such as a new radio, television, vacation, and passes to nightclubs. These *premios* (prizes) were given by the government, at one's work site, as incentives and gifts to loyal revolutionaries. When this source of diversion and consumption dried up during the Special Period, individuals found other sources. While I certainly agree that consumerism seems to have exploded in Cuba in recent years, especially relative to outsider images of socialist practice as one of Spartan simplicity and lack of style, the implicit argument against the desire for diversion and consumption must be challenged because it pathologizes individuals who use clothing, hairstyles, jewelry, and new experiences to restyle themselves (as cosmopolitan and therefore) as important subjects. Further, this is incongruous with Cuba's culture of creative and productive consumption. Various changes in economy and national identity have constantly conditioned recastings of Cuban nationalism and therefore masculinity and femininity.

Here I have discussed the controversial choices that Cuban sex laborers make, given not only their limited repertoire of agency but also the sexual scripts imbricated with the historic fear or obsession with black and otherwise "tropical" sexuality. Earlier I explored revolutionary policies that sought to prevent just this sort of expression as it was deemed exploitative to the nation and to the individual. Not only is sex labor characterized as indicative of a lack of local sovereignty and of moral degradation, but scholars and popular observers deride what they see as a commoditization of humanity that reinscribes for them "savage" hypersexuality served up at auction. That is, it points to always already *queer* gender and sexuality. Increasingly influenced by the exigencies of the global market, new ways of self-making are emerging among Cubans who already have access to a wide repertoire of cultural idioms of identity. Similar processes are taking place throughout the Caribbean, and other sites around the globe where black and brown bodies are required for the sex market, and where black and brown *persons* use their bodies to meet their own needs. As I have pointed out, these choices are "forced" to the degree that black and brown men have been effectively excluded from various avenues, are already seen to be "sexual machines," and to which there is a willing market for the performance and play of Caribbean masculinity.

ONE NIGHT DURING MY first research trip to Cuba, my respondent Herman—who was agitated after learning that his brother had been denied entry into England after leaving Spain where he was supposed to be visiting his fiancée—began talking about leaving the island for the United States as a *balsero* (a rider in an inner tube). I asked why he would do this when he had things in Cuba that poor people around the world would envy, such as education, housing, and national belonging. I was (and still am) enamored of the gains that the Revolution had made, and saddened by what appeared to be a lag in the revolutionary resolve of young people. After a long pause, during which he seemed to be gazing for the answer in the distant horizon, he said simply:

"You have good tennis shoes. I want good tennis shoes too." Herman's long-ing for good tennis shoes should not be read as frivolous or indicative of false consciousness. Young Cubans who have been educated to believe in their own value as agents are understandably very frustrated by the lack of what appears to them, from their observation of foreigners, to be basic—nice cloth-ing, some jewelry, and the opportunity to travel to other countries "freely." Months later, when I asked Herman about his plans, he laughed and said that he had been "depressed and desperate" when we talked last, and he was "trying to find a solution." He had realized that he should plan more care-fully how to leave the island legally, especially since he felt he would quickly become homesick and need to return to see his family. He had heard that a cruise ship was coming to Havana to hire, and had already taken a test and presented his credentials to the Cuban officials in charge of prescreening. I gave him one of my shirts to wear to the interview for good luck. Herman had not left the island, however, when we last corresponded in 2002. Instead, he was awaiting a visa to visit Canada as the fiancée of a young woman he met at a conference in Havana.

¡Vamos a Vencer!

(We Will Win!)

Finally, I have sought to study—it is my current work—the way a human being turns him or herself into a subject. . . . Thus it is not power, but the subject, which is the general theme of my research. [But] while the human subject is placed in relations of production and of signification, he is equally placed in power relations which are very complex.

—MICHEL FOUCAULT, "The Subject and Power"

IN HIS CHAPTER in *No Guarantees: In Honour of Stuart Hall*, James Clifford defends "the constitutive role of cultural, ethnic, and racial identification in contemporary politics" (2000: 96), noting that "identity politics" is currently being "attacked from all sides" (94). He writes, following Stuart Hall, that "human beings become agents, capable of effective action, only when they are actively sustained in place through social and historical connections and disconnections" (96). For Hall, this relational positioning is the work of culture, ensuring that "as subjects, social actors function by taking up the discourses of the present and the past" (Hall 1998: 291, and quoted in Clifford 2000: 96). In this book, I have attempted to show this. At the center of my work in *¡Venceremos?*, which is an offering of initial notes describing scenes of subject formation and reformation—is a question gleaned from Hall's project of critical cultural studies, and black queer feminist analysis: how can we contribute to progressive strategies for the material and psychic liberation of marginal communities and marginal subjects? Following Audre Lorde, it pursues the site of erotic subjectivity, and transcendent erotics and politics, which are useful tools being fashioned by marginalized subjects.

I realize that the fact that most of the tools my respondents use are not organized or respectable is an issue that may disquiet many of the scholars and activists with whom I would normally share agreement and common projects. Legitimate anxieties around both "politics" writ large, and the respectability of a black subject that has just recently been recognized as more than an object, too often write over the personal and intimate—especially when this involves sexual intimacy, sexual commerce, and personal matters not easily counted either to a totalizing "evil" extrinsic force or to a pathological, inherited moral failing. Living is messy business and we should not attempt to sanitize or depoliticize it with these "just so" stories, for the sake of elegance. These anxieties around representation (of black people as decent, clean, and hardworking, and of black scholars as "serious" academics) are impelled by long-standing psychosexual racist logics that continue to circulate and that are given torque in this moment by the continued commoditization of black bodies and by attacks on black studies. I hope that in my work I have shown that inhering in these small, intimate, troubled spaces is a powerful and virtually unexplored ground for political possibilities.

There is a profound and widespread bawdy/body tradition in black diaspora cultures, which is represented prominently in carnivals and festivals, house parties, rum house "limes," and other more quotidian practices. The concepts of liminality, transcendence, and communitas that are used to describe ritual and celebration in small-scale societies (and sometimes in industrial ones) are familiar topics in anthropology. To bring these concepts to bear on the imaginations of those subjects marginalized within contemporary societies is to push past the conventions of the "savage slot" (Trouillot 2003). Here, "the native" is not noble, insolent, or merely a hapless victim, but rather an agent with a limited repertoire of actions doing the best that he or she can.

I am also aware, of course, that some, for example, eminent theorists of the black Atlantic, Cuban revolutionaries, and liberals and neoliberals of many descriptions, to name a few, would rather abandon what they refer to as "race" altogether (the scare quotes around the concept signaling their distance) by arguing that it entraps and provides no way out of the morass of "raciologi-cal thinking." While I sympathize with the ethic that underlies this as one facet of a utopic vision, it does not seem to emerge from a commitment to on-the-ground research or real-life strategies and tactics. While this stream of criticism is very helpful in thinking about the consequences of raciology, what is more important is to help people negotiate the current conjuncture, which is constitutive of particular sets of historical, cultural, and political economic events and rhetorics—the politics of (cultural) "identity."

Black cultural criticism that targets what Paul Gilroy brilliantly distilled as "the fundamental, time-worn assumption of homogeneous and unchang-ing black communities whose political and economic interests were readily knowable and easily transferred from everyday life into their expressive cul-tures" (1993a: 6) has made signal contributions to the emerging subfield of black diaspora studies. Still, cultural expressions, styles, and the uses to which these are put do not emerge out of cultural, historical, and political-economic vacuums. My respondents do share a dynamic, contested, transnational, multi-lingual, and polyglot blackness. They make themselves into certain types of subjects who are recognized and accorded respect, or reputation, based on the successful (re)interpretation and deployment of subjectivities or identi-ties, rhetorics, styles, and symbols that have profound historical, cultural, and affective resonance. To wit, the tradition of critical, progressive black feminist and black queer artists, activists, and scholars, who point out the ways in which the assumption of racial and gender homogeneity benefits heteropa-triarchy, is to launch arguments (which seek to go beyond mere critique) not from a position *against* race, but rather *for* more capacious, humane, and sus-tainable blacknesses.

¡Adelante! But Which Way?

The Revolution, likely unwittingly but nonetheless accountable, recuperated pre-revolutionary racial and sexual ideologies. What have been missing are the reparative and affirmatively acting policies that would begin to address the historically entrenched inequities wrought by the Cuban slave state, which persist despite the lifting of legal barriers, and have intensified since the Spe-cial Period.[1] Though after the Rectification campaign, the Mariel boatlift, and the Special Period, Cuba is now finally reconsidering in public forums the handling of issues of race and sexuality by the Revolution, it is important to note that the discussion of the issue of sexuality is much more amplified and at a much higher level than is the discussion on race. We must therefore ask difficult questions around pervasive racial and gender ideologies and pernicious social practices that operate—in silence—beyond the purview of top-down juridical remedies. While one might argue that protest politics in Cuba will finally bring the island in line with its laudable ideals and de jure equality, a combination of the insights of my respondents and real engagement with the consequences of such a move—in some ways against current Revolutionary ideology—do not recommend certain brands of (black) nationalist and "gay and lesbian rights" politics and protest postures, but instead call for a critical engagement with issues of racial, gender, and sexual politics on the island from the bottom up. I have argued that erotic subjectivity, which insists on everyday erotic and sensuous practices as a ground for a liberatory politics, is deployed as a way to express and increase personal freedom and thereby influence cultural and personal openings in Cuban society from a position within and supportive of the revolutionary process. Gestures and actions like those analyzed here are of the utmost importance.

Most Cubans are loyal to the revolutionary project, which liberated the majority from deplorable material conditions and provided the promise of a new society to which they could contribute and benefit. At the same time, this loyalty is constantly tested. Cubans suffer the effects of both global political-economic shifts and local mismanagement. In addition to a centralized, socially conservative, and often inefficient government that is currently reevaluating its commitment to delivering the full complement of social welfare on which the people have come to depend, Cubans must contend with regional pressures of global economic readjustments that press economic reforms within Cuba. They also suffer under the effects of *el bloqueo*—the fifty-one-year-old unilateral embargo by the United States (unprecedented in United States history), which was initiated by the John F. Kennedy administration; made more severe by the Helms-Burton Act of 1996 under President Bill Clinton;[2] intensified by the George W. Bush administration; and at the time of this writing, left in place by President Barack H. Obama.

On the surface, the comments and viewpoints expressed by everyday Cubans reify Marxist ideology. The public transcript of socialist Cuba reads the history of the island and the political tensions with the United States as a battle between capitalism and socialism, imbued with moral rhetorics that cast capitalism as an evil (alas, apparently now seen as a "necessary evil," at least in part) that seeks to destroy what it cannot control. The biblical metaphor of David versus Goliath—the small socialist nation doing battle with the mammoth superpower—is invoked to describe the class struggle between rich empire and poor island nation. But the fact that it seems to be true that global capital, set in motion and protected by United States state apparatus, has as its imperative the consumption of every meter of the earth, and the fact that the economic and social capital that Cuban Americans wield drives this nonsensical and inhumane embargo, is not to say, however, that class is the primary axis of power that subsumes others, like race and gender and sexuality.

"This conga going down La Rampa is not a gay pride march"

John D'Emilio convincingly argues that the emergence of homosexuality as a category of identification in the North is associated with the growth of capitalism. It seems evident that capitalism—or more to the point, the so-called free labor system—"has allowed large numbers of men and women in the late twentieth century to call themselves gay . . . [and] to organize politically on the basis of that identity" (1993: 468). There is no denying the advances that the gay liberation movement and gay rights have made in the United States in terms of meeting goals of increased visibility and legal protection. This is especially true for middle-class white gay men, and to a lesser extent, middle-class white lesbians and middle-class people of color. To wit, the uneven access to capital also helps account for some of the differences between racial and class groups, and the differences between gender normative and non-gender normative folks with respect to "coming out" in the North. Capitalism is not, however, the only issue apropos of the contradictory push of individuals. For D'Emilio the push has been at once away from family and toward other sorts of reproductive activities in factories, offices, and the like and what he calls "the elevation of the family to ideological preeminence" (1993: 474).[3] However, this view deserves rethinking given the current political and social conditions in the United States and elsewhere. For Cuban revolutionaries there has been a push toward labor collectives and families as smaller units organized around and in the service of the constitution of communism. The revolutionary Cuban government has worked hard to curtail any organized identitarian movement in Cuba, which they see as a threat to their socialist and nationalist projects.

In spring 2009, Dixie Edith reported that "100 people filed through 23rd street, the principal artery of the Cuban capital, accompanied by zanqueros [stilt-walking clown characters], bands and drums, to the rhythm of the conga, to open the celebration of the Worldwide Day Against Homophobia and Transphobia, which this year centers on the family."[4] She wrote that Mariela Castro Espín, the director of CENESEX and organizer of the activities, hastened to explain that "this conga going down la Rampa is not a Gay Pride march" but rather commemorates the day that the World Health Organization eliminated homosexuality from its list of mental illnesses. Castro said that the activities were meant "to call attention to the reality of silence, lack of knowledge, fear and bad interpretations that bring hatred, lack of respect, loneliness and a lack of love between people [due to] repudiation." This event is part of an educational strategy that grows each year, according to the CENESEX Sexual Diversity Project staff member Dixie Edith. During the event Ricardo Alarcon, president of the Cuban parliament, addressed the large crowd of supporters. In his speech he stated that the island had made "a number of advances in the rights of sexual minorities, even though this was a complex and long process to be completed."[5] Moreover, Dr. Alberto Roque, a collaborator in the Sexual Diversity Project of CENESEX and director of the event's panel "Sexual Diversity in the Cuban Family," talked about intolerance and lack of understanding along with the daily suffering and maladjustment in families when they take on "rigid cultural norms that condition their structure and functioning." Roque, who is a long-time advocate for sexual diversity and for the recognition of the particular difficulties that non-heteronormative individuals face, hastened to add that the intent of the panel was "not to question the legal model of family traditionally accepted by our society" but rather to make visible and to legitimate other family models that are also valid and that form part of our diverse reality."[6]

For a number of years, Mariela Castro has advocated for sexual education and tolerance for transgender, gay, and lesbian Cubans. She has also called on the gay and lesbian community in Cuba to push for greater integration, rather than what she characterizes as self-isolation through organizing separate groups. While one can be forgiven for appreciating this as a "go slow" rhetoric—the less powerful "telling their stories" within contexts in which they make claims to familyhood and citizenship, Cuba's recognition of non-heteronormative Cubans at this level is unprecedented in the Caribbean region. And it is more, according to my respondents, than they had ever expected, especially from a Castro. Under Mariela Castro CENESEX has been at the forefront of the public campaign to change attitudes about sexuality and gender identity in Cuba.

A draft proposal from the FMC and CENESEX has been presented to the Political Bureau of the Communist Party to amend the Family Code of 1975. The amendment would stipulate that the family has the responsibility and duty to accept and care for all of its members, regardless of their gender and sexual orientation, and would recognize the rights of any woman to assisted reproductive service (something that is presently under way). Sex-reassignment surgeries have been performed in Cuba since 2007, and thus covered by the comprehensive universal healthcare system. Castro also states that she has the support of her uncle, Fidel Castro, who typically, she says, has asked a barrage of questions, some of which she has no answers for presently. In the meantime, Yaineris, Delores, las Krudas, and a number of my respondents may not be able to join the conga line—they have each emigrated. And Lili appears to be on the forefront of another level of this public discourse, preferring, of course to make her arguments loudly and glamorously on the street.

Erotic Redux

Erotic subjectivity—deeper understandings and compulsions of the body and soul, simultaneously embodying and invoking sex and death—works toward not only transgressing but also transcending and finally transforming hegemonies of global capital, the state, and bourgeois, limited, and limiting notions of gender, sexuality, or blackness, for example. For Lorde, the erotic is not only about the power of one's own sexual energy, but instead includes and goes well beyond it to a site of knowledge production and energy that is alternative to regimes of the state and received culture. It is the deep subjective, which she recognizes as "a lens through which we scrutinize all aspects of our existence" (1984: 57), as Delores and other respondents did in groups large and small, local and transnational. Through friendships and collective discussion, these folks "evaluate those aspects honestly in terms of their relative meaning within their lives . . . not settling for the convenient, the shoddy, the conventionally expected, nor the merely safe" (1984: 57). We can see in one performance Octavio responding to cultural expectations and interpellations in two very distinct ways—accommodation and resistance, thereby demonstrating how transgression can only take place within the frame(s) that one already inhabits. Delores does not move "outside" ideology when she, like La Krudas, lays claim to the vindication of the new global women. She is precisely responding to local Cuban cultural tropes, the formal ideologies forged by the Cuban Revolution, black feminisms, and queer liberation. The stories of Yaineris, Delores, Cole, and Octavio/Lili show us that in order to move beyond individual transgression, or momentary transcendence, recontextualization must take place, in conversation with others. Thus, we must not sit easily after we have dug to the messy level of erotics where we find "opposition" and "transgression." These acts of self-making, cultivating spaces of critical enunciation, transgressing the hegemonic, and transforming the standard dehumanizing practices of black genocide, create a counterpublic in which new forms of art, affective and erotic relations, and rules of public and private engagement not only inform all our choices, as Audre Lorde suggests, but in fact may condition new choices and new politics.

Sí. ¡Venceremos! But with No Guarantees

And quite likely in a manner that does not look as we expect it should.

As we continue to witness the various levels and paces of change in Cuba—changes as seen through the apparatus of the Cuban state and global imperatives, individual desire, the arts and performance, and the networks between friends both local and global—what is most clear is that change is inevitable. Moreover, change in Cuba will most probably take a shape that is very different from what casual observers and politicos on the north side of the Florida Straits forecast. Contemporary Cuba is but one example of the global participation of individuals embedded in particular circumstances of history, culture, and political economy. The fact that many of these subjects are black, and some queer, requires particular forms of self-making that have been honed throughout history and reinterpreted today because of rapidly morphing demands and expectations. Individuals get on with their lives. They deal with situations in which they are embedded, making choices according to what they view as their possibilities. Those around them, including the scaffoldings of power, may or may not cooperate with their individual projects. Most times, in fact, individuals and groups are caught in conjunctures of intentions that necessitate the composition of a new strategy, or the on-the-fly performance of new tactics. The self-making presented in this book, therefore represents agency *akimbo*—often off balance, tenuous, and clumsy looking at times. I am precisely not claiming that this is a sufficient or final step. It is, however, a requisite part of our new toolkit. It is a crucial line in the architecture of resistance.

Notes

Introduction

1. I borrow this term from Kofi Annan's report to the United Nations, "In Larger Freedom: Towards Development, Security and Human Rights for All" (2005).

2. "Queer" does not only capture the sense of the non-normative status of men and women who identify with or are identified as homosexual and those whose gender self-identification is not resonant with the sex assigned to them at birth. But also, and more pointedly, for my respondents "queerness is essentially about . . . an insistence on potentiality or concrete possibility for another world" (Muñoz 2009: 1). No term, even those that may seem self-evidently Cuban, is perfectly stable or synchronous with dynamic self-identification on the ground. Likewise, black identity or identification holds no mystical, transhistorical, or biological valence here. "Black" refers to a set of complex and deeply held translocal historical, political, and affective ties among individuals, movements, and texts—to, from, and beyond "African descent." This is true regardless whether their "official" local color category is *moro/a*, *jaba/o*, *mulata/o*, or other categories of nonwhite and non-Asian. See also Sawyer 2006; Telles 2006.

3. See Sherry B. Ortner's *Making Gender: The Politics and Erotics of Culture* (1996: 12).

4. A number of important ethnographic works on Cuba's Special Period are emerging, including Fernandes 2006, 2010; Brotherton 2005; Ryer 2000; and Hernandez-Reguant 2009. While illuminating in a

number of ways, this body of work does not offer a thoroughgoing analysis of race. The political scientist Mark Sawyer's *Racial Politics in Post-Revolutionary Cuba* (2006) is the first book to analyze contemporary Cuban racial ideologies and attitudes.

5. In addition to my innumerable informal talks with individuals in Cuba, I have formally interviewed more than fifty-two respondents whose ages range from nineteen to sixty-five. Each of these respondents identifies as Afro-Cuban or black. Twenty-two respondents self-identify as male, and twenty are (biologically and socially) female. Six females identify as lesbian, and three as bisexual. Several members of the male group report recurrent homosex, although only a few identify as gay or bisexual. Roughly two-thirds of the respondents are drawn from professional, artist/intellectual, and emergent middle classes in Havana. All translations of the interview materials, song lyrics, and poetry are mine, unless otherwise noted, and the names of the respondents have been changed—in many cases to the names that the respondents themselves chose. To ensure privacy, situations and subjects have been "ambiguated," and no photos of key research respondents appear.

6. See Jacqui Alexander's theorization of pedagogies of crossing in her book of the same title (2005).

7. Personal communication with the late Margaret Dalton in 2000.

8. Whereas the "intersectional" approach advanced by the critical race theorist Kimberly Crenshaw (1989) and others refers most centrally to juridical or otherwise formal structures that are rearticulated by groups and individuals for particular ends; for the literary theorist Hortense Spillers (1984) the notion of "the interstices" also suggests both historically and culturally constructed subjectivities, and deep wells of consciousness out of which interactions emerge.

9. See Faye V. Harrison's *Outsider Within: Reworking Anthropology in the Global Age* (2008) and her edited collection *Decolonizing Anthropology: Moving Further toward an Anthropology for Liberation* (1991), apropos the politics of ethnographic methodology and representation followed in this book. Martin Manalansan (2003) and others demonstrate the profound potential of ethnographies of non-heteronormative subjects at the moment of transnational, neoliberal encroachment. Recently, Gloria Wekker's *Politics of Passion: Women's Sexual Culture in the Afro-Surinamese Diaspora* (2006) and Lisa Rofel's *Desiring China: Experiments in Neoliberalism, Sexuality, and Public Culture* (2007) have provided sterling examples of queer (and in Wekker's case, black diasporic) anthropological perspectives on deeply imbricated erotic, political, and existential desire and self-making.

10. This shift toward black Cuban as agent has been pioneered by Cuban scholars and artists. Among them, for example, Betancourt Bencomo 1959; Morejón 1988; C. Moore (1988, 2008), Fernández Robaina 1990, 2009; Sarduy and Stubbs 1998, 2000; and Fowler 2002.

11. A number of scholars have already demonstrated, for example in work in Brazil, Nicaragua, Mexico, and the United States, that theories of male sexual behavior and sexual identification cannot be uncritically trafficked across borders—or time, as the historian George Chauncey (1994) makes clear. See especially Mott 1988; Green 2000; Parker 1991, 1999; Lancaster 1992; and Gutmann 1996, 1997.

12. These are the acronyms for, respectively, Gay and Lesbian Alliance Against Defamation; Parents and Friends of Lesbians and Gays; National Gay and Lesbian Task Force; Human Rights Campaign, and Gay Men's Health Crisis. LOGO is the name of a gay- and lesbian-oriented cable television corporation.

13. These acronyms represent the National Association for the Advancement of Colored People; Congress of Racial Equality; Historically Black Colleges and Universities; and Black Entertainment Television.

14. Carlos Moore's early polemical work (1988) is part of a critical political and intellectual black diasporic project, dating back to W. E. B. Du Bois, Edward W. Blyden, St. Clair Drake, and others. This project is evident also in the work of, for example, Abdias Nascimento (1989) and Walter Rodney (1969, 1981), which inspired my desire to research black diasporas. For the next wave of foundational theorization of black diaspora, "articulation," and "hybridity," see Hall 1980, 1990, 1991a, 1991b; Gilroy 1993a, 1993b; Carby 1998, 1999; Mercer 1994; and Edwards 2003. The fact that diaspora is also about relationality and the reimagination of various, often contradictory, "traditions" is well illustrated and theorized in the work of the anthropologists Gordon 1998; Clarke 2004; Thomas 2004; and Brown 2005, among others. Two stellar works on South Asian diasporas/transnational flows, by Inderpal Grewal (2005) and Gayatri Gopinath (2005), and another on Filipino diasporas by Martin Manalansan (2003), inspire crucial sutures across region, race, and ethnicity.

15. The analytic frame in this book owes a tremendous debt to foundational black queer literature and analysis, found in a number of key anthologies, such as *Home Girls: A Black Feminist Anthology* (B. Smith 1983) and *Brother to Brother: New Writing by Black Gay Men* (Hemphill 1991), and E. Patrick Johnson and Mae G. Henderson's more recent collection, *Black Queer Studies* (2005). See also, e.g., Lorde 1978, 1983, 1984; Hemphill 1991, 2000; B. Smith 1983, 1998; Beam 1981, 1986; Cohen 1997, 1999a, 1999b, 2004; Battle and Bennett 2000; Ferguson 2004; McBride 2005. On black queer diasporas, I follow Alexander 1997, 2005; Walcott 2005; Wekker 2006; Glave 2008; Wright and Schuhmann 2008; and Tinsley 2008. Key examples of queer-of-color theory that have greatly influenced the analysis in this book include Muñoz 1999, 2009; Rodriquez 2003; Manalansan 2003; and Gopinath 2005.

16. Here I follow Paul Gilroy's homophonic and political engagement with Bob Marley's metaphor of the "small axe" chopping down a big tree, in his *Small Acts*

(1993b). "Boasteth thyself, evil man, playing smart and not being clever. I say you're working inequity to achieve vanity, yeah. But the goodness of Jah endureth forever. . . . If you are a big tree, we are the small axe, sharpened to cut you down, ready to cut you down. These are the words of my master, telling me that no weak heart shall prosper" (from the song "Small Axe" on *Burnin'* by Robert Nesta [Bob] Marley, 1973).

17. To wit, a number of sterling queer theory texts have probed the meanings and potential pitfalls of "normalcy" and homonormativity, including Duggan 2002, 2003, 2004; Warner 1993, 2000; and Halberstam 1998, 2005.

18. For excellent arguments in this mien, see Hartman 1997 and Wilderson 2003.

Chapter 1. Looking (at) "Afro-Cuba(n)"

1. "Old Man" refers to the former president, Fidel Castro Ruz. The narratives of exile are often stunningly personalized and centered on "Castro."

2. See Nicolás Guillén's "Tengo" in his *Antologia mayor* (1967).

3. For an excellent (and rare) discussion of color and diasporic belonging, identification, and scholarly demeanor, see Jemima Pierre's "'I Like Your Colour!' Skin Bleaching and Geographies of Race in Urban Ghana" (2008).

4. See Helg 1995; Ferrer 1999; de la Fuente 2001; Guridy 2010.

5. On "Afro-kitsch," see Diawara 1992.

Chapter 2. Discursive Sleight of Hand

1. This was during the late 1990s when the U.S. dollar was accepted as legal tender in Cuba. This issue will be discussed more thoroughly in the next chapter.

2. The popular Cuban rap group Orishas, now residing in France, recorded a song proclaiming what is quintessentially Cuban experience in their opinion: "A lo Cubano, mujeres, ron, tobacco Habano" (2000).

3. While this was true for some time, it is currently not the case. At present, the island itself—people, sun, and sand—is the top commodity.

4. This particular kind of "whitening" or blanquemiento (Wade 1993) is more precisely phrased as "mulatáje"—or mixing to produce mulata/os (rather than European/Indian mestizos) in Cuba.

5. And lest I overstate the participation of Latin Americanist scholars in this regard, I want here to point out that there is a veritable métissage/mestizáje/Creole/hybridity scholarship industry, in at least three languages, some of which unconsciously capitulates to similar othering projects.

6. The cigarette-smoking women to whom he refers are proper ladies, white women, but pre-revolutionary images of negras smoking cigars remains one of the most

enduring racialized images of Cuba, and a popular souvenir item in tourist markets.

7. This ideology holds that the condition of blacks is not due to any historical or structural system of oppression but rather wholly an effect of an essential nature of indolence, laziness, and tendency to succumb to sexual and other appetites. We will return to analyze this theme in chapter 4.

8. See chapter 7, "The Racist Massacre of 1912," in Helg's *Our Rightful Share* (1995) in which she describes the siege. She notes that "evidently, the exact balance of the racist massacre of 1912 will never be known. Official Cuban sources put the toll at more than 2,000. US citizens living in Oriente put it at 5,000–6,000" (225). This was carried out in collaboration with the United States government, and in many ways in the defense of interests of the United States.

9. In this essay, Thompson does not detail the Louisiana practice of plaçage, which allowed for the social movement and flexibility denied to enslaved women, whose mixedness was less phenotypically appreciable or whose racial lineage was not as clearly tied to whiteness. As she notes, however, "free men of color often felt that this status came at their expense" (2001: 242).

10. The position of the mulata fina, or light-skinned mulata with long, straighter hair, was constantly invoked thusly in my interviews and participant observations. Please see Nadine Fernandez (1999) for more on this contemporarily. See Martinez-Alier (1974) for historical dimensions.

11. Here I mean, of course, "known" to have been penetrated or habitually penetrated. This is distinct from the occasional penetration of another man, as we will see in chapter 5.

12. The interview presented here is actually a composite of three conversations with Jaime, during which he was uncharacteristically uncomfortable and not completely forthcoming. In fact, although he knew that I wished to extensively interview someone who had experienced life in the UMAP camps, he did not offer that he had been there until his lover brought it up in another conversation after a few months of acquaintance.

13. Courtney, his lover of twelve years, remarked in an aside that "exotic means that he has a very big dick."

14. See Salas (1979) for more on this statute of the Ministry of Culture, which like the PC, (Communist Party), have policies barring homosexuals. In practice, this bar is not in effect in Cuban cultural institutions.

15. Fidel Castro, interview with Carmen Lira Saade, "Soy el responsable de la persecución a homosexuales que hubo en Cuba: Fidel," *Periódico La Jornada*, August 31, 26. http://www.jornada.unam.mx/2010/08/31/index.php?section=mundo&article=026e1mun.

Chapter 3. Erotics and Politics of Self-Making

1. There is widespread absenteeism by workers at state jobs in Cuba. The pay is low, and demanding in many cases. Also, the historical fact and current perception of some that sexual minorities—and in certain workplaces women and blacks, to a lesser degree—are targeted for harassment and ill treatment is another reason for the lack of interest in some forms of labor.

2. Lili and others explained to me that "because we are both black" and familiar with each other, using the term "negro" or "negrito" is not considered rude. In many white and mestizo families, the darker-haired or darker-eyed member is often called negrita or negrito as a term of endearment. However, this should not be uttered outside of one's group. Perhaps because Lili was flirting and unsure of my own gendered sexual preferences (beyond being gay), she used various terms of endearment that play with particular styles and "positions." *Machito* at once conveys a playful or youthful masculinity and fondness.

3. Although there are post-operative transsexuals living in Havana, to my knowledge I was not acquainted with any of these individuals.

4. I have argued that being mulata/o is in fact one of a number of ways of being black. At the same time, everyday differences in treatment between dark-skinned black (negro) blacks and apparently "mixed" and lighter-skinned (black) individuals are startlingly apparent—especially women, who pay a particularly high social cost for dark skin, broad features, and kinky hair.

5. This is the inverse within (neo)liberal states, including most dramatically the United States, which privileges social rights like "free expression" and "free association" while not recognizing economic rights (for example, universal healthcare, free higher education, land rights) in international treaties or domestic law.

6. I should note here that Wilderson is talking about black Americans. Since the foundation of his argument is the relationship of blackness to chattel slavery and de jure discrimination, we can extend this to Cuba.

7. Although I hasten to add that any threat—especially from going against ideological state apparatus—implies the potential for force or other material consequences, threat of force is not necessarily the motivation. This human faculty, which resists various of the slings and arrows of social circumstance, can be operationalized as personal agency. Personal agency is the spark that ignites self-making strategies. It is democratically available at the same time that it is universally constrained. Put differently: while personal agency is available to everyone, it is also everywhere constrained and conditioned by particular contingencies of culture, power, and history.

8. Although it is unlikely that Yaineris and Cole have had a sexual relationship, given Yaineris's openness with me about several romantic encounters with women and a few men, it really makes no difference to my argument whether they have

actually sexually consummated their relationship. The attraction between them is erotic nonetheless in terms of their shared close, affectionate, and intimate friendship and Cole's professed sexual attraction.

9. M. Jacqui Alexander in "Remembering This Bridge Called My Back, Remembering Ourselves" in her *Pedagogies of Crossing* (2005), offers another way to see the wide-ranging processes of friendship between women. She honors the work of the important volume published by Kitchen Table / Women of Color Press and offers an archeology of experiences and knowledges that seem to ineluctably connect to this consideration of friendship. In remembering her own longing and desire she acknowledges her debt to women from Sistren, CAFRA (Caribbean Association for Feminist Research and Action), and the Boston Women's Health Book Collective as examples of "the plain courage and determination of a bunch of different women all tied to some kind of cultural inheritance, sometimes at a cost, sometimes isolated from it, at times yearning for it" (260).

10. To briefly summarize, this stream of standpoint epistemology holds that shared positions of disempowerment within hierarchies of power, which can be understood as a perspective from which one both sees and is seen, produces unique and often oppositional knowledges, and this positioning in the political economy constitutes them as certain types of subjects—in this case, as black women. Patricia Hill Collins, herself intimately associated with standpoint theory, assays it as "one important source of analytic guidance and intellectual legitimization for African-American women" (1990: 201). In the absence of a sustained movement or group consciousness, however, Collins herself asks, "Are group based identities that emerge from standpoint theory and the politics they generate still empowering?" (203).

11. Gloria Wekker in *The Politics of Passion: Women's Sexual Culture in the Afro-Surinamese Diaspora* (2006) uses the busy, exciting intersection called Heiligeweg in Paramaribo, Suriname, as a name for the *jouissance* of sexual climax.

12. Mohanty uses Toni Morrison's *Beloved*, among other texts, to argue for a cognitivist notion of identity or experience, in which we understand cultural and political positions as theories that neither come from some mystical essence nor are completely unknowable. In holding that "both the essentialism of identity politics and the skepticism of the postmodernist position seriously underread the real epistemic and political complexities of our social and cultural identities" (1993: 51), he calls for a reevaluation of the relation between personal experience and public meanings. Mohanty's cognitivist conception of experience would allow us to "see experience as a source of both real knowledge and social mystification" (54).

13. See, for example: Barbara Ransby 2003; Hazel Carby 1998, 1999; Combahee River Collective 1983; Chela Sandoval 2000; Hortense Spillers 1984, 1987; Julia Sudbury 1998.

Chapter 4. De Cierta Manera

1. These time frames are unavoidably imprecise. The current period seems, for many, like a continuation of the Special Period because the economy has yet to perform as it did before the Special Period.

2. Although these determinations are notoriously idiosyncratic, the actor does not appear to me to be jabao, but rather mulato atrasado, like Domingo. The important point here is that Gómez was savvy enough to cast someone who is obviously black/Afro-Cuban, but not negro, which would have been too shocking for audiences, and for ICAIC. That González and other commentators have called the actress who plays Yolanda "blanca" was quite interesting to me during my first viewing of the film. To my North American eyes, she seemed herself what people in Cuba would call mulatta fina. This points to the inexact "art" of color/race typology in Cuba, as well as the different colorings of foreign perspectives in Cuba.

3. See especially Rolando's 1996 film *Raíces de mi corazón*.

4. For more on machista ideology and masculine performance in Latin America, see Rafael Ramirez (1999), Matthew Gutmann (1996, 1997), Roger Lancaster (1992), and Richard Parker (1999). These works carefully distinguish historical discourses and processes on the ground from the popular myth of "machismo," which I argue is shrouded in race and class hegemonies. They have provided persuasive analyses of discourses and practices of masculinities in Puerto Rico, Mexico, Nicaragua, and Brazil, respectively. Their work exemplifies what Keith Nurse has called the erosion of the myth of unproblematic masculinity and the interrogation of "masculinism embedded in . . . modernity . . . and one of the core features of the global problematique" (2004: 4).

5. See Alejandra Bronfman (2004) for an analysis of the construction of Cuban rac(ism) through social science scholarship.

6. For more on these emerging cooperatives, see Premat 2009.

7. Alexander's work focuses on the Bahamas, a small nation with neocolonial relations to not only the United Kingdom but also to the United States, where the sovereign archipelago of the Bahamas is often openly referred to as its "backyard."

8. The quote here is from material reprinted in *Granma*, July 6, 1975. Regarding the feminist movement in the North, the force of United States capitalist hegemony—primarily through the United States blockade—is understood not to generally undermine the socialist project but rather specifically marshal coordinated attacks on a number of particular sites. One of these is the cultural imperatives of liberal feminism, which were said to threaten the "new" Cuban family.

9. On this view, see especially Gilliam 1991.

10. As both a political commitment and a scholarly choice, this position at the interstices of so-called identity-based and humanist movements makes for a strategic

locus for on-the-ground politics and academic work that in fact attends to multiply constituted identities—including sexuality, class, nation, and the consideration of history and material conditions. Perhaps the most well-known stream of black feminism is that which privileges the unique positionality of black women to self-define and self-valuate their own lived experiences (see Collins 1990), which is of vital import as among the first steps toward more radical black feminist politics (see, e.g., Joy James 2000). Black feminism's engagement with Third World feminism is crucial in our world in which racisms and sexisms and classisms are multiple, and do not fall easily on either side of the falsely dichotomous poles of white/black, or even north/south. Indigenous Caribbean Feminism builds on the tradition of scholarship and transnational activism of individuals like Claudia Jones (see Carole Boyce Davies 2007). This echoes Gilliam's call for a more "unified approach" (1991) as an alternative to what she calls "sexualism" in liberal feminism.

11. Hernandez-Reguant's important collection (2009) features a number of the important emerging scholars of Cuba's Special Period. Ethnographic works on Special Period Cuba have commented on numerous economic, social, and political changes during this period, such as sex tourism (Cabezas 1998; Fosado 2004; Allen 2007; Stout 2008), media and art (Fernandes 2006; Hernandez-Reguant 2009), and medicine (Brotherton 2005).

12. See Lynn Bolles (1983a, 1983b) and Helen Safa (1995) for comparisons from the Caribbean and Central America.

13. Before the Revolution these independent black institutions in Cuba had contact with similar racial uplift groups in the Caribbean and the United States and Africa—both in terms of historical connection and real circulation of ideas and strategies. See Guridy 2010.

14. Theorizations of the politics of gender, sexuality, (and black) respectability by Peter Wilson (1973) and others point out that differences in performances of gender and sexuality are not neutral but rather are read on a stratified pole defined (at least) by class and color. For Wilson, this pole positions oppositional reputation on one side and whitened respectability on the other. The experiences of my respondents and the demands of the current moment, however, suggest a more complex scheme. In departing from the binarism of Wilson, which is still quite helpful in identifying the elementary forms of respectability and reputation, Edmund Gordon (1997) puts forth a more complex perspective on black masculinity. His "Cultural Politics of Black Masculinity" sees a "cultural repertoire" of black masculinity that may include characteristics of respectability or reputation at particular points in life rather than dichotomous nodes.

15. This should not be read as if departing from the insistence of black feminist works that intimate, interpersonal, and even psychic hurts in the home are often the most political. And this is in no way to wax nostalgic for the bad old days of

the black patriarch. In fact, not only is patriarchy in any form ethically corrupt, but it also reflects an uneven representation of the black patriarch's control of black communities, which after all, still reside with white heteropatriarchy. This should not be read as if departing from the insistence of black feminist works that intimate, interpersonal, and even psychic hurts in the home are often the most political.

16. In the mid-1990s, recognition of "bisexual behavior" without bisexual identity or non-identifying men who take part in homosex—now referred to as MSM, or "men who have sex with men"—fueled talk of polysexual and or polyamorous men as vectors of disease in the United States, and led to much-needed research funding for studies on AIDS and male sexuality, which have not borne out the "common sense" assumption that non-gay identifying men who have sex with men are the major cause of escalating rates of HIV infection among heterosexual practicing women. This recent discourse around the so-called down low has been raised to the level of a cultural and racial crisis by pundits in the United States. Tanya Saunders's work (2009a, 2009b) finally sheds light on female sexualities missing from the literatures on contemporary Cuban society.

17. As Ian Lumsden (1996) and others have shown, Cubans use several descriptors to reference their sexual behavior. The completo (complete, or "'versatile'"), may be the penetrator or the penetrated. The pasivo (passive) is always the penetrated partner. And the activo (active) is the penetrator. In older parlance, this last category is also known as el bugarrón (the fucker). The comments of early respondents who held that younger men were more likely to identify as completo than either of the exclusive categories was confirmed by those I interviewed and observed, and by their acquaintants. As my twenty-year-old respondent Giovanni—who is entendido (por no dicho, understood but undeclared to be homosexual)—expressed: "The problem is . . . I know that getting fucked does not make me any less of a man . . ." He continues, laughing, but very seriously drawing the line that will allow him to save face: "W . . . well . . . maybe this makes me a little bit more of his woman . . . but only in bed, not in the street."

18. I make the point here that we must pay closer attention to the subjectivities of researchers and the ways that various researchers are perceived by their respondents, as well as their level of cultural immersion, intimacy, and time, to render a verdict on how much to accept reports of rigidified "macho" or insertive sexual behaviors.

19. This vision of masculinity rests on a concept of male sexual drive as domineering, nearly uncontrollable, and in need of outlets for the expression of putatively rapacious masculine sexuality, which demands acts that are improper to expect one's wife or a woman of high class or color status to do. In addition, the class honor and respect of the individual and the family is an important commod-

ity whose value must be protected through proper gender performance in the street. A partner with a low race/color or class status would be cause for great social anxiety, despite claims of racial pluralism and the end of racism in Cuba. Nadine Fernandez documents this in her study "Race, Romance, and Revolution: The Cultural Politics of Interracial Encounters in Cuba" (1996a). Low racial- and sexual-status bugarrónes are sought to penetrate higher-status men. For a man of high status to allow another man of similar status to penetrate him, however, would constitute utter failure, and a social crisis. Masculine failure is to "act like a woman." Women of high status are expected to be penetrated by high- or higher-status men. Lower-status men being penetrated is not at all remarkable since the understanding in this logic, regardless of who is being penetrated, is that the high-status man has unlimited access to the bodies of darker, poorer others. Machista society requires allowances—different "shades," if you like—for male-to-male sex, and encourages sex with individuals of lower class and racial status.

20. Having sexual contact with another male "as a youth," that is, "as a boy not knowing anything" was very common. In fact adult masturbation seemed a much bigger taboo than sex between preadolescent boys.

Chapter 5. Friendship as a Mode of Survival

1. As recorded in, respectively, Toni Morrison's *Beloved*; Gloria Naylor's *Women of Brewster Place*; Ntozake Shange's *For Colored Girls Who Have Considered Suicide When the Rainbow Is Enuf*, and Alice Walker's *The Color Purple*. See also Farah Griffin's *Beloved Sisters and Loving Friends: Letters from Rebecca Primus of Royal Oak, Maryland, and Addie Brown of Hartford, Connecticut, 1854–1868*, which tells of an intimate friendship between two black women across class differences and geography.

2. See Sidney Mintz (1985) and Richard and Sally Price (1991).

3. Wekker reports that there are same-gender men who are also called mati, although there appears to be no scholarly work on this population.

4. This quote from the theatrical version, staged in Austin Texas in 2006.

5. Lee Edelman's *No Future: Queer Theory and the Death Drive* (2004) is perhaps the most forceful and eloquent recent example of this anti-relationality and anti-futurity stream of work. On the other hand, José Esteban Muñoz is equal to the task of countering this impulse in his *Cruising Utopia: The Then and There of Queer Futurity* (2009).

6. The mood and style of this opening of the section is an homage to the party scene in Audre Lorde's "Tar Beach," found in *Homegirls: A Black Feminist Anthology* (Smith 1983: 146). Excerpted from her *Zami: A New Spelling of My Name—A Biomythography* (Lorde 1983).

7. In 1999 my friends and colleagues in Cuba, Joseph Mutti and Llane Alexis, asked me to collaborate on a team research project commissioned by the United Nations Research Institute on Social Development (UNRISD), "Between the Devil, But the Deep Blue Sea: HIV/AIDS and Tourism in Cuba" (2000). Much of the research for this section of the current chapter was carried out under the aegis of this project.

8. Public health decisions are political and ethical judgments based on local history, politics, and culture just as much (or more than) they are on medical or epidemiological measures. As in the case of tuberculosis, for example, the Cuban state views HIV as a medical condition for which an individual bears social responsibility. The system of quarantining infected bodies along with heightened surveillance was initiated consistent with the local understanding that community rights take precedence over the rights of the individual to privacy and self-determination in healthcare.

   In terms of civil and political rights (stressed by liberal values), the forced quarantining of infected individuals was a violation of privacy, on a dangerously slippery slope to the wearing down of other rights. The notion of personal privacy in the United States and Western Europe is sacrosanct. Still, the closing of public baths frequented by men who have sex with men in San Francisco and New York City in the 1980s, while not a "quarantine" of infected individuals, is one illustration of how fear of HIV has, in cases, overridden civil liberties concerns, even in the United States. See P. Sean Brotherton (2008) for a full analysis of the healthcare system of Cuba.

9. A key criterion for living outside the sanatoria is disclosure of one's sexual partners and providing the health authorities with the "confidence" that one is sexually responsible. Those who are newly diagnosed as HIV positive are advised by their physician to undergo an eight-to-twelve-week education and observation period (now known as an "orientation period") at one of the nation's sanatoria. According to Dr. Rosabal of the sanatorium in Santiago de las Vegas, the object is to ensure that the patient is in good health—physically and mentally—and to make sure that they know how to protect others as well as themselves. Still, those deemed a "public danger" through their sexual behavior are required to remain in the sanatoria.

10. "In the decade since effective drug treatments for AIDS dramatically cut death rates across the country, black Americans continue to get infected and die at alarming rates. For example, one in five black men in New York City between the ages of forty and forty-nine has HIV or AIDS, and in the population overall, black men die at a rate six times that of white men. Recently released statistics show an AIDS epidemic among black gay and bisexual men that outstrips anything seen in the worst-hit parts of sub-Saharan Africa. Nearly 50 percent of black gay and bisexual men in some of our nation's cities are estimated to be infected with HIV" (Black AIDS Institute 2005: 3).

11. I refer here to the infamous Tuskegee syphilis experiment; but I am also thinking of historical cases of forced sterilization of black women and other women of color in the United States and Puerto Rico, for example, and the continuing lack of representations of blacks in key clinical trials in the United States on one hand, and proliferation of "race drugs" on the other.

12. The AIDS epidemic claimed an estimated twenty-four thousand lives in the Caribbean in 2005, making it the leading cause of death among adults aged fifteen to forty-four. More than twenty thousand people died of AIDS in 2006 in this region. The estimated national adult-HIV prevalence surpasses 1 percent in Barbados, Dominican Republic, Jamaica, and Suriname; 2 percent in the Bahamas, Guyana, and Trinidad and Tobago; and exceeds 3 percent in Haiti. In Cuba, which has the lowest HIV prevalence in the Americas, prevalence is yet to reach 0.2 percent (UNAIDS and WHO 2008).

13. In the United States, the history of AIDS is marked by various reinscriptions of pathology and disgust on three already subaltern categories of folks. While the last "H" (hemophiliacs) of the early "four H's" litany of high-relative-incidence of HIV infection were cast as "innocent victims," the other three were not talked about in terms of innocents but rather as "risk groups" to be avoided: heroine users, which stood in for all intradermal drug users; Haitians, as people "needing to be sent back to where they came from," and homosexuals, vilified as deserving of "god's curse."

14. We have come to know this as the linchpin of neoliberalism. Concomitantly, there was increased investment in modes of surveillance and containment in the United States and increased political intervention in Central America (Nicaragua) and the Caribbean (Grenada), for example. We now understand these interventions as part and parcel of the expansion of global markets for the export of goods from the center to the periphery, and cheap labor and raw materials from the opposite direction.

15. One can also understand this as "within the Revolution, everything [is possible]." In any event, this quote is much more complex than at first blush. In other contexts, this quote and the "words to intellectuals" has been read as a rhetorical exclusion or tacit threat.

16. Dr. Armando Alvarez, interviewed by Joseph Mutti, spring 2001.

17. Conner Gorry (Oxfam Programa Conjunto Cuba). "Cuba's HIV/AIDS Strategy: An Integrated, Rights-Based Approach," Havana, 2008. http://www.oxfam.org.uk/resources/policy/health/downloads/rr_cuba_hiv_aids_strategy.pdf.

18. In 2004, I had been surprised and horrified to receive an e-mail memorandum from the National Science Foundation Graduate Research Fellowship Office (which had funded my dissertation research), informing fellows working in Cuba that their grants were no longer tenable there.

19. Marc Perry (2004), Sujatha Fernandes (2006), and others have already provided excellent analyses of these issues.

Chapter 6. ¡Hagamos un Chen!

1. The "world's oldest profession" did not disappear, but it had been limited to small sex-for-commodity exchanges with Soviet and Eastern European functionaries visiting the island prior to the Special Period. By 2000, intermittent crackdowns and harassment—especially of black men and young women, had dramatically reduced the obviousness of the sex trade in Havana's streets.

2. I include the term "survival" here in an effort not only to reflect the reports of sex laborers about their motivations, especially at the height of the Special Period when food was scarce, but more pointedly to capture the affect of desperation that some reported, even when their material survival, as such, was not in danger. I have seen no evidence of Cubans engaging in sex work in order to take care of basic survival or subsistence.

3. This was out of the ordinary, in any case, because in 1999 when we met, no one else I talked to reported quoting prices to Pepes (customers). They depended on "in kind" gifts and parting donations. Ramon seemed to be reaching toward a model of charging for discrete sex acts for money transactions.

4. The title here comes from the song "Hagamos un chen" on the album *Tremendo Delirio* (1997) by David Calzado and Charenga Habanera (my translation):

And how we make change, change, change, change!
How do you want to pay, mamí?
By check or in cash?
We will make a successful business transaction

Give me love in a bottomless sack
Give me caresses, tenderness and sex
So hard, so tender that time is held up
I will give in to you, take you inside
I will be a volcano that will shake your body
I must fulfill your love's fury
And after the fire I am going to caress you

Our transaction will be so fulfilling
But first, we sign a contract for this love exchange
It is very important to know the form of payment.
We will be multimillionaires.
Who can say it is otherwise?
Why is the business of feelings only possible if it springs from inside?
And if I have what you like,

And you have what is worth my while,
And now if nothing detains us:
"We make change"

And when we make change, change, change!
How would you like to pay, mamí
In check, or cash?
(. . . if you'd like to have a receipt . . .)
And what did you say?
That you want to pay with a card of what? Credit?
You are crazy
This is not taken here

5. I pointed out to her later that although she and I were certainly not romantically involved, we often "went around" together. One important difference was the degree to which she served as a host, and our shared preference for local (that is, often off limits to tourists) forms of diversion that cost nothing, or very little.

6. This account describes the gay party scene before the delegalization of the U.S. dollar in 2004. The parties have become more diffuse now, and of course more expensive.

7. This is not to say the work is not being produced. However, it is found under rubrics like black studies, diaspora studies, and area studies (especially in the Caribbean, as I have cited previously).

8. See Terry McMillan's novel *How Stella Got Her Groove Back* (and the subsequent film rendition from 1998). While there has been recent controversy over this travelogue as literature, there was surprising silence apropos of the elements of the consumption of the Third World other.

9. My emphasis on the clichéd phrase "tall, dark, and handsome" is meant to underscore the fact that Roberto—with his square jaw, full features, wide shoulders, and height of six feet two inches—so well reflected notions of masculine attractiveness."

Coda

1. I can advocate affirmative actioning and other reparative policies here without automatically parroting rhetorics of "multiculturalism" and "diversity," as is the fashion vis-à-vis debates on affirmative action in the United States, because Cuba is already self-consciously diverse. This is good to think with, and instructive for places such as the United States where, while aesthetic forms of diversity and multiculturalism enjoy wide acceptance because it is good for business and good for personal education and the broadening of a liberal education that we hold valuable, there is little discussion of the original raison d'être of these affirmative action policies, reparation, or at least an attempt at "redress" of the material effects of slavery and Jim Crow.

2. The pressure from Cuban American groups was intensified after Cuba's act of shooting down an airplane belonging to the Miami-based Cuban exile group Brothers-to-the-Rescue, which flew illegally in Cuban air space. This tragedy cost the lives of the pilots. The Helms-Burton Act places restrictions on trade with nations that do business with Cuba, allows campaigning against Cuban interests among other nations, strengthens the embargo of United States shipments to Cuba, and sought to end remittances. This final provision of the act was routinely suspended by President Clinton.

3. D'Emilio points this out in order to direct gay and lesbian activists and historians of the 1980s in the United States toward "political lessons" that now seem to need updating, given recent tense play of accommodation and resistance to the state-recognized formalization of same-sex relationships.

4. E-mail from Dixie Edith (Diversidad Sexual CENESEX), May 18, 2009, to Sexual Diversity Listserv, "RE: REPORTAJE ESPECIAL."

5. Ibid.

6. Ibid.

References

Aggleton, Peter. 1999. *Men Who Sell Sex: International Perspectives on Male Prostitution and HIV/AIDS*. Philadelphia: Temple University Press.

Alea, Tomás Gutiérrez. 1983. *Hasta cierto punto*. Havana: Instituto Cubano del Arte e Industrias Cinematográficos.

Alexander, M. Jacqui. 1994. "Not Just (Any) Body Can Be a Citizen: The Politics of Law, Sexuality, and Postcoloniality in Trinidad and Tobago and the Bahamas." *Feminist Review* 48:5–23.

———. 1997. "Erotic Autonomy as a Politics of Decolonization: An Anatomy of Feminist and State Practice." In *Feminist Genealogies, Colonial Legacies, Democratic Futures*, ed. M. Jacqui Alexander and Chandra Mohanty. New York: Routledge.

———. 2005. *Pedagogies of Crossing: Meditations on Feminism, Sexual Politics, Memory, and the Sacred*. Durham: Duke University Press.

Allen, Jafari Sinclaire. 2000. "Caminos de Macho." Paper presented at the American Anthropological Association conference, November, San Francisco.

———. 2003. *Counterpoints: Black Masculinities, Sexuality, and Self-Making in Contemporary Cuba*. New York: Columbia University Press.

———. 2007. "Means of Desire's Production: Male Sex Labor in Cuba." *Identities* 14 (1–2): 183–202.

———. 2009. "Looking Black at Revolutionary Cuba." *Latin American Perspectives* 36 (1): 53–62.

Almaguer, Tomas. 1998. "Chicano Men: A Cartography of Homosexual Identity and Behavior." In *Social Perspectives in Lesbian and Gay Studies*, ed. Peter M. Nardi and Beth Schnieder. New York: Routledge.

Almendros, Néstor, and Orlando Jiménez-Leal. 1974. *Improper Conduct*. CineVista Video.

Alonso, Jorge. 1990. *Cuba: La rectificación*. Guadalajara, Mexico: University of Guadalajara.

Althusser, Louis. 1968. "Ideology and Ideological State Apparatuses (Notes Towards an Investigation)." In *Media and Cultural Studies: Keyworks*, ed. Meenakshi Gigi Durham and Douglas Kellner. Hoboken, N.J.: Wiley-Blackwell.

Altman, Dennis. 1996. "Rupture or Continuity? The Internationalization of Gay Identities." *Social Text*, no. 48 (autumn): 77–94.

Annan, Kofi. 2005. "In Larger Freedom: Towards Development, Security and Human Rights for All." Report of the Secretary-General, United Nations. http://www.un.org/largerfreedom/.

Anzaldúa, Gloria. 1999. *Borderlands/La Frontera: The New Mestiza*. San Francisco: Aunt Lute.

Aparicio, Frances R., and Susana Chavez-Silverman. 1997. *Tropicalizations: Transcultural Representations of Latinidad*. Hanover, N.H.: University Press of New England.

Appadurai, Arjun. 1991. "Global Ethnoscopes. Notes and Queries for a Transnational Anthropology." In *Recapturing Anthropology: Working in the Present*, ed. R. G. Fox. Santa Fe, N.M.: School of American Research.

———. 1996. *Modernity at Large: Cultural Dimensions of Globalization*. Minneapolis: University of Minnesota Press.

Arandia, Gisela. 2005. "Somos o no somos." *La Gaceta de Cuba*, no. 1 (January–February): 59.

Arenas, Reinaldo. 1994. *Before Night Falls: A Memoir*. Trans. Dolores M. Koch, New York: Penguin Books.

Arguelles, L., and B. R. Rich. 1984. "Homosexuality, Homophobia, and Revolution: Notes Toward an Understanding of the Cuban Lesbian and Gay Male Experience, Part I." *Signs* 9 (4): 683–99.

Armstead, Ronni. 2007. "'Growing the Size of the Black Woman': Feminist Activism in Havana Hip Hop." *NWSA Journal* (19) 1: 106–17.

Azicri, Max. 1988. *Cuba: Politics, Economics, and Society*. London: Pinter.

———. 2000. *Cuba Today and Tomorrow: Reinventing Socialism*. Gainesville: University Press of Florida.

Balderston, Daniel, and Donna J. Guy. 1997. *Sex and Sexuality in Latin America*. New York: New York University Press.

Baldwin, James. 1948. *Another Country*. New York: Dell Publishing.

Bamboleo. 1999. *Ya no hace falta*. Ahi Nama (compact disc).

Baraka, Amiri. 2000. "Cuba Libre." In *The LeRoi Jones/Amiri Baraka Reader*. 2nd ed. New York: Thunder's Mouth Press.

Barnet, Miguel. 1966. *Biografía de un cimarron*. Havana: Instituto de Ethnologia y Folklore.

———. 1995. *Cultos afrocubanos: La Regla de Ocha, la Regla de Palo Monte*. Havana: Ediciones Union Artex.

Barthes, Roland. 1975. *The Pleasure of the Text*. Trans. Richard Miller. New York: Hill and Wang.

Batalla, Bonfil. 1996. *Mexico Profundo: Reclaiming a Civilization*. Austin: University of Texas Press.

Battle, Juan, and Michael Bennett. 2000. "Research on Lesbian and Gay Populations Within the African American Community: What Have We Learned?" *African American Research Perspectives* 6 (2): 35–47.

Battle, J., et al. 2003. *Say It Loud, I'm Black and I'm Proud: Black Pride Survey 2000*. New York: National Gay and Lesbian Task Force.

Beam, Joseph, ed. 1986. *In the Life: A Black Gay Anthology*. Boston: Alyson Publishing.

———. 1991. "Brother to Brother: Notes from the Heart." In *Brother to Brother: New Writing by Black Gay Men*, ed. Essex Hemphill and Joseph Beam. Boston: Alyson Publishing.

Behar, Ruth. 1995. *Puentes a Cuba/Bridges to Cuba*. Ann Arbor: University of Michigan Press.

———. 1996. *The Vulnerable Observer: Anthropology that Breaks Your Heart*. Boston: Beacon.

Bejel, Emilio. 2003. *Gay Cuban Nation*. Chicago: University of Chicago Press.

Bell, Shannon. 1997. *Reading, Writing, and Rewriting the Prostitute Body*. Bloomington: Indiana University Press.

Benitez-Rojo, Antonio. 1992. *The Repeating Island: The Caribbean and the Postmodern Perspective*. Durham: Duke University Press.

Berlant, Lauren Gail. 2000. *Intimacy*. Chicago: University of Chicago Press.

Bersani, Leo. 1999. *Homos*. Cambridge: Harvard University Press.

Betancourt Bencomo, Juan Rene. 1959. "Fidel Castro y la integración nacional." *Bohemia* (Havana), February 15, 66, 122–23.

Black AIDS Institute. 2005. "The Time is Now! The State of AIDS in Black America. A Black AIDS Institute Report." http://www.blackaids.org.

Boellstorff, Thomas. 2007. "Queer Studies in the House of Anthropology." *Annual Review of Anthropology* 36 (October): 17–35.

Bolles, A. Lynn. 1983a. "Economic Crisis and Female Headed Households in Jamaica." In *Women and Change in Latin America*, ed. June Nash and Helen Safa. South Hadley, Mass.: Bergin and Garvey.

———. 1983b. "Kitchens Hit by Priorities: Working Class Women Confront the IMF." In *Women and Change in Latin America*, ed. June Nash and Helen Safa. South Hadley, Mass.: Bergin and Garvey.

Bourdieu, Pierre, and Loïc Wacquant. 1999. "On the Cunning of Imperialist Reason." *Theory, Culture and Society* 16 (1): 41–58.

Boyce Davies, Carole. 1999. "Beyond Unicentricity: Transcultural Black Intellectual Presences." *Research in African Literatures* 30 (2): 96–109.

———. 2007. *Left of Karl Marx: The Political Life of Black Communist Claudia Jones.* Durham: Duke University Press.

Brand, Dionne. 1997. *In Another Place, Not Here.* New York: Grove Press.

Brandon, George. 1993. *Santeria from Africa to the New World: The Dead Sell Memories.* Bloomington: Indiana University Press.

Brennan, Denise. 2004. *What's Love Got to Do with It? Transnational Desires and Sex Tourism in the Dominican Republic.* Durham: Duke University Press.

Bridgforth, Sharon. 2004. *Love/Conjure/Blues.* Washington: Redbone Press.

Brock, Lisa, and Digna Casteneda Fuentes. 1998. *Between Race and Empire: African-Americans and Cubans before the Cuban Revolution.* Philadelphia: Temple University Press.

Brock, Lisa, Digna Casteneda Fuentes, and Otis Cunningham. 1991. "Race and Cuban Revolution: A Critique of Carlos Moore's 'Castro, the Blacks, and Africa.'" *Cuban Studies* 21:171–86.

Bronfman, Alejandra. 2004. *Measures of Equality: Social Science, Citizenship, and Race in Cuba, 1902–1940.* Chapel Hill: University of North Carolina Press.

Brotherton, Pierre Sean. 2005. "Macroeconomic Change and the Biopolitics of Health in Cuba's Special Period." *Journal of Latin American and Caribbean Anthropology* 10 (2): 339–69.

———. 2008. "'We Have to Think Like Capitalists but Continue Being Socialists': Medicalized Subjectivities, Emergent Capital, and Socialist Entrepreneurs in Post-Soviet Cuba." *American Ethnologist* 35:259–74.

Brown, Jacqueline Nassy. 2005. *Dropping Anchor, Setting Sail: Geographies of Race in Black Liverpool.* Princeton: Princeton University Press.

Buck-Morss, Susan. 1986. "The Flaneur, the Sandwichman and the Whore: The Politics of Loitering." *New German Critique* 39:99–140.

Butler, Judith. 1990. *Gender Trouble: Feminism and the Subversion of Identity.* New York: Routledge.

Cabezas, Amalia. 1998. "Discourses of Prostitution: The Case of Cuba." In *Global Sex Workers: Rights, Resistance, and Redefinition,* ed. Kamala Kempadoo and Jo Doezema. New York: Routledge.

Cabrera, Lydia. 1959. *La sociedad secreta Abaku: Narrado por viejos adeptos.* Havana: Ediciones Universal.

———. 1969. "Ritual y simbolos de la iniciación en la sociedad secreta Abakuá." *Journal de la Société des Américanistes* 58:139–71.

———. 1979. *Reglas de Congo. Palo Monte Mayombe.* Miami: Peninsular Print.

Calzado, David, and Charanga Habanera. 1997. *Tremendo delirio*. Universal Latino (compact disc).

Carby, Hazel. 1998. *Race Men*. Cambridge: The President and Fellows of Harvard University.

———. 1999. *Cultures in Babylon: Black Britain and African America*. London: Verso.

Carrillo, Héctor. 2003. *The Night Is Young: Sexuality in Mexico in the Time of AIDS*. Chicago: University of Chicago Press.

Casal, Lourdes. 1979. "Race Relations in Contemporary Cuba." In *The Position of Blacks in Brazilian and Cuban Society*, ed. Anani Dzidzienyo and Lourdes Casal. London: Minority Rights Group.

———. 1980. "Revolution and Conciencia: Women in Cuba." In *Women, War and Revolution*, ed. Carol R. Berkin and Clara M. Lovett. New York: Holmes and Miers.

Castillo Bueno, Maria de los Reyes. 2000. *Reyita sencillamente*. Durham: Duke University Press.

Castro, Fidel. 1967. *Aniversarios del triunfo de la Revolución Cubana*. Havana: Editora Política.

———. 1983. *La historia me absolverá*. Havana: Ediciones Ciencias Sociales.

———. 1990. *The Rectification Process Is Not Something New*. Havana: José Martí.

———. 1996. *Cuba at the Crossroads*. New York: Ocean Press.

———. 1996. Speech delivered at the closing session of Seventeenth Congress of the Central Organization of Cuban Trade Unions (April 30, 1996). Castro Speech Database. http://lanic.utexas.edu/la/cb/cuba/castro.html.

Cerrutti Costa, Luis B. 1973. *Socialismo y tercer mundo*. Buenos Aires: Ediciones Rancagua.

Chauncey, George. 1994. *Gay New York: Gender, Urban Culture, and the Making of the Gay Male World, 1890–1940*. New York: Basic Books.

Chauncey, George, and E. A. Povenelli. 1999. "Thinking Sexuality Transnationally: An Introduction." *GLQ: A Journal of Lesbian and Gay Studies* 5 (4): 439–49.

Clarke, Kamari. 2004. *Mapping Yoruba Networks: Power and Agency in the Making of Transnational Communities*. Durham: Duke University Press.

Clarke, Kamari, and Deborah A Thomas. 2006. *Globalization and Race: Transformations in the Cultural Production of Blackness*. Durham: Duke University Press.

Clifford, James. 2000. "Taking Identity Politics Seriously: 'The Contradictory, Stony Ground.'" In *Without Guarantees: In Honour of Stuart Hall*, ed. Paul Gilroy, Lawrence Grossberg, and Angela McRobbie. London: Verso.

Cohen, Cathy. 1997. "Punks, Bulldaggers and Welfare Queens: The Real Radical Potential of 'Queer' Politics" in *GLQ: A Journal of Lesbian and Gay Studies* 3:437–85.

———. 1999a. *The Boundaries of Blackness: AIDS and the Breakdown of Black Politics*. Chicago: University of Chicago Press.

———. 1999b. "What Is This Movement Doing to My Politics?" *Social Text* 61:111–18.

———. 2004. "Deviance as Resistance: A New Research Agenda for the Study of Black Politics." *Du Bois Review* 1 (1): 27–45.

Cole, Johnnetta. 1986. *Race Toward Equality*. Havana: José Martí.

Collins, Patricia Hill. 1990. *Black Feminist Thought, Consciousness, Knowledge, and the Politics of Empowerment*. Boston: Heinemann.

———. 1998. *Fighting Words: Black Women and the Search for Justice*. Minneapolis: University of Minnesota Press.

Comaroff, Jean. 1985. *Body of Power, Spirit of Resistance: The Culture and History of a South African People*. Chicago: University of Chicago Press.

Comaroff, Jean, and John Comaroff. 1991. *Of Revelation and Revolution: Christianity, Colonialism, and Consciousness in South Africa*. Chicago: University of Chicago Press.

Combahee River Collective. 1983. "Combahee River Collective Statement." In *Home Girls: A Black Feminist Anthology*, ed. Barbara Smith. New York: Kitchen Table Press.

Connell, R. W. 1987. *Gender and Power: Society, the Person, and Sexual Politics*. Stanford: Stanford University Press.

———. 1991. "The State, Gender, and Sexual Politics: Theory and Approach." In *Power/Gender: Social Relations in Theory and Practice*, ed. Lorraine Radtke and Hendrikus J. Stam. Thousand Oaks, Calif.: Sage.

———. 1996. "New Directions in Gender Theory, Masculinity Research, and Gender Politics." *Ethnos* 61 (3–4): 157–76.

Coronil, Fernando. 1995. Introduction to Fernando Ortiz, *Cuban Counterpoint: Tobacco and Sugar*. Durham: Duke University Press.

———. 1997. *The Magical State*. Chicago: University of Chicago.

Cossman, Brenda. 2007. *Sexual Citizens: The Legal and Cultural Regulation of Sex and Belonging*. Stanford: Stanford University Press.

Crenshaw, Kimberlé Williams. 1994. Mapping the Margins: Intersectionality, Identity Politics, and Violence against Women of Color." In *The Public Nature of Private Violence*, ed. Martha Albertson Fineman and Rixanne Mykitiuk. New York: Routledge.

Croucher, Sheila L. 1997. *Imagining Miami: Ethnic Politics in a Postmodern World*. Charlottesville: University of Virginia Press.

Cruz-Malavé, Arnaldo, and Martin F. Manalansan, eds. 2002. *Queer Globalizations: Citizenship and the Afterlife of Colonialism*. New York: New York University Press.

Cvetkovich, Ann. 2003. *An Archive of Feelings: Trauma, Sexuality, and Lesbian Public Cultures*. Durham: Duke University Press.

Daniel, Yvonne. 1995. *Rumba: Dance and Social Change in Contemporary Cuba*. Bloomington: Indiana University Press.

Davis, Angela. 1981. *Women, Race, and Class*. London: The Women's Press.

———. 1998. *Blues Legacies and Black Feminism: Gertrude "Ma" Rainey, Bessie Smith, and Billie Holiday*. New York: Vintage.

de Certeau, Michel. 1984. *The Practice of Everyday Life*. Trans. S. Rendall. Berkeley: University of California Press.

D'Emilio, John. 1993. "Capitalism and Gay Identity." In *The Lesbian and Gay Studies Reader*. New York: Routledge.

———. 1997. *Intimate Matters: A History of Sexuality in America*. Chicago: University of Chicago Press.

de la Fuente, Alejandro. 1998. "Race, National Discourse, and Politics in Cuba." *Latin American Perspectives* 25 (3): 43–69.

———. 2001. *A Nation for All: Race, Inequality, and Politics in Twentieth-Century Cuba*. Chapel Hill: University of North Carolina Press.

De Veaux, Alexis. 2004. *Warrior Poet: A Biography of Audre Lorde*. New York: W. W. Norton.

Diawara, Manthia. 1992. "Afro-kitsch." In *Black Popular Culture*, ed. Gina Dent, 285–91. Seattle: Bay Press.

———. 1998. *In Search of Africa*. Cambridge: Harvard University Press.

Doezema, Jo. 1998. "Forced to Choose: Beyond the Volunteer v. Forced Prostitution Dichotomy." In *Global Sex Workers: Rights, Resistance, and Redefinition*, ed. K. Kempadoo and Jo Doezema. New York: Routledge.

Dominguez, Jorge. 1978. *Cuba: Order and Revolution*. Cambridge: Harvard University Press.

Dominguez, Virgina R., and Yolanda Prieto. 1987. "Sex, Gender, and the Revolution: The Problem of Construction and the Construction of a Problem." *Cuban Studies* 17:1–24.

Dowsett, G. W. 1996. *Practicing Desire: Homosexual Sex in the Era of AIDS*. Stanford: Stanford University Press.

Du Bois, W. E. B. 1903. *The Souls of Black Folk: Essays and Sketches*. Chicago: A.C. McClurg and Co.

Duggan, Lisa. 1994. "Queering the State." *Social Text* 39:1–14.

———. 2002. "The New Homonormativity: The Sexual Politics of Neoliberalism." In *Materializing Democracy: Toward a Revitalized Cultural Politics*, ed. Russ Castronovo and Dana D. Nelson. Durham: Duke University Press.

———. 2003. *The Twilight of Equality? Neoliberalism, Cultural Politics and the Attack on Democracy*. Boston: Beacon Press.

Ebron, Paulla A. 2002. *Performing Africa*. Princeton: Princeton University Press.

Edelman, Lee. 2004. *No Future: Queer Theory and the Death Drive*. Durham: Duke University Press.

Edwards, Brent Hayes. 2003. *The Practice of Diaspora: Literature, Translation, and the Rise of Black Internationalism*. Cambridge: Harvard University Press.

Engels, Frederick. 1968. "The Origin of the Family, Private Property and the State." In *Karl Marx and Frederick Engels: Selected Works*. Moscow: Russia Progress Publishers.

Fairley, Jan. 2006. "Dancing Back to Front: Reggaeton, Sexuality, Gender and Transnationalism in Cuba." *Popular Music Journal* 25 (3): 471–88.

Farmer, Paul. 1992. *AIDS and Accusation: Haiti and the Geography of Blame*. Berkeley: University of California Press.

Ferguson, Roderick A. 2004. *Aberrations in Black: Toward a Queer of Color Critique*. Minneapolis: University of Minnesota Press.

Fernandes, Sujatha. 2005. "Transnationalism and Feminist Activism in Cuba: The Case of Magín." *Politics and Gender* 1 (3): 431–52.

———. 2006. *Cuba Represent! Cuban Arts, State Power, and the Making of New Revolutionary Cultures*. Durham: Duke University Press.

Fernandez, Nadine T. 1996a. "Race, Romance, and Revolution: The Cultural Politics of Interracial Encounters in Cuba." Ph.D. diss., University of California, Berkeley.

———. 1996b. "The Color of Love: Young Interracial Couples in Cuba." *Latin American Perspectives* 23 (1): 99–117.

———. 1999. "Back to the Future? Women, Race, and Tourism in Cuba." In *Sun, Sex, and Gold: Tourism and Sex Work in the Caribbean*, ed. K. Kempadoo. Lanham, Md.: Rowman and Littlefield.

———. 2010. *Revolutionizing Romance: Interracial Couples in Contemporary Cuba*. New Brunswick, N.J.: Rutgers University Press.

Fernández Robaina, Tomás. 1994. *El negro en Cuba: Apuntes para la historia de la lucha contra la discriminacion racia*. Havana: Editorial de Ciencias Sociales.

Ferrer, Ada. 1999a. "Cuba, 1898: Rethinking Race, Nation, and Empire." *Radical History Review* 73:22–46.

———. 1999b. *Insurgent Cuba: Race, Nation, and Revolution, 1868–1898*. Chapel Hill: University of North Carolina Press.

Findlay, Eileen. 1999. *Imposing Decency: The Politics of Sexuality and Race in Puerto Rico, 1870–1920*. Durham: Duke University.

Formell, Juan, and Los Van Van. 2003. *En el malecon de la Habana: Concierto en vivo*. Universal Latino (compact disc).

Fosado, Gisela C. 2004. "The Exchange of Sex for Money in Contemporary Cuba: Masculinity, Ambiguity and Love." Ph.D. thesis, University of Michigan.

Foucault, Michel. 1972. *The Archaeology of Knowledge; and, the Discourse on Language*. New York: Pantheon Books.

———. 1973. *The Birth of the Clinic: An Archaeology of Medical Perception*. New York: Penguin.

———. 1979. *Discipline and Punish: The Birth of the Prison*. Trans. A. Sheridan. New York: Penguin.

———. 1980. *The History of Sexuality*. Vols. 1 and 2. Trans. Robert Hurley. New York: Vantage.

———. 1983. "The Subject and Power. Afterword." In *Michel Foucault: Beyond Structuralism and Hermeneutics*, ed. Hubert L. Dreyfus and Paul Rabinow. 2nd ed. Chicago: University of Chicago Press.

———. 1986. "Of Other Spaces." *Diacritics* 16 (1): 22–27.

———. 1997. "Friendship as a Way of Life." In *The Essential Works of Foucault, 1954–1984. Volume One—Ethics: Subjectivity and Truth*, ed. Paul Rabinow. New York: New Press.

Fowler, Victor. 1998. *La maldición una historia del placer como conquista*. Havana: Editorial Letras Cubanas.

———. 2002. "A Traveler's Album: Variations on Cubanidad." *boundary 2* 29 (3): 106–119.

Fraser, Nancy. 1992. "Rethinking the Public Sphere: A Contribution to the Critique of Actually Existing Democracy." In *Habermas and the Public Sphere*, ed. Craig Calhoun. Cambridge: MIT Press.

Freyre, Gilberto. 1964. *The Masters and the Slaves: A Study in the Development of Brazilian Civilization*. New York: Random House.

Fusco, Coco. 2001. "Hustling for Dollars: Jineteras in Cuba." In *The Bodies That Were Not Ours, and Other Writings*. New York: Routledge.

Gilliam, Angela. 1991. "Women's Equality and National Liberation." In *Third World Women and the Politics of Feminism*, ed. Chandra Talpade Mohanty, Ann Russo, and Lourdes Torres. Bloomington: Indiana University Press.

Gilroy, Paul. 1993a. *The Black Atlantic: Modernity and Double Consciousness*. Cambridge: Harvard University Press.

———. 1993b. *Small Acts: Thoughts on the Politics of Black Cultures*. London: Serpent's Tale.

———. 2000. *Against Race: Imagining Political Culture beyond the Color Line*. Cambridge: Harvard University Press.

Gilroy, Paul, Lawrence Grossberg, and Angela McRobbie. 2000. *Without Guarantees: In Honour of Stuart Hall*. London: Verso.

Ginsberg, Faye, and Rayna Rapp. 1995. *Conceiving the New World Order: The Global Politics of Reproduction*. Berkeley: University of California Press.

Glave, Thomas. 2008. *Our Caribbean: A Gathering of Lesbian and Gay Writing from the Antilles*. Durham: Duke University Press.

Gómez, Sara. 1974. *De cierta manera*. Havana: Instituto Cubano del Arte e Industrias Cinematográficos.

González, Tomás. 1993. "Sara, One Way or Another." In *AfroCuba: An Anthology of Cuban Writing on Race, Politics and Culture*, ed. Pedro Peréz Sarduy and Jean Stubbs. Melbourne: Ocean Press.

Gopinath, Gayatri. 2005. *Impossible Desires: Queer Diasporas and South Asian Public Cultures*. Durham: Duke University Press.

Gordon, Edmund T. 1997. "Cultural Politics of Black Masculinity." *Transforming Anthropology* 6:36–53.

———. 1998. *Disparate Diasporas*. Austin: University of Texas Press.

———. 1999. "Cultural Politics of Black Masculinity." *Transforming Anthropology* 6:36–53.

Gramsci, Antonio, and Quentin Hoare. 1971. *Selections from the Prison Notebooks*, ed. Geoffrey Nowell Smith. New York: International Publishers.

Green, James Naylor. 2000. *Beyond Carnival: Male Homosexuality in Twentieth-Century Brazil*. Chicago: University of Chicago Press.

Grewal, Inderpal. 2005. *Transnational America: Feminisms, Diasporas, Neoliberalisms*. Durham: Duke University Press.

Grewal, Inderpal, and Caren Kaplan, eds. 1994. *Scattered Hegemonies: Postmodernity and Transnational Feminist Practices*. Minneapolis: University of Minnesota Press.

Grub, Eveho. 2000. *Black Cuban, Black American: A Memoir*. Houston: Arte Publico Press.

Guanche Perez, Jesús. 1993. "La antropología cultural en Cuba durante el presente siglo." *Interciencias* 18 (4): 176–83.

Guillén, Nicolás. 1967. *Antologia mayor*. Havana: José Martí.

———. 1995. *The Great Zoo and Other Poems*. Havana: José Marti.

Gupta, Akhil, and James Ferguson. 1992. "Beyond 'Culture': Space, Identity and the Politics of Difference." *Cultural Anthropology* 7 (1): 6–23.

Guridy, Frank Andre. 2010. *Forging Diaspora: Afro-Cubans and African Americans in a World of Empire and Jim Crow*. Chapel Hill: University of North Carolina Press

Gutmann, Matthew C. 1996. *The Meaning of Macho: Being a Man in Mexico*. Berkeley: University of California Press.

———. 1997. "The Ethnographic (G)ambit: Women and the Negotiation of Masculinity in Mexico City." *American Ethnologist* 24 (4): 833–55.

Guy, Donna J. 1994. "Future Directions in Latin American Gender History." *The Americas: A Quarterly Review of Inter-American Cultural History* 51 (1): 1–9.

Guy-Sheftall, Beverly. 1995. *Words of Fire: An Anthology of African-American Feminist Thought*. New York: New Press.

Gwaltney, John. 1980. *Drylongso: A Self-Portrait of Black America*. New York: Vintage.

Halberstam, Judith. 1998. *Female Masculinity*. Durham: Duke University Press.

———. 2005. *In a Queer Time and Place: Transgender Bodies, Subcultural Lives*. New York: New York University Press.

Hale, Charles. 2006. "Activist Research v. Cultural Critique: Indigenous Land Rights and the Contradictions of Politically Engaged Anthropology." *Cultural Anthropology* 21 (1): 96–120.

———. 2008. *Engaging Contradictions: Theory, Politics, and Methods of Activist Scholarship*. Berkeley: University of California Press.

Hall, Stuart. 1980. "Race, Articulation and Societies Structured in Dominance." In *Sociological Theories: Race and Colonialism*. Paris: UNESCO.

———. 1986. "Gramsci's Relevance for the Study of Race and Ethnicity." *Journal of Communication Inquiry* 10 (2): 5–27.

———. 1989. "Then and Now: A Re-evaluation of the New Left (discussion)." In *Out of Apathy: Voices of the New Left Thirty Years On*, ed. Oxford University Socialist Group. London: Verso.

———. 1990. "Cultural Identity and Diaspora." In *Identity, Community, Culture, Difference*, ed. Jonathan Rutherford. London: Lawrence and Wishart.

———. 1991a. Introduction to *Gramsci's Political Thought* by Roger Simon. London: Lawrence and Wishart.

———. 1991b. "The Local and the Global: Globalization and Ethnicity." In *Culture, Globalization, and the World-System: Contemporary Conditions for the Representation of Identity*, ed. Anthony King. London: Macmillan.

———. 1998. "Subjects in History: Making Diasporic Identities." In *The House That Race Built: Original Essays by Toni Morrison, Angela Y. Davis, Cornel West, and Others on Black Americans and Politics in America Today* by Wahneema H. Lubiano. New York: Vintage Books.

Hall, Stuart, and Tony Jefferson. 1990. *Resistance through Rituals: Youth Subcultures in Post War Britain*. New York: Routledge.

Hall, Stuart, David Morley, and Kuan-Hsing Chen. 1996. *Stuart Hall: Critical Dialogues in Cultural Studies*. London: Routledge.

Hammonds, Evelynn. 1997. "Black (W)holes and the Geometry of Black Female Sexuality." In *Feminism Meets Queer Theory*, ed. Elizabeth Weed and Naomi Schor. Bloomington: Indiana University Press.

Hanchard, Michael. 1998. *Orpheus and Power: The Movimento Negro of Rio de Janeiro and São Paulo, Brazil, 1945–1988*. Princeton: Princeton University Press.

———. 2006. *Party/Politics: Horizons in Black Political Thought*. Oxford: Oxford University Press.

Hanerz, Ulf. 1989. "Notes on the Global Ecumene." *Public Culture* 1 (2): 66–75.

Hanh, Thich Nhat. 1989. *The Moon Bamboo*. Berkeley: Parallax Press.

Harrison, Faye V. 2008. *Outsider Within: Reworking Anthropology in the Global Age*. Urbana: University of Illinois Press.

———. 1991. *Decolonizing Anthropology: Moving Further toward an Anthropology for Liberation*. Washington, D.C.: Association for Black Anthropologists.

———. 1995. "The Persistent Power of 'Race' in the Cultural and Political Economy of Racism." *Annual Review of Anthropology* 24:47–74.

Hartman, Saidiya. 1997. *Scenes of Subjection: Terror, Slavery, and Self-Making in Nineteenth-Century America*. New York: Oxford University Press.

Harvey, David. 1989. *The Condition of Postmodernity: An Enquiry into the Origins of Cultural Change*. New York: Oxford University Press.

Hebdige, Dick. 2001. *Subculture: The Meaning of Style*. London: Taylor and Francis.

Helg, Aline. 1995. *Our Rightful Share: The Afro-Cuban Struggle for Equality, 1886–1912*. Durham: Duke University Press.

Hemphill, Essex. 1991. *Brother to Brother: New Writing by Black Gay Men*. With introduction by Jafari Sinclaire Allen. Washington, D.C.: Redbone Press.

———. 2000. *Ceremonies: Prose and Poetry*. San Francisco: Cleis Press.

Herdt, Gilbert H. 1990. *Intimate Communications: Erotics and the Study of Culture*. New York: Columbia University Press.

Hermanos de Causa. 2003. *Tengo. La Causa Nostra*. Vol. 1 (compact disc).

Hernandez-Reguant, Ariana. 2005. "Cuba's Alternative Geographies." *Journal of Latin American and Caribbean Anthropology* 10 (2): 275–313.

———. 2009. *Cuba in the Special Period: Culture and Ideology in the 1990s*. New York: Palgrave Macmillan.

Hodge, Derrick G. 2001. "Colonization of the Cuban Body: The Growth of Male Sex Work in Havana." *NACLA Report on the Americas* 34:20–28.

Hooker, Juliet. 2005. "Beloved Enemies": Race and Official Mestizo Nationalism in Nicaragua." *Latin American Research Review* 40 (3): 14–39.

———. 2009. *Race and the Politics of Solidarity*. New York: Oxford University Press.

hooks, bell. 1989. *Talking Back: Thinking Feminist, Thinking Black*. Boston: South End Press.

———. 1990. *Yearning: Race, Gender, and Cultural Politics*. Boston: South End Press.

———. 1994. *Outlaw Culture: Resisting Representations*. New York: Routledge.

Howe, C. 2002. "Undressing the Universal Queer Subject: Nicaraguan Activism and Transnational Identity." *City and Society* 14 (2): 237–79.

Incite! Women of Color Against Violence. 2007. *The Revolution Will Not be Funded: Beyond the Non-profit Industrial Complex*. Boston: South End Press.

James, C. L. R. 1963. *Beyond a Boundary*. New York: Pantheon Books.

James, Conrad. 2003. "Georgina Herrera and the Pleasures of Maternity." *Bulletin of Latin American Research* 22 (4): 475–83.

James, Joy. 2000. "Radicalizing Feminism." In *The Black Feminist Reader*, ed. Joy James and T. Denean Sharpley-Whiting. Malden, Mass.: Blackwell.

Jameson, Fredric. 1991. *Postmodernity, or the Cultural Logic of Late Capitalism*. Durham: Duke University Press.

Johnson, E. Patrick. 2001. "'Quare' Studies, or (Almost) Everything I Know about Queer Studies I Learned from My Grandmother." *Text and Performance Quarterly* 21:1–25.

Johnson, E. Patrick, and Mae Henderson. 2005. *Black Queer Studies: A Critical Anthology*. Durham: Duke University Press.

Joy, James. 2000. "Radicalizing Feminism." In *The Black Feminist Reader*, ed. Joy James and T. Denean Sharpley-Whiting. Malden, Mass.: Blackwell Publishers.

Kelley, Robin D. G. 1994. *Race Rebels*. New York: Free Press.

———. 1997. *Yo' Mama's Disfunktional! Fighting the Culture Wars in Urban America*. New York: Beacon.

———. 1998. "Check the Technique: Black Urban Culture and the Predicament of Social Science." In *Near Ruins: Cultural Theory at the End of the Twentieth Century*, ed. Nicolas Dirks. Minneapolis: University of Minnesota Press.

———. 2002. *Freedom Dreams: The Black Radical Imagination*. Boston: Beacon Press.

Kempadoo, Kamala. 1999. Introduction to *Sun, Sex, and Gold: Tourism and Sex Work in the Caribbean*. Lanham, Md.: Rowman and Littlefield.

———. 2004. *Sexing the Caribbean: Gender, Race and Sexual Labor*. New York: Routledge.

Kempadoo, Kamala, and Jo Doezema. 1998. *Global Sex Workers: Rights, Resistance, Redefinition*. New York: Routledge.

Kennedy, Elizabeth, and Madeline Davis. 1993. *Boots of Leather, Slippers of Gold: The History of a Lesbian Community*. New York: Routledge.

Kincaid, Jamaica. 1988. *A Small Place*. New York: Farrar, Straus, and Giroux.

Klak, Thomas C. 1998. *Globalization and Neoliberalism: The Caribbean Context*. Lanham, Md.: Rowman and Littlefield.

Knight, Franklin. 1974. *The African Dimension in Latin American Societies*. Oxford: Oxford University Press.

Kulick, Don, and Margaret Willson, eds. 1995. *Taboo: Sex, Identity and Erotic Subjectivity in Anthropological Fieldwork*. London: Routledge.

Kutzinski, Vera. 1993. *Sugar's Secrets: Race and the Erotics of Cuban Nationalism*. Charlottesville: University of Virginia Press.

Lancaster, Roger. 1986. Comment on Arguelles and Rich's "Homosexuality, Homophobia, and Revolution: Notes toward an Understanding of the Cuban Lesbian and Gay Male Experience, Part II." *Signs* 12 (1): 188–92.

———. 1992. *Life Is Hard: Machismo, Danger, and the Intimacy of Power in Nicaragua*. Berkeley: University of California.

———. 1995. "'That We Should All Turn Queer?' Homosexual Stigma in the Making of Manhood and the Breaking of a Revolution in Nicaragua." In *Conceiving Sexuality: Approaches to Sex Research in a Postmodern World*, ed. Richard Parker. New York: Routledge.

Las Krudas. 2003. *CUBENSI*. Independent (compact disc).

Lash, Scott. 1998. "Reflexive Modernization: The Aesthetic Dimension." In *Theory, Culture and Society* 10:1–23.

Lash, Scott, and John Urry. 1994. *Economies of Signs and Spaces*. London: Sage.

Lavie, Smadar, and Ted Swedenburg. 1996. *Displacement, Diaspora, and Geographies of Identity*. Durham: Duke University Press.

Leiner, Marvin. 1994. *Sexual Politics in Cuba: Machismo, Homosexuality, and AIDS*. Boulder, Colo.: Westview.

Lewis, Oscar, Ruth M. Lewis, and Susan M. Rigdon. 1977. *Neighbors: Living the Revolution: An Oral History of Contemporary Cuba.* Urbana: University of Illinois Press.

Lipsitz, George. 1998. *The Possessive Investment in Whiteness: How White People Profit from Identity Politics.* Philadelphia: Temple University Press.

Lockwood, Lee. 1990. *Castro's Cuba, Cuba's Fidel.* Boulder, Colo.: Westview.

Lorde, Audre. 1978. *The Black Unicorn.* New York: Norton.

———. 1982. *Zami: A New Spelling of My Name.* Berkeley: Crossing Press.

———. 1983. *Zami: A New Spelling of My Name.* Trumansburg, N.Y.: Crossing Press.

———. 1984. *Sister Outsider: Essays and Speeches.* Trumansburg, N.Y.: Crossing Press.

Lowe, Lisa, and David Lloyd. 2007. *The Politics of Culture in the Shadow of Capital.* Durham: Duke University Press.

Lumsden, Ian. 1996. *Machos, Maricones, and Gays: Cuba and Homosexuality.* Philadelphia: Temple University Press.

Manalansan, Martin F. 2003. *Global Divas: Filipino Gay Men in the Diaspora.* Durham: Duke University Press.

———. 2005. "Race, Violence, and Neoliberal Spatial Politics in the Global City." *Social Text* 84/85:141–56.

———. 2006. "Queer Intersections: Sexuality and Gender in Migration Studies." *International Migration Review* 40 (1): 224–49.

Martí, José. 1891. *Nuestra América.* Mexico: El Partido Liberal.

Martinez-Alier, Verena. 1974. *Marriage, Class and Colour in Nineteenth-Century Cuba: A Study of Racial Attitudes and Sexual Values in a Slave Society.* London: Cambridge University Press.

Marx, Karl. 1858. "The Grundrisse." In *The Marx-Engels Reader,* ed. Robert C. Tucker. 2nd ed. New York: W. W. Norton.

———. 1867. *Capital, Volume One.* In *The Marx-Engels Reader,* ed. Robert C. Tucker. 2nd ed. New York: W. W. Norton.

———. 1888. "Theses on Fuerbach." In *The Marx-Engels Reader,* ed. Robert C. Tucker. 2nd ed. New York: W. W. Norton.

Massey, Doreen. 1994. *Space, Place, and Gender.* Minneapolis: University of Minnesota Press.

Matory, J. Lorand. 1994. *Sex and the Empire That Is No More: Gender and Politics of Metaphor in Oyo Yoruba Religion.* Minneapolis: University of Minnesota Press.

McBride, Dwight A. 2005. Why I Hate Abercrombie & Fitch: Essays on Race and Sexuality. New York: New York University Press.

Medin, Tzvi. 1990. *Cuba: The Shape of Revolutionary Consciousness.* Boulder, Colo.: Lynne Rienner Publishers.

Mercer, Kobena. 1994. *Welcome to the Jungle: New Positions in Black Cultural Studies.* London: Routledge.

Mesa Logo, Carmelo. 1974. *Cuba in the 1970s: Pragmatism and Institutionalization.* Albuquerque: University of New Mexico Press.

———. 1993. *Cuba after the Cold War*. Pittsburgh: University of Pittsburgh Press.

Mintz, Sidney. 1985. *Sweetness and Power: The Place of Sugar in Modern History*. New York: Viking.

Mohammed, Patricia. 1998. "Towards Indigenous Feminist Theorizing in the Caribbean." *Feminist Review* 59:6–33.

Mohanty, Sataya P. 1993. "The Epistemic Status of Cultural Identity: On *Beloved* and the Postcolonial Condition." *Cultural Critique* 24 (spring): 41–80.

Molyneux, Maxine. 1996. *State, Gender and Institutional Change in Cuba's "Special Period": The Federacion de Mujeres Cubanas*. London: Institute of Latin American Studies.

Moore, Carlos. 1988. *Castro, the Blacks, and Africa*. Los Angeles: University of California Center for African American Studies.

———. 2008. *Pichon: Race and Revolution in Castro's Cuba: A Memoir*. Chicago: Chicago Review Press.

Moore, Robin. 1997. *Nationalizing Blackness: Afrocubanismo and Artistic Revolution in Havana, 1920–1940*. Pittsburgh: University of Pittsburgh Press.

Moraga, Cherríe, and Gloria Anzaldúa. 1983. *This Bridge Called My Back: Writings of Radical Women of Color*. New York: Kitchen Table Press.

Morejón, Nancy, 1988. *Fundación de la imagen*. Havana: Editorial Letras Cubanas.

Morley, Dave. 1996. *Stuart Hall: Critical Dialogues in Cultural Studies*. London: Routledge.

Morrison, Toni. 2004. *Beloved*. New York: Viking International.

Mott, Luiz Barros. 1988. *Escravidão, homossexualidade e demonologia*. São Paulo: Ícone.

Moynihan, Daniel Patrick. 1995. "The Negro Family: The Case for National Action." Office of Policy Planning and Research. http://www.dol.gov/oasam/programs/history/webid-meynihan.htm.

Mullings, Leith. 1996. *On Our Own Terms: Race, Class and Gender in the Lives of African-American Women*. New York: Routledge.

———. 2005. "Interrogating Racism: Toward an Antiracist Anthropology." *Annual Review of Anthropology* 34:363–84.

Muñoz, José Esteban. 1996. "Ephemera as Evidence: Introductory Notes to Queer Acts." *Women and Performance: A Journal of Feminist Theory* 8 (2): 5–16.

———. 1999. *Disidentifications: Queers of Color and the Performance of Politics*. Minneapolis: University of Minnesota Press.

———. 2009. *Cruising Utopia: The Then and There of Queer Futurity*. New York: New York University Press.

Nascimento, Abdias do. 1989. *Brazil: Mixture or Massacre? Essays in the Genocide of a Black People*. Dover, Mass.: Majority Press.

Nash, Gary B. 1995. "The Hidden History of Mestizo America." *The Journal of American History* 82 (3): 941–64.

Nassy Brown, Jacqueline. 2005. *Dropping Anchor, Setting Sail: Geographies of Race in Black Liverpool*. Princeton: Princeton University Press.

Norman, Brian. 2007. "'We' in Redux: The Combahee River Collective's Black Feminist Statement." *differences* 18 (2): 103–32.

Nurse, Keith. 2004. *Masculinities in Transition: Gender and the Global Problematique. In Interrogating Caribbean masculinities: Theoretical and Empirical Analyses*. Kingston: The University of the West Indies Press.

Omise'eke, Natasha Tinsley. 2008. *Black Atlantic, Queer Atlantic: Imagining the Middle Passage as Queer Borderwaters. GLQ: A Journal of Lesbian and Gay Studies* 14 (2–3): 191–215.

Orishas. 2000. *A lo cubano*. Universal Latino Records (compact disc).

Ortiz, Fernando. 1913. *Entre cubanos: psicología tropical*. Habana: Editorial de Ciencias Sociales.

———. 1940. *Los factores humanos de la cubanidad*. Havana: Imprenta Molina.

———. 1957. "Origen geográfico de los Afro-Cubanos." *Revista Bimestre Cubana* 2:226–48.

———. 1987. *Los negros brujos*. Havana: Editorial de Ciencias Sociales.

———. 1995a. *Los negros esclavos*. Havana: Cubanas Ediciones.

———. 1995b. *Cuban Counterpoint: Tobacco and Sugar*. Durham: Duke University Press.

Ortíz, Ricardo L. 2007. *Cultural Erotics in Cuban America*. Minneapolis: University of Minnesota Press.

Ortner, Sherry B. 1996. *Making Gender: The Politics and Erotics of Culture*. Boston: Beacon Press.

Oxfam International. 2008. "Cuba's HIV/AIDS Strategy: An Integrated, Rights-Based Approach." http://www.medicc.org/ns/assets/documents/Cuban%20HIV%20Strategy.pdf.

Padilla, Mark. 2007. *Caribbean Pleasure Industry: Tourism, Sexuality, and AIDS in the Dominican Republic*. Chicago: University of Chicago Press.

Parker, Richard. 1991. *Bodies, Pleasure and Passions: Sexual Culture in Contemporary Brazil*. New York: Beacon.

———. 1999. *Beneath the Equator: Cultures of Desire, Male Homosexuality and Emerging Gay Identities in Brazil*. New York: Routledge.

Parker, Richard, and John Gagnon. 1995. *Conceiving Sexuality: Approaches to Sex Research in a Postmodern World*. London: Routledge.

Parker, Richard, and D. Easton. 1998. "Sexuality, Culture, and Political Economy: Recent Developments in Anthropological and Cross-Cultural Sex Research." *Annual Review of Sex Research* 9:1–19.

Parker, Richard, Regina Maria Barbosa, and Peter Aggleton, eds. 2000. *Framing the Sexual Subject: The Politics of Gender, Sexuality, and Power*. Los Angeles: University of California Press.

Perry, Marc David. 2004. "Los Raperos: Rap, Race, and Social Transformation in Contemporary Cuba." Ph.D. thesis, University of Texas, Austin.

Pheterson, Gail, ed. 1989. *Vindication of the Rights of Whores: The International Movement for Prostitutes' Rights*. Seattle: Seal Press.

Pierre, Jemima. 2008. "'I Like Your Colour!' Skin Bleaching and Geographies of Race in Urban Ghana." Feminist Review 90 (1): 9–29.

Premat, Adrian 2009. "State Power, Private Plots and the Greening of Havana's Urban Agriculture Movement." *City and Society* 21 (1): 28–57.

Price, Richard, and Sally Price. 1991. *Two Evenings in Saramaka*. Chicago: University of Chicago Press.

Puar, Jasbir K. 2002. "Circuits of Queer Mobility: Tourism, Travel, and Globalization." *GLQ: A Journal of Lesbian and Gay Studies* 8 (1–2): 101–37.

Qurioga, José. 2000. *Tropics of Desire: Interventions from Queer Latino America*. New York: New York University Press.

Ramírez, Rafael. 1999. *What It Means to Be a Man: Reflections on Puerto Rican Masculinity*. New Brunswick, N.J.: Rutgers University Press.

Ransby, Barbara. 2003. *Ella Baker and the Black Freedom Movement: A Radical Democratic Vision*. Chapel Hill: University of North Carolina Press.

Reddock, Rhoda. 1990. "Feminism, Nationalism, and the Early Women's Movement in the English Speaking Caribbean (with special reference to Jamaica and Trinidad and Tobago)." In *Caribbean Women Writers: Essays from the First International Conference*, ed. Selwyn Reginald Cudjoe. Wellesley, Mass.: Calaloux Publications.

———, ed. 2004. *Interrogating Caribbean Masculinities: Theoretical and Empirical Analyses*. Kingston, Jamaica: University of West Indies Press.

———. 2009. *Identidad afrocubana: cultura y nacionalidad*. Santiago de Cuba: Editorial Oriente.

Robinson, Cedric. 2000. *Black Marxism: The Making of the Black Radical Tradition*. Chapel Hill: University of North Carolina Press.

Rodney, Walter. 1969. *The Groundings With My Brothers*. London: Bogle-L'Ouverture Publications.

———. 1973. *How Europe Underdeveloped Africa*. Washington, D.C.: Howard University Press.

———. 1981. *How Europe Underdeveloped Africa*. Washington, D.C.: Howard University Press.

———. 1996. *Groundings with My Brothers*. Chicago: Research Associates School Times Publications.

Rodriguez, Juana Maria. 2003. *Queer Latinidad: Identity Practices, Discursive Spaces*. New York: New York University Press.

Rofel, Lisa. 1999. *Other Modernities: Gendered Yearnings in China after Socialism*. Berkeley: University of California.

———. 2007. *Desiring China: Experiments in Neoliberalism, Sexuality, and Public Culture*. Durham: Duke University Press.

Rosendahl, Mona. 1998. *Inside the Revolution: Everyday Life in Socialist Cuba*. Ithaca: Cornell University Press.

Ryer, Paul. 2000. "Millenniums Past Cuba's Future." *Public Culture* 12 (2): 499.

Safa, Helen Icken. 1995. *The Myth of the Male Breadwinner: Women and Industrialization in the Caribbean*. Boulder, Colo.: Westview Press.

Safa, Helen Icken, and June Nash. 1976. *Sex and Class in Latin America: Women's Perspectives on Politics, Economics, and the Family in the Third World*. New York: Praeger Publishers.

———. 1986. *Women and Change in Latin America*. South Hadley, Mass.: Bergin and Garvey.

Salas, Luis. 1979. *Social Control and Deviance in Cuba*. New York: Praeger Publishers.

Sandoval, Chela. 2000. *Methodology of the Oppressed*. Minneapolis: University of Minnesota Press.

Sarduy, Pedro, and Jean Stubbs. 1998. *Afrocuba: Una antologia de escritos cubanos sobre raza, politica y cultura*. San Juan: Editorial de la Universidad de Puerto Rico.

———. 2000. *Afro-Cuban Voices: On Race and Identity in Contemporary Cuba*. Gainesville: University Press of Florida.

———. 2002. *AfroCuba: An Anthology of Cuban Writing on Race, Politics and Culture*. New York: Ocean Press.

Saunders, Tanya. 2009a. "Grupo OREMI: Black Lesbians and the Struggle for Safe Social Space in Havana." *Souls* 11 (2): 167–85.

———. 2009b. "Black Lesbians and Racial Identity in Contemporary Cuba." *Black Women, Gender, and Families* 4 (1).

———. 2009c. "La Lucha Mujerista: Krudas Cubensi and Black Feminist Sexual Politics in Cuba." *Caribbean Review of Gender Studies* 3:1–20.

Sawyer, Mark. 2006. *Racial Politics in Post-Revolutionary Cuba*. New York: Cambridge University Press.

Schwartz, Rosalie. 1997. *Pleasure Island: Tourism and Temptation in Cuba*. Lincoln: University of Nebraska Press.

Scott, David. 1991. "That Event, This Memory: Notes on an Anthropology of African Diasporas in the New World." *Diaspora* 1 (3): 261–84.

———. 1999. *Refashioning Futures: Criticism after Postcoloniality*. Princeton: Princeton University Press.

Scott, James. 1985. *Weapons of the Weak: Everyday Forms of Peasant Resistance*. New Haven: Yale University Press.

———. 1990. *Domination and the Arts of Resistance: Hidden Transcripts*. New Haven: Yale University Press.

Scott, Joan. 1986. "Gender as a Useful Category of Historical Analysis." *American Historical Review* 91 (5): 1053–75.

Sierra Madero, Abel. 2002. *La nación sexuada: Relaciones de género y sexo en Cuba, 1830–1855*. Havana: Editorial de Ciencias Sociales.

———. 2003. "La policía del sexo: La homofobia en Cuba en el siglo XIX." *Revista Sexología y Sociedad* 21 (9): 21–44.

———. 2004. "Cuba." In *GLBTQ: An Encyclopedia of Gay, Lesbian, Bisexual, Transgender, and Queer Culture*. www.glbtq.com.

Smith, Barbara, ed. 1983. *Home Girls: A Black Feminist Anthology*. New York: Kitchen Table Press.

———. 1998. *The Truth That Never Hurts: Writings on Race, Gender, and Freedom*. New Brunswick, N.J.: Rutgers University Press.

Smith, Lois M. 1992. "Sexuality and Socialism in Cuba." In *Cuba in Transition: Crisis and Transformation*, ed. Sandor Halebsky and John M. Kirk. Boulder: Westview Press.

Spillers, Hortense J. 1984. "Interstices: A Small Drama of Words." In *Black, White, and in Color: Essays on American Literature and Culture*. Chicago: University of Chicago Press.

———. 1987. "Mama's Baby, Papa's Maybe: An American Grammar Book." *Diacritics* 17 (2): 64–81.

Spivak, Gayatri Chakravorty. 1988. *In Other Worlds: Essays in Cultural Politics*. New York: Routledge.

Stack, Carol B. 1997. *All Our Kin*. Boulder, Colo.: Westview Press.

Stoler, Laura Ann. 1995. *Race and the Education of Desire: Foucault's History of Sexuality and the Colonial Order of Things*. Durham: Duke University Press.

Stout, Noelle M. 2008. "Feminists, Queers and Critics: Debating the Cuban Sex Trade." *Journal of Latin American Studies* 40 (4): 721–42.

Sudbury, Julia [Julia Chinyere Oparah]. 1998. *Other Kinds of Dreams: Black Women's Organisations and the Politics of Transformation*. London: Routledge.

Telles, Edward E. 2006. *Race in Another America: The Significance of Skin Color in Brazil*. Princeton: Princeton University Press.

Thomas, Deborah A. 2004. *Modern Blackness: Nationalism, Globalization and the Politics of Culture in Jamaica*. Durham: Duke University Press.

Thompson, E. P. 1964. *The Making of the English Working Class*. New York: Pantheon Books.

Thompson, Shirley. 2001. "'Ah Toucoutou, ye conin vous': History and Memory in Creole New Orleans." *American Quarterly* 53 (2): 232–66.

Trinh, T. Minh-Ha. 1989. *Woman, Native, Other: Writing Postcoloniality and Feminism*. Bloomington: Indiana University Press.

Trouillot, Michel-Rolph. 1991. "Anthropology and the Savage Slot." In *Recapturing Anthropology*, ed. R. G. Fox. Santa Fe, N.M.: School of American Research Press.

———. 1992. "The Caribbean Region: An Open Frontier in Anthropological Theory." *Annual Review of Anthropology* 21:19–42.

———. 1995. *Silencing the Past: Power and the Production of History*. Boston: Beacon.

———. 2003. *Global Transformations: Anthropology and the Modern World*. New York: Palgrave Macmillan.

Turner, Victor Witter. 1982. *From Ritual to Theatre: The Human Seriousness of Play*. New York: Performing Arts Journal Publications.

Twinam, Ann. 1999. *Public Lives, Private Secrets: Gender, Honor, Sexuality, and Illegitimacy in Colonial Spanish America*. Stanford: Stanford University Press.

Ulysse, Gina A. 2007. *Downtown Ladies Informal Commercial Importers, a Haitian Anthropologist, and Self-making in Jamaica*. Chicago: University of Chicago Press.

UNAIDS and WHO [Joint United Nations Programme on HIV/AIDS and World Health Organization]. 2008. "Caribbean AIDS Epidemic Update: Regional Summary." http://data.unaids.org/pub/Report/2008/jc1528_epibriefs_caribbean_en.pdf.

United Nations Development Program. 1999. *Human Development under Transition*. New York: United Nations.

Urrutia, Gustavo E. 1937. *Puntos de vista del nuevo Negro*. Havana: Imprenta El Score.

Urry, John. 1990. *The Tourist Gaze: Leisure and Travel in Contemporary Societies*. London: Sage.

Vance, C. S. 1984. *Pleasure and Danger: Exploring Female Sexuality*. Boston: Routledge and Kegan Paul.

———. 1991. "Anthropology Rediscovers Sexuality: A Theoretical Comment." *Sociological and Scientific Medicine* 33 (8): 875–84.

Vargas, João Costa. 2003. "The Inner City and the Favela: Transnational Black Politics." *Race and Class* 44 (4): 19–40.

———. 2004. "Hyperconsciousness of Race and Its Negation: The Dialectic of White Supremacy in Brazil." *Identities* 11 (4): 443–70.

Visweswaran, Kamala. 1994. *Fictions of Feminist Ethnography*. Minneapolis: University of Minnesota Press.

Wade, Peter. 1993. *Blackness and Race Mixture: The Dynamics of Racial Identity in Colombia*. Baltimore: Pluto Press.

———. 1997. *Race and Ethnicity in Latin America*. Baltimore: Pluto Press.

———. 2001. "Racial Identity and Nationalism: A Theoretical View from Latin America." *Ethnic and Racial Studies* 24 (5): 845–65.

Walcott, Rinaldo. 2005. "Outside in Black Studies: Reading from a Queer Place in the Diaspora." In *Black Queer Studies: A Critical Anthology*, ed. E. Patrick Johnson and Mae G. Henderson. Durham: Duke University Press.

———. 2009. "Reconstructing Manhood; or, the Drag of Black Masculinity." *Small Axe: A Caribbean Platform for Criticism* 28 (March): 75–89.

Walker, Alice. 1982. *The Color Purple*. New York: Pocket Books.

Warner, Michael. 1993. *Fear of a Queer Planet: Queer Politics and Social Theory*. Minneapolis: University of Minnesota Press.

———. 2000. *The Trouble with Normal: Sex, Politics, and the Ethics of Queer Life*. Cambridge: Harvard University Press.

Weeks, J. 1985. *Sexuality and Its Discontents: Meanings, Myths, and Modern Sexualities*. London: Routledge and Kegan Paul.

Wekker, Gloria. 2006. *The Politics of Passion: Women's Sexual Culture in the Afro-Surinamese Diaspora*. New York: Columbia University Press.

Weston, Kath. 1991. *Families We Choose: Lesbians, Gays, Kinship*. New York: Columbia University Press.

Wilderson, Frank III. 2003. "Gramsci's Black Marx: Whither the Slave in Civil Society?" *Social Identities: Journal for the Study of Race, Nation and Culture* 9 (2): 225–40.

Williams, Brackette. 1991. *Stains on My Name, War in My Veins: Guyana and the Politics of Cultural Struggle*. Durham: Duke University Press.

Williams, Raymond. 1961. *The Long Revolution*. New York: Anchor Books.

———. 1977. *Marxism and Literature*. Oxford: Oxford University Press.

Wilson, Peter J. 1969. "Reputation and Respectability: A Suggestion for Caribbean Ethnology." *Man* 4:37–53.

———. 1973. *Crab Antics: A Caribbean Study of the Conflict between Reputation and Respectability*. New Haven: Yale University Press.

Wing, Adrien Katherine. 2000. *Global Critical Race Feminism: An International Reader*. New York: New York University Press.

Wolf, Eric. 1982. *Europe and the People without History*. Berkeley: University of California Press.

Wright, Michelle, and Antje Schuhmann. 2008. *Blackness and Sexualities*. Berlin: Lit Verlag.

Young, Allen. 1981. *Gays under the Cuban Revolution*. San Francisco: Grey Fox Press.

Index

homophilia, 49, 149

homophobia, 67, 90, 126, 145, 149, 172, 191. *See also* heterosexism

"homosex," 126–27

homosexuality, 10, 69; capitalism and, 190; Castro and, 68–69, 72–73. *See also* gay men; lesbians; queer: queerness

Hooker, Juliet, 55–56

hooks, bell, 50, 82–83

Howe, Cymene, 12

human rights, 72, 81, 95, 130, 200n5, 206n8. *See also* rights

hyperconscious negation of race (Costa Vargas), 6, 55, 62

Ian (respondent), 142

identities, 33, 57, 92–93, 119, 173, 184; cognitivist notion of experience and, 201n12; women's, 99

identity: movements based in, 191, 202n10; politics, 186–88; positions, 93

interpellation, 24–25, 37, 65, 93, 95, 160–61, 163, 193

intersectional approach, 12, 106, 117, 196n8

interstices, 135, 196n8

interstitial analysis, 9, 10

"in the life," 134–35, 141, 144

Jaime (respondent), 70–72

James, Conrad, 116

James, Joy, 98

jineteras (female sex workers), 36, 160

Johnson, E. Patrick, 133

Juan (respondent), 128

Kelley, Robin D. G., 40, 74, 83–84, 180–81

Kempadoo, Kamala, 16–17, 110, 129, 131

Kincaid, Jamaica, 28–29

Kutzinski, Vera, 61

Lao (respondent), 29, 31–32, 34

"larger freedom," 80, 130–31; invoking, 1–3, 5, 8–10, 17

Latin America, 11, 22, 46–48, 54–57, 60; gender in, 125, 176, 202n4

lesbians, 11, 136–37, 144, 149–50, 153; friendship and, 89, 93, 131–32, 137. *See also* CENESEX; Delores; Oremi

liberalism, 107

Lili (respondent), 74–80, 192–93

Liolvys (respondent), 24, 34

Lombroso, Cesare, 44

Lorde, Audre, 16, 30, 81, 84, 97–98, 130, 141; on "deep longing within," 96, 130; on desirè, 12; on the erotic, 3, 12, 96–97, 130, 192–93; on home, 134; on "house of difference," 98; on loving friendship, 131; on "Zami," 133

Los Cocos (HIV sanatorium), 142–43

love, 94; revolutionary, 36; sex and, 133

loving, 144, 155. *See also* friendship

Lozano, Compañero, 36–37, 121–24

luchando (struggling/fighting/hustling), 21, 101, 120, 122, 125, 162, 180

Lucumí, 32, 59, 121, 123–24, 149

Lumsden, Ian, 166

Maceo, Antonio, 124

machismo, 13, 50–51, 166, 168, 171, 181, 202n4; "*yo soy macho*," 125–28

machista, 51, 90, 103, 118–19, 166, 174, 179, 202n4

Magia (performer), 116

Malécon, 35–37, 75, 173–74

Manalansan, Martin, 159

Marcos (respondent), 35–36

maricones, 68, 70–72, 75, 77, 127–28, 181

Marilisa (respondent), 138–39

Wilson, Phil, 144

women: agency of, 30, 113; black, 117; Cuban Revolution and making new, 109–13; identities of, 99; New Woman, 67, 99, 109, 111; rights of, 112, 114–15, 156, 192; status in socialist revolution of, 111–17. *See also* feminism; lesbians

women's bodies as battlegrounds of honor and shame, 60–61

women who have sex with women, 68, 129

Yaineris (respondent), 33–34, 89–90, 92, 136–39, 149–50, 193

YaYa, 33–34, 93, 152

"yo no me parezco a nadie" (I'm like no other), 138–41

Yoruba. *See* Lucumí

Young, Allen, 68

JAFARI S. ALLEN is an assistant professor of African
American studies and anthropology at Yale
University.

Library of Congress Cataloging-in-Publication Data
Allen, Jafari S.
¡Venceremos? : the erotics of black self-making in Cuba /
Jafari S. Allen.
p. cm.—(Perverse modernities)
Includes bibliographical references and index.
ISBN 978-0-8223-4932-7 (cloth : alk. paper)
ISBN 978-0-8223-4950-1 (pbk. : alk. paper)
1. Blacks—Cuba. 2. Gay men, Black—Cuba. 3. Sex role—
Cuba. 4. Identity (Psychology)—Cuba. I. Title. II. Series:
Perverse modernities.
F1789.N3A45 2011
305.896'07291—dc22
2011010728